Financial Institutions and Markets

Financial Institutions and Markets

The Financial Crisis—An Early Retrospective

Edited by

Robert R. Bliss and George G. Kaufman

palgrave
macmillan

FINANCIAL INSTITUTIONS AND MARKETS: THE FINANCIAL CRISIS—AN EARLY
RETROSPECTIVE
Copyright © Robert R. Bliss and George G. Kaufman, 2010.

First published in 2010 by
PALGRAVE MACMILLAN®
in the United States – a division of St. Martin's Press LLC,
175 Fifth Avenue, New York, NY 10010.

Where this book is distributed in the UK, Europe and the rest of the world,
this is by Palgrave Macmillan, a division of Macmillan Publishers Limited,
registered in England, company number 785998, of Houndmills, Basingstoke,
Hampshire RG21 6XS.

Palgrave Macmillan is the global academic imprint of the above companies
and has companies and representatives throughout the world.

Palgrave® and Macmillan® are registered trademarks in the United States, the
United Kingdom, Europe and other countries.

ISBN: 978–0–230–10835–6

Library of Congress Cataloging-in-Publication Data is available from the
Library of Congress.

A catalogue record of the book is available from the British Library.

Design by MPS Limited, A Macmillan Company

First edition: December 2010

10 9 8 7 6 5 4 3 2 1

Printed in the United States of America.

Contents

List of Figures

List of Tables

About the Contributors

Sujit Chakravorti is a Senior Economist in the financial markets group at the Federal Reserve Bank of Chicago. Chakravorti's research focuses on the economics of payments and the evolving structure of global financial markets. Before joining the Chicago Fed, Chakravorti worked at the Dallas Fed. Prior to joining the Federal Reserve System, he worked at KPMG as an international economist, advising foreign governments on financial market policy. In addition, he has been a visiting scholar at the De Nederlandsche Bank (Dutch central bank), European University Institute, the International Monetary Fund, and the University of Granada. Chakravorti received a BA degree in Economics and genetics from the University of California-Berkeley and MA and PhD degrees in Economics from Brown University.

Gilles Chemla is the Head of the finance group at Imperial College Business School, a Research Director at Centre National de la Recherche Scientifique at the University of Paris-Dauphine, and a Research Affiliate at the Centre for Economic Policy Research. He has taught at the London School of Economics and the University of British Columbia and has worked for BNP Paribas and as an independent consultant.

Gillian G. H. Garcia was an Assistant Professor at the University of California at Berkeley until she went to Washington to work on the U.S. banking and thrift crises of the 1980s and early 1990s. In Washington she worked for the U.S. General Accountability Office and the Senate Banking Committee, where she participated in the enactment of reform legislation (the Financial Institutions Reform Recovery and Enforcement Act [FIRREA], and the FDIC Improvement Act [FDICIA]). She then went to the IMF to help resolve the financial crises in East Asia and advise the fund on issues relating to deposit insurance.

Dr. Garcia has also been a distinguished professorial lecturer at Georgetown University, a National Fellow at the Hoover Institute at Stanford University, a Visiting Scholar at the Office of the Comptroller of the Currency, the Congressional Research Service, the Federal Reserve Bank of Chicago, and De Nederlandsche Bank in Amsterdam. Now retired, she currently teaches from time to time at the University of Maryland, consults for developing countries and the Financial Services Volunteer Corp, and writes and presents papers on financial-sector policy issues. She has published six books and a number of articles—especially on deposit insurance and banking reform for the United States and the European Union.

Giorgio Di Giorgio is Professor of Monetary Economics and Dean of the Faculty of Economics at Università LUISS Guido Carli, Rome. After a obtaining his BA at Università La Sapienza, Rome, he received a PhD in Economics at Columbia University. His research focuses on monetary policy, financial intermediation theory, and financial regulation. Professor Di Giorgio published several papers in academic journals and as chapters of edited books, and he is a former Editor of the *Journal of Banking and Finance.* He also served as an adviser to the Italian Ministry of the Treasury (1997–2002), as Deputy Rector for international relations (2003–2005), and is now an independent director of asset management and listed companies in Italy.

Jeffery W. Gunther is Vice President of the Federal Reserve Bank of Dallas, where he oversees analysis of financial institutions and their supervisory environment. His primary focus involves the detection of emerging risks to the banking system. Gunther received a PhD in Economics from Southern Methodist University in 1995.

Maximilian J. B. Hall graduated with a first class honors degree in Economics from Nottingham University in 1975. He received a PhD from the same university in 1978. He joined the staff of the Economics Department of Loughborough University in 1977 and is currently Professor of Banking and Financial Regulation in that department. Professor Hall has published nine books (one coauthored) in the areas of money, banking, and financial regulation and has contributed chapters to a further 12 books. He has three entries in the New Palgrave Dictionary of Money and Finance published by Macmillan in 1992; and he has also acted as Managing Editor for a further two books, including *Regulation and Supervision of Banks* (four volumes) published by Edward Elgar in July 2001.

Ruth Judson is an Economist in the Division of Monetary Affairs at the Federal Reserve Board. Her work covers a range of topics, including demand for broad money, the link between inflation and growth, and the implementation of monetary policy. Together with Richard Porter, she was a primary contributor to the joint U.S. Treasury-Federal Reserve program, examining the international use and counterfeiting of U.S. currency. In connection with the project, she has worked extensively on the measurement of currency flows using U.S. currency data as well as other sources. She holds an AB in Russian Civilization from the University of Chicago and a PhD in Economics from MIT.

George G. Kaufman is the John F. Smith Professor of Economics and Finance at Loyola University Chicago and consultant to the Federal Reserve Bank of Chicago. He has published widely on financial markets and institutions and authored and edited numerous books in the field including *Global Financial Crises* (Kluwer: 2000); *Asset Price Bubbles* (MIT Press: 2003); *Systemic Financial Crises* (World Scientific: 2005); and the annual *Research in Financial Services* (JAI/Elsevier Press: 1989–2003). Dr. Kaufman is coeditor of the *Journal of Financial Stability* and a founding editor of the *Journal of Financial Services Research*. He is the former President of the Western Finance Association, the Midwest Finance Association, and the North American Economic and Finance Association. He serves as cochair of the Shadow Financial Regulatory Committee. Kaufman holds a PhD in Economics from the University of Iowa.

Philip Molyneux is currently Professor in Banking and Finance and Head of Bangor Business School at Bangor University. Between 2002 and 2005 he has acted as a member of the ECON Financial Services expert panel for the European Parliament. His most recent coauthored texts are: *Thirty Years of Islamic Banking* (Palgrave Macmillan: 2005), *Shareholder Value in Banking* (Palgrave Macmillan: 2006), and *Introduction to Banking* (FT Prentice Hall: 2006). He recently coedited (with Berger and Wilson) the *Oxford Handbook of Banking* (Oxford University Press). His main research interests focus on the structural features of banking systems, modeling bank performance, Islamic banking, and wealth management. He has recently held Visiting Professorships at Bocconi University, Erasmus University, and Bolzano Free University (Italy). He has acted as a consultant to New York Federal Reserve Bank, World Bank, European Commission, UK Treasury; Citibank Private Bank, Bermuda Commercial Bank, McKinsey's, Credit Suisse, and various other international banks and consulting firms.

Robert R. Moore is a Research Officer in the Financial Industry Studies Department of the Federal Reserve Bank of Dallas. He has published various articles on banking and financial markets in academic, trade, and Federal Reserve publications. Dr. Moore joined the Federal Reserve Bank of Dallas in 1991. Before joining the Federal Reserve, he was an Assistant Professor of Economics at Tulane University. He received a BA in Economics from the University of Missouri, where he was elected to Phi Beta Kappa. He received a PhD in Economics from the University of Wisconsin.

Adrian Pop holds a PhD from the University of Orleans, France. In 2006, he obtained the prize for the "Best PhD Thesis 2006" in Banking & Monetary

Economics awarded by Banque de France. He is currently Associate Professor of Banking and Finance at the University of Nantes and Research Consultant to the French Banking Commission (Banque de France). He is also the Head of the Executive Part-time MBA Program at the Institute of Banking & Finance. His main research interests include the role of market discipline in banking regulation and supervision, Basel II, capital standards, procyclicality, stress testing, financial crises, informational content of security prices, early warning systems, credit derivatives, Islamic banking, and Too Big To Fail issues in banking.

Diana Pop received a PhD from the University of Orleans, France. She is currently Associate Professor of Finance in the Economics Department of the University of Angers. Her main research interests are in the area of emerging markets finance and regulation, mergers and acquisitions and corporate restructuring, and corporate governance. She has a contributed chapter in *Financial Development, Integration and Stability: Evidence from Central, Eastern and South-Eastern Europe,* published by Edward Elgar in November 2006.

Richard Porter received a PhD in Economics from the University of Wisconsin at Madison. Currently, he is Vice President and Senior Policy Advisor in the financial markets group of the Federal Reserve Bank of Chicago. Before joining the Bank, Porter served as an economist at the Board of Governors of the Federal Reserve System for over three decades. He was the recipient of a special achievement award from the Board in 1982 and a certificate of appreciation in special recognition of efforts and superior contributions for the International Currency Audit Program to the law enforcement responsibilities of the USSS in 2000. In May 2004 he was privileged, along with Peter Tinsley and Dale Henderson, to have the Board of Governors sponsor a festschrift-type conference entitled in his honor.

David J. Reiss is Professor of Law at Brooklyn Law School and has also taught at Seton Hall Law School. His research focuses on the secondary mortgage market. Previously, he was an associate at Paul, Weiss, Rifkind, Wharton & Garrison in its Real Estate Department and an associate at Morrison & Foerster in its Land Use and Environmental Law Group. He was also a law clerk to Judge Timothy Lewis of the United States Court of Appeals for the Third Circuit. He received his BA from Williams College and his JD from the New York University School of Law.

Richard Rosen is an Economic Advisor and Senior Economist at the Federal Reserve Bank of Chicago. In that position, he focuses on financial intermediation including the future of banking, bank regulation, and the housing markets. Prior to coming to the Chicago Fed, Dr. Rosen taught in the Finance Departments at the Kelley School of Business at Indiana University, the Wharton School at the University of Pennsylvania and the School of Business at Georgetown University. He has also worked on the Board of Governors of the Federal Reserve System. He received a BA from Swarthmore College and a PhD in Economics from Princeton University.

Guido Traficante is an Economist at the Development and Strategy Department of Eni and a Research Fellow at Università LUISS Guido Carli, Rome. After a BA at Università LUISS Guido Carli, Rome, he got a PhD in Economics at Tor Vergata University in Rome. His research focuses on monetary and fiscal policy, International Macroeconomics and Finance. Dr. Traficante was Research Fellow at the University of California Santa Cruz during the academic year 2005–2006 and has been a teaching assistant since 2004.

Santiago Carbó has a BA in Economics (Universidad de Valencia, Spain), a PhD in Economics and an MS in Banking and Finance (University of Wales, Bangor, UK), and Full Professor of Economics at the University of Granada (Spain). He was Dean of the School of Economics and Business of the University of Granada during 2006–2008. He has been the Head of Financial System Research of the Spanish Savings Banks Research Foundation (Funcas) since 1996. He is also Consultant at the Federal Reserve Bank of Chicago since 2008. He has been (and in some cases still is) consultant for public institutions such as the European Central Bank, the European Commission, the Spanish Ministry of Science and Innovation, the Spanish Ministry of Labour, and the Institute of European Finance) and for leading economic consulting companies. He has published widely in peer-reviewed publications. He has given conferences, lectures, and seminars at international institutions (G-20, World Bank, World Savings Banks Institute), central banks and government bodies (European Central Bank, Federal Reserve Board, Bank of Spain, Spanish Antitrust Authority), several banks of the Federal Reserve System, and universities.

Part I

Financial Crises across Countries

1

Banking from Riches to Rags: Ignoring the Supervisory Red Flags and Thwarting Prompt Corrective Action

*Gillian G. H. Garcia**

Introduction

The Federal Deposit Insurance Corporation Improvement Act (FDICIA) of 1991 was enacted 19 years ago. In one of its major provisions— prompt corrective action (PCA)—Congress mandated that supervisors place a series of increasingly severe restrictions on the activities of a troubled bank or thrift if it did not correct its weaknesses but continued instead to deteriorate. Congress hoped that supervisors would correct weaknesses as soon as they perceived them in order to reverse an institution's path to destruction. On those—it was hoped rare—occasions when such correction failed, a nonviable institution was to be closed and resolved once its tangible equity capital declined to, or below, 2 percent of its assets. Congress intended that closing an institution promptly before it became insolvent would prevent serious losses to the deposit insurance funds.

At the time, those that commented on the Act were optimistic that it would prevent a future recurrence of the losses that were incurred by the bank and thrift insurance funds during the banking and thrift crises of the 1980s and early 1990s. "Never again" became a Congressional slogan. Not everyone was so confident. Carnell (1993) wondered if regulators would be willing to forgo their culture of ad hoc discretion. Kaufman (2002, 2004) and Eisenbeis and Wall (2002) warned that the failures that were occasionally occurring during the late 1990s and early 2000s were proving to be unexpectedly expensive, suggesting that PCA was not working in the way it was intended.

Failures became frequent again in 2008 and 2009 (fig. 1.1), and they were expensive (table 1.1). The losses rendered the Federal Deposit Insurance Corporation's (FDIC) Deposit Insurance Fund (DIF) technically insolvent in 2009, and it became dependent on its full faith and credit guarantee from the U.S. Treasury while it waited for increased and prepaid premiums from the banking industry to restore its financial integrity.

In the final months of 2009, the U.S. Congress again considered bills to reform the financial sector in an effort to discourage another financial crisis as vicious as the receding one. While not the most important of the needed reforms, much of the discussion, and dissent, over the financial reform proposal (2009) and the House and the Senate bills concern the reallocation of supervisory powers for banks, thrifts, and their holding companies. In addition, in typical Washington fashion in the aftermath of a crisis, the reforms would create new oversight agencies. All three proposals, for example, provide for a new body to oversee systemic risk and another to protect the consumer from abusive bank practices. All three proposals would abolish the Office of Thrift Supervision (OTS). The Senate bill proposes to create a new supervisor that would take over the bank-by-bank supervisory responsibilities of the Federal Reserve (the Fed), the Office of the Comptroller of the Currency (OCC), the FDIC, and the OTS.[1] In contrast, the House bill and Administration proposals would not consolidate these supervisory responsibilities, which would remain as they were—except that the OCC would take over the OTS's responsibilities.[2] Agencies that are at risk of having their remit (clout) reduced are naturally resisting these proposals and are lobbying hard,[3] as is the banking industry.[4] In addition, the reform proposals would impose additional regulations but ignore problems that exist in the implementation of existing regulations. But supervision is given short shrift.

To throw some light on this controversy, this paper examines performance by the four bodies (the FDIC, the Fed, the OCC, and the OTS) in their oversight responsibilities. To do so, it relies on the Material Loss Reviews (MLRs) conducted by the inspectors general (IGs) of the federal agencies responsible for supervising the institutions that failed in the calendar years 2007, 2008, and 2009—the years in which failures of insured banks and thrifts escalated from the zero readings recorded for 2005 and 2006. In doing so, it recognizes that the IGs may not have complete command over the causes of the institutions' failures nor over the supervisory deficiencies that enabled them. Nevertheless, the MLRs are revealing. They show that supervision was deficient, so much so that it contributed to the thwarting of prompt corrective action.

On its Web site, the FDIC's IG explains his MLR responsibilities as follows:

> Section 38(k) of the Federal Deposit Insurance Act states that when the Deposit Insurance Fund incurs a material loss with respect to an insured depository institution, the IG of the appropriate Federal banking agency shall make a written report to that agency reviewing the agency's supervision of the institution (including the agency's implementation of prompt corrective action provisions of section 38), which shall ascertain why the institution's problems resulted in a material loss to the Deposit Insurance Fund; and make recommendations for preventing any such loss in the future. A loss is material if it exceeds the greater of $25 million or 2 percent of an institution's total assets at the time the FDIC was appointed receiver.[5]

This chapter's Section 2 presents data on numbers of failures for the years 2001 through November 2009 and the material losses incurred by each supervisor. The following four sections analyze, in turn, the MLRs of the four federal supervisors. Section 7 generalizes and concludes.

1. Bank and Thrift Failures and Material Losses

Figure 1.1 shows the number of bank and thrift failures by month for the years 2001 through November 2009. (There were 16 more failures through

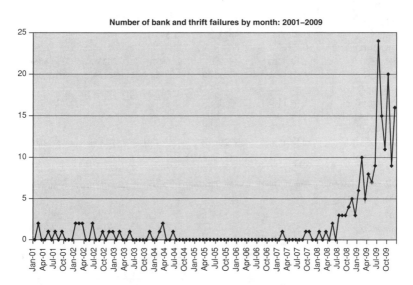

Figure 1.1   Number of bank and thrift failures by month: 2001–2009

the third Friday in December.) There were few failures early in the decade and none in 2005 and 2006, but their numbers escalated thereafter to peak (so far) at 24 in July 2009.

Table 1.1 shows the numbers of failures of insured banks and thrifts and their material losses for the years 2007 through mid-December 2009, distributed according to their federal supervisor. During this three-year

Table 1.1   Failures and material losses: 2007–2009[a]

	FDIC	FED	OCC	OTS	Total
2009[a]					
Number of institutions[b]	5.039	858	1,505	773	6,995
Their deposits[b] ($bn)	$1,733bn	$962bn	$4,142bn	$713bn	$6,617bn
Number of failures	77	16	29	20	142
Assets of ML institutions ($m)	$9,568m	$8,036m	$5,916m	$541m	$24,061m
Estimated material losses[d] ($m)	$2,802m	$2,227m	$1,317m	$138m	$6,514m
Number of MLR[4]	20	2	6	2	30
Assets of ML institutions reviewed[d] ($m)	$9,568m	$2,229m	$5,916m	$541m	$18,254m
Estimated losses reviewed[d] ($m)	$2,802m	$338m	$1,317m	$168m	$4,625m
2008					
Number of institutions[b]	5,163	874	1,515	809	7,203
Their deposits[b] ($m)	$1,642m	$857m	$3,597m	$923m	$5,886m
Number of failures[c]	15	1	8	6	30
Number of material losses & reviews[d]	11	1	1	4	17
Assets of MRL institutions[d] ($m)	$11,349m	$229m	$2.1bn	$78.6bn	$92,278m
Estimated material losses[d] ($m)	$3,354m	$72m	$214m	$12.9bn	$16,540m
2007					
Number of institutions[b]	5,215	888	1,676	815	7,350
Their deposits[b] ($bn)	$1,645bn	$831bn	$3,274bn	$945bn	$5,530bn

(Continued)

Table 1.1   Continued

	FDIC	FED	OCC	OTS	Total
Number of failures[c]	2	0	0	1	3
Number of material losses & reviews[d]	0	0	0	1	1
Assets of MRL institutions[d]	0	0	0	$25bn	$25bn
Estimated material losses[d]	0	0	0	$108m	$108m
2007–2009[a]					
Number of failures: total	94	17	37	24	168
Number of MLRs	31	3	7	7	48
Assets of MLR institutions	$20,917m	$2,458m	$8,016m	$104,141m	$135,532m
Estimated material losses	$6,156m	$410m	$1,531m	$13,176m	$21,273m
Material losses as % assets	29.4%	16.7%	19.1%	12.7%	16.7%

Notes: [a] Data through December 20, 2009.
[b] Numbers and deposits of institutions are taken from FDIC Summary of Deposit data for National Totals by Charter Class. FDIC data include FDIC-supervised savings banks. OTS data include federally chartered and OTS-supervised savings associations. Data are for June of each year.
[c] FDIC Historical Statistics (2009) on Failures and Assistance Transactions, which include cases of assistance under a systemic risk determination.
[d] Author's analysis of MLRs by the FDIC, the Fed, the OCC, and the OTS, as published by December 20, 2009.

period there were 175 bank and thrift failures. Material losses on 48 of the failures on which MLRs had been published through December 20, 2009, were estimated at $21.3 billion—62 percent attributable to the OTS. Estimated material losses over the three-year period show a loss rate of 29.4% for the FDIC, 16.7% for the Fed, 19.1% for the OCC, and 12.7% for the OTS. Clearly OTS's experience stands out. OCC's performance, however, is worse than it looks because the large troubled banks it oversees were not allowed to fail, and their losses were thus not recorded; instead the national mega banks and regional banking powerhouses were rescued by the Troubled Asset Relief Program (TARP). The Fed's record also looks stronger than it should because its IG had managed to report only three MLRs by mid December 2009, and losses on the eight pending MLRs are estimated to be higher, bringing its overall loss rate on MLR banks to 28.2%. This percentage is comparable to that of the FDIC, whose IG had completed 31 reviews.

Tolstoy in his novel *Anna Karenina* writes, "Happy families are all alike; every unhappy family is unhappy in its own way." This paper questions whether, similarly, banks of different sizes with different supervisors fail for different reasons, or *whether* there are universal flags that signal failure for all banks, regardless of their size or supervisor. Fisher (2009, p. 2) reports that Paul Volcker sees universal themes among bank failures, commenting, "In his day he knew a bank was headed for trouble when it grew too fast, moved into a fancy new building, placed the chairman of the board as head of the art committee, and hired McKinsey & Co. to do an incentive compensation study for senior officers."

2.   FDIC Material Loss Reviews

2.1   The causes of failure

FDIC MRLs are required to be issued within six months after the material loss becomes apparent. As serious exercises in analysis that span between 30 and 60 pages, they are published prominently in a separate section of the Web site (www.fdicoig.gov). The FDIC's IG issued no MLRs for banks that failed in 2007, but has recorded 11 for banks that failed in 2008 and 20 for banks that failed in 2009 through the third week of December.

Table 1.2 summarizes the causes of failure as recorded in these 31 MLRs. It shows that high-loss failures among FDIC-supervised banks occurred in 15 states, particularly in states that have experienced heavy real estate development in recent years—especially Georgia with seven MLRs and California with five. Twenty-one of the FDIC's MLRs were for banks that belonged to a single-bank holding company, while another four were for two-bank holding companies. Eighteen of the failures were at new banks—those less (and often much less) than ten years old. Twenty-four of the MLR banks exaggerated their capital levels by maintaining inadequate loan loss reserves. Thirty MLRs mention fast, aggressive growth as a critical factor contributing to failure. Undue concentration of assets was emphasized in 25 MLRs. Asset concentration was not so much in risky types of home mortgages, which were mentioned in only six MLRs or in mortgage backed securities, but rather in excessive acquisition, development and construction (ADC) lending, which was criticized in 27 MLRs, and overlending for commercial real estate (CRE), which was cited in 22 MLRs.

Management is well-recognized as a crucial determinant of a bank's success or failure. FDIC auditors criticized a lack of board leadership and/ or weak management in 30 of the 31 MLRs and cited poor underwriting and credit administration in 30 MLRs. In all cases, the failed banks pursued

Table 1.2 Causes of failure among banks supervised by the FDIC

Institution	Structure			C	Assets							Management				E		Liquidity		
	1	2	3	4	5	6	7	8	9	10	11	12	13	14	15	16	17	18	19	20
MLRS [a]	STT	BHC	NEW	ILL	FGR	CON	RHM	ADC	CRE	DOM	WBM	IRC	UCA	RIC	IRS	VLR	MIR	VNF	BRD	FHLB Adv
2009																				
America West Bank	UT	1	X	X	X	X		X	X	X	X	X	X		X	X	X	X	X	
Great Basin Bank	NV	1		X	X	G			X		X	X	X		X	X	X			
Strategic Capital Bank	IL	1	X	X	X	X	X		X	X	X	X	X		X	X		X	X	X
American Southern Bank	GA	1	X		X	X		X	X	X	X	X	X	X		X		X	X	
Westsound Bank	WA	1	X	X	X	X		X	X		X	X	X	X	X	X	X	X	X	
First, Beverley Hills	CA	1	C	X	X	X		X	X		X	X	X	X	X		X	X		X
New Frontier	CO	1	X		X	X		X			X	X	X	X	X	X	X	X		X
Cape Fear	NC	1	X		X	X		X			X	X	X		X			X	X	
First City, Stockbridge	GA	1		X	X	X		X	X			X	X			X		X		
Security Savings	NV	1	X	X	X	X		X	X	X	X	X	X		X	X	X	X	X	X

(Continued)

Table 1.2 Continued

Institution	Structure			C		Assets						Management					E	Liquidity		
	1	2	3	4	5	6	7	8	9	10	11	12	13	14	15	16	17	18	19	20
	STT	BHC	NEW	ILL	FGR	CON	RHM	ADC	CRE	DOM	WBM	IRC	UCA	RIC	IRS	VLR	MIR	VNF	BRD	FHLB Adv
MLRS																				
2009[a]																				
Freedom Commerce	GA	1	X	X	X	X		X	X		X	X	X		X			X		X
Heritage Community	IL	1			X	X		X	X	X	X	X	X	X	X	X	X			
Sherman County	NB	1		X		X					X	X	X		X	X		X	X	
Corn Belt	IL	1		X	X					X	X	X	X		X	X		X	X	X
FirstBank Fin. Services	GA	1	X	X	X	X		X	X		X	X	X		X	X	X	X	X	X
Silver Falls Bank	OR	0	X	X	X	X	X	X			X	X	X		X		X	X		
Alliance Bank	CA	1			X	X		X	X	X	X	X	X		X	X		X	X	X
Magnet Bank	UT	0	X	X	X	X		X	X	X	X	X	X	X	X	X		X	X	
1st Centennial Bank	CA	1		X	X	X		X	X		X	X	X		X		X	X	X	X
Bank of Clark County	WA	1	X	X	X	X		X	X		X	X	X					X	X	X
Total for 2009: 20			12	15	19	19	2	16	16	7	19	19	20	6	17	14	8	18	13	10
Failed in 2008																				
Haven Trust	GA	3	X	X	X	X		X	X	X	X	X	X		X	X	X	X	X	X

Bank	State		1 STT	2 BHC	3 NEW	4 ILL	5 RG	6 CON	7 RHM	8 ADC	9 CRE	10 DOM	11 WBM	12 IRC	13 UCA	14 RIC	15 IRS	16 VLR	17 MIR	18 NCF	19 BD	20 FHLB
Community Bank	GA	1		X	X	X			X		X	X	X		X			X	X	X	X	X
Franklin Bank	TX	2	X	X	X	X		X	X	X	X	X	X	X	X	X	X	X	X	X	X	X
Security Pacific	CA	2	X	X	X	X		X			X	X	X	X	X			X		X	X	X
Freedom Bank	FL	0		X	X	X		X	X	X	X	X	X	X	X	X	X	X	X	X	X	X
Alpha Bank	CA	0	X	X	X	X	X	X			X	X	X	X	X	X	X	X	X	X	X	X
Main Street Bank	MI	1	X	X	X	X	X	X	X	X	X	X	X		X	X	X	X	X	X	X	X
Silver State Bank	NV	2		X	X	X	X	X	X		X	X	X	X	X		X	X	X	X	X	X
Integrity Bank	GA	1	X	X	X	X		X			X	X	X	X	X		X	X	X	X	X	X
Columbian Bank	KS	2		X	X	X	X	X		X	X	X	X	X	X	X	X	X	X	X	X	X
First Priority Bank	FL	0	X	X	X	X		X		X	X	X	X	X	X	X	X	X	X	X	X	X
Total for 2008:		6	9	11	11	4	11	6	5	11	11	11	4	10	7	7	9	11	11	11	11	11
Number of MLRs for 2008 and 2009[a]: 31	GA7 CA5 11	18	24	30	30	6	27	22	12	30	31	27	10	27	15	27	24	21	21	21	21	21

Notes: [a] Through December 15, 2009. **Key—Structure:** (1) STT=State; (2) BHC=Bank Holding Company; (3) NEW=Institution less than 10 years old. **Capital:** (4) ILL=Inadequate loan loss reserves. **Assets:** (5) RG=Fast rate of growth; (6) CON=Concentrated lending; (7) RHM=Risky home mortgage loans; (8) ADC=Acquisition development and construction lending; (9) CRE=Commercial real estate. **Management:** (10) DOM=Dominant owner, board member, or manager; (11) WBM=Weak board or management; (12) IRC=Inadequate risk controls; (13) UCA=Weak underwriting/credit administration; (14) RIC=Risky incentive compensation; (15) IRS=Inadequate response to supervisory concerns; (16) VLR=Violated laws/regulatio ns. **Earnings:** (17) Misused interest reserves. **Liquidity:** (18) Non core funds; (19) Brokered deposits; (20) FHLB advances.

a problematic business model—funding risky long-term assets with volatile short-term funds. A dominant individual was prominent in 12 of the failures. Inadequate control over risks was blamed in all 31 MLRs. Weak incentive compensation systems that encouraged risky lending were criticized in ten reviews. Inadequate response to concerns expressed by examiners by the failed banks' boards and managers was featured in 27 reports. In 21 cases the boards of directors and managers violated laws and/or regulations. With regard to earnings, banks were criticized for exaggerating earnings, and therefore capital, in 15 MLRs through their abuse of interest reserves.[6] Supervisors and their auditors criticized 27 failed banks for jeopardizing their liquidity by funding long-term assets from volatile noncore sources, such as brokered deposits (cited in 24 MLRs) and Federal Home Loan Bank (FHLB) advances (mentioned in 21 reviews).

In short, the MLRs attribute the 31expensive failures to long-recognized problematic behavior. An Office of Inspector General (OIG) report in 2003, which summarized failures from 1994 through 2003, summarizes four stages of deterioration: (1) weak corporate governance, (2) poor risk management, (3) lending concentration, and (4) failure. The 2009 MLRs reflect these concerns and show little that is new. But supervisors let the banks pursue this well-worn path to failure.

Fast growth, especially in lending for acquisition, development, construction, and for commercial real estate were cited in 27 and 22, of the 31 MLRs, respectively. Management was weak, unable to handle the risks the institutions faced, maintained poor underwriting and credit administration policies and practices, was often dominated by one individual, ignored supervisory concerns, and violated laws and regulations.

Banks exaggerated their earnings and capital by holding insufficient reserves against loan losses, misusing interest reserves, violating accounting rules, and delaying reporting adverse changes. The failed institutions relied on volatile, wholesale sources of funds and were often dependent on brokered deposits and FHLB advances.

2.2   FDIC supervision

Table 1.3 reports the office of the FDIC's IG assessment of the FDIC's supervision of state nonmember banks' high-cost failures. The 31 MLR banks failed with $21 billion in assets and cost the DIF $6.16 billion—a loss rate of 29.4 percent, which is high by historical standards—resolution costs averaged 12 percent of assets from 1980 through 1994 and peaked at 25 percent in 1986 (FDIC, 1998, p. 98–99).

Auditors showed that MLR banks were funding their assets, which were largely risky long-term assets, from volatile, noncore sources. While banks

Table 1.3 FDIC supervision banks failing with material losses

MLRs	1 Year open	2 Change	3 Date failed	4 Assets $m	5 Est. loss $m	6 PCA failed	7 Supervision slow and ineffective	8 Bank allowed to ignore	9 Enforcement actions
Failed in 2009									
America West Bank	2000	2005	5/09	310	119	X	X	X	2:2
Great Basin Bank	1993		4/09	229	39	X	X	X	2:1
Strategic Capital Bank	1999	2004	5/09	537	172	X			0:1
American Southern Bank	2005		4/09	113	42	X	X	X	0:1
Westsound Bank	1999		5/09	324	106	X	X	X	4:1
First, Beverley Hills	1980	2004	4/09	1.3bn	394	X	X		0:1
New Frontier	1998		4/09	1.8bn	609	X	X	X	1:1
Cape Fear	1998		4/09	467	131	X	X	X	3:1
First City Stockbridge	2001		3/09	291	102	X	X	X	1:1
Security Savings	1960	2004	2/09	202	59	X	X	X	1:0
Freedom Commerce	2004		3/09	176	36	X	X	X	0:1
Heritage Community	1969		2/09	228	42	X	X	X	1:1
Sherman County	1932		3/09	127	28	X	X	X	1:1
Corn Belt	1946	1973	3/09	262	101	X	X	X	4:1
FirstBank Fin. Services	2002		2/09	325	112	X	X	X	1:1
Silver Falls Bank	2000		2/09	139	49	X	X	X	1:1
Alliance Bank	1980		2/09	1.2bn	206	X	X	X	1:1
Magnet Bank	2005		1/09	286	119	X	X		2:1

(Continued)

Table 1.3 Continued

MLRs	1 Year open	2 Change	3 Date failed	4 Assets $m	5 Est. loss $m	6 PCA failed	7 Supervision slow and ineffective	8 Bank allowed to ignore	9 Enforcement actions
1st Centennial Bank	1990		1/09	784	215	X			2:0
Bank of Clark County	1999		2/09	468	121	X	X	X	2:2
Total for 2009: 20				**9,568**	**2,802**	**20**	**18**	**15**	**29:20**
Failed in 2008									
Haven Trust	2000		12/08	576	207	X	X		2:0
Community Bank	1946		11/08	653	218	X	X	X	1:1
Franklin Bank	1987		11/08	4.9bn	1.5bn	X	X	X	1:1
Security Pacific	1981	2004	11/08	540	208	X	X	X	0:1
Freedom Bank	2005		10/08	276	93	X	X	X	2:1
Alpha Bank	2006		10/08	335		X	X	X	0:2
Main Street Bank	2004		10/08	102	36	X	X	X	0:2
Silver State Bank	1996	1999	9/08	1.9bn	505	X	X	X	1:2
Integrity Bank	2000		8/08	1.1bn	295	X	X		0:3
Columbian Bank	1978	1990	8/08	726	62	X	X	X	0:1
First Priority Bank	2003		8/08	241	72	X	X	X	1:1
Total for 2008: 11				**11,349**	**3,354**	**11**	**11**	**9**	**8:15**
Overall Total for 2008 and 2009: 31	**1932–2006**			**20,917m**	**6,156m** **29.4%**	**31**	**29**	**24**	**37:35**

Key: (1) Year opened; (2) Year of change of control; (3) Month/year closed; (4) Size (assets); (5) Estimated loss; (6) PCA failed; (7) Follow up/enforcement was slow and/or ineffective; (8) Bank allowed to ignore supervisory concerns; (9) Enforcement actions—informal: formal.

can delay reporting inadequate capital, market discipline can force risky institutions to default through shortages of liquidity. FDICIA contains a provision to prevent weak institutions from dodging this discipline by funding themselves with high-rate brokered deposits, as they had done during the bank and thrift crises of the 1980s and early 1990s.[7] Only well-capitalized banks are permitted to court brokered deposits (unless the FDIC grants a waiver). Yet 27 of the MLR banks relied on volatile sources of funding, 24 of them using high percentages of brokered deposits. Although these institutions were able to maintain well-capitalized designations and so could continue to garner brokered deposits until the last minute, the FDIC Risk Management manual urges examiners not to wait for the PCA restriction on brokered deposits to be triggered, but rather to question the safety and soundness of relying on volatile sources of funding, particularly among new institutions. Yet even after it revised its business plan in 2004, FDIC examiners allowed Main Street Bank to draw 67 percent of its funding from brokered deposits.

Lender of last resort provisions have long been made available to prevent sound banks from failing for lack of liquidity. This is one of the purposes of Federal Reserve discount window lending. Banks became reluctant to use Fed loans during the 1990s, fearing that their borrowing would become public knowledge and that this would tarnish their reputation. Instead, banks came to rely more and more on FHLB advances, which had became available to banks, as well as to savings institutions, that joined the system in the 1990s. Table 1.3 shows that auditors noted heavy reliance on FHLB advances at 21 of the MLR banks. While the FDIC does not discourage the use of FHLB advances in a well-managed funding program, its guidance cautions against abuse of the system, particularly against replacing brokered deposits with advances when a bank's capital level had declined to prevent it from raising brokered deposits. This was the situation at Main Street Bank (MSB) in 2008, which was able to obtain FHLB advances even though it was operating under a Cease and Desist order. FHLB advances represented 31 percent of the estimated loss to the FDIC when MSB failed. FHLB advances are collateralized, as such they increase failure costs to the FDIC when a bank fails because they subordinate the FDIC's position to that of the FHLB at resolution. Advances also subsidize risk taking, because they relax the market discipline that fear of illiquidity imposes. While the FDIC's guidance in the 2000 Risk Manual states that there should be restrictions on advances to institutions without adequate capital, the MLR for MSB could not find any such guidance or regulations to implement this sensible precaution.

In general, the IG auditors considered that the FDIC's examiners almost always identified the failed banks' problems, and reported them to the board and senior management, but failed to follow up to ensure that they were corrected. They were almost universally slow and ineffective in their follow up and enforcement. In 24 cases the board of directors and senior managers were allowed to ignore the many warnings that examiners gave.

Auditors, summarizing, for example, their audit (FDIC OIG, 2009, AUD-09-023, p. 2) of Silver Falls Bank, which was chartered in 2000 and failed in February 2009, noted that "[T]he FDIC has authority to take a wide range of supervisory actions. Earlier supervisory actions may have been warranted to address Silver Fall's elevated risk profile before the problem became severe in 2008." They explained the examiners' delay in taking urgent action as follows: "[B]ecause the bank was reporting high net income and capital along with a low level of adversely classified assets, examiners did not take additional supervisory actions to help address the bank's risks prior to 2008." Similarly, characterizing the supervisory oversight of Haven Bank and Trust, which was founded in 2000 and failed in December 2008, as inadequate, auditors reported (FDIC OIG, 2009, AUD-09-017, p. 17) that "Haven's apparently high level of earnings and apparently adequate capital levels along with an expectation by regulators that bank ownership would infuse capital when needed as they had done in the past, combined to delay effective supervisory actions."

Seven MLR were for de novo banks, which the Fed defines as banks five or less years old and 18 were for banks less than ten years old. Researchers at the OCC and the FDIC have long recognized that new banks fail at higher rates than established banks (De Young and Hassan, 1997) and that they invest in risky real estate assets (Yom, 2003). They are therefore supposed to be given especial attention by examiners and careful off-site monitoring. Extending de novo oversight from three to seven years as recently proposed may not be enough to contain the risks that new institutions pose. One wonders why the researchers' cautionary findings were not forcefully conveyed to examiners, why the OIG's 2003 analysis had scant effect, and why the OIG and researchers at the different regulatory agencies had apparently had such little impact on supervisory practices. The FDIC issued guidance on concentrated commercial real estate lending in December 2006 (FDIC, 2006). This guidance prescribed extra scrutiny of CRE lending but not restrictions on it.[8]

2.3   Peer group analysis

Analysis by comparing a bank with its peer group, appears to weaken the case for remedial action. In boom times, it is a systemic problem when many banks are growing fast, using volatile sources of funding, and investing in risky real estate assets. The banking system is not being supervised adequately when only those institutions that exceed peer group averages are criticized for their behavior.

2.4   Prompt corrective action

Auditors universally judged that the prompt corrective action provisions of the 1991 FDICIA were ineffective. The audit reports typically explained that this was because prompt corrective actions were triggered when banks breached capital thresholds and that capital is a lagging indicator. Referring to the failure of the long-established Community Bank (1946–2008) auditors wrote (AUD-09-016, p. 19), "PCA's focus is on capital, and capital can be a lagging indicator of an institution's financial health as was the case with Community." The audit (FDIC OIG, 2009, AUD-09-021, p. 17) of MagnetBank, chartered in 2005 and failed in 2009, reported that it delayed reporting its decreases in capital, thus thwarting supervisory action and prolonging its access to brokered deposits, which it needed to maintain its liquidity.

Repeatedly the MLRs show that institutions reported artificially high capital levels almost until they failed. They did this by using, for example, interest reserves to make underperforming loans appear to be current, thus avoiding putting aside reserves against them and exaggerating earnings and overestimating capital. Failed banks made inaccurate call reports and ignored supervisory warnings.

One of the notable facts that appeared from reading the reports is that reports of examination and informal enforcement actions failed to remedy the troubled banks' problems and that supervisors refrained from issuing formal enforcement actions almost until the institution failed. The OIG had warned earlier in 2003 that "PCA's focus is on capital, and because capital can be a lagging indicator of an institution's financial health, a banks' capital can remain in the 'well to adequate' range long after its operations have begun to deteriorate from problems with management, asset quality, or internal controls." Registered capital can fall precipitately—MagnetBank's status, for example, fell from well-capitalized to critically under-capitalized between late 2007 and September 2008.

Occasionally an MLR pointed out that supervisors also had discretionary powers to discipline banks through formal and/or informal enforcement actions under FDICIA, but did not use them. The OIG report on MSB notes that, while the primary focus of section 38 of the FDI Act is on capital, as it noted in its 2003 report (FDIC OIG 2003), actions based on other (noncapital) indicators are possible under sections 38 and 39 of the act. Noncapital triggers include problems with (1) operations and management; (2) asset quality, earnings, stock valuation; and/or (3) compensation—all problems documented in the MLRs. The MSB audit notes that "the RM Manual and FIAP Manual have procedures to address section 39 provisions. . . . We found no documented indication that DSC [Department of Supervision and Consumer Protection] considered using noncapital provisions in its supervision of MSB" (p. 23).

The MLRs typically reported that PCA was properly executed, which is surprising because it manifestly failed to achieve its purposes. Institutions maintained their well-capitalized status by overstating their earnings and capital almost until they failed, so the graduated corrective measures were not applied, and institutions continued to garner brokered deposits and rely on FHLB advances. Supervisors refrained from using their discretionary PCA powers to reign in errant banks, as was occasionally noted in the MLRs.

3.   Federal Reserve Material Loss Reviews

One Fed-supervised bank failed with a material loss to the FDIC in 2008, and ten failed with material losses during the first nine months of 2009. The Fed's IG has released only three MLRs on its web site (www.federalreserve.gov/oig), which states that another eight reviews are pending.[9] The FDIC provided a wealth of information on the causes of failure and supervisory deficiencies that it perceived in the 26 MLRs it had conducted through mid-December 2009. The Fed's three MLRs, in contrast, are more summary in nature. The results of these reviews are presented in tables 1.4 and 1.5.

3.1   Causes of failure

The Fed's IG emphasized the decline in the real estate markets as a prime cause of failures among the banks the Fed supervised and noted, for example, in its section on the causes of the failure, "the root causes of Country's failure were (1) a precipitous decline in the local real estate market. . . ." But such analysis misses the point that banks should have been managed to weather a market decline.

The Fed's IG, like the FDIC's (table 1.3), found that all three failed banks maintained inadequate reserves for losses on their assets that were unduly concentrated. One bank focused on residential mortgages and mortgage-backed securities; all three held large portfolios of acquisition, development, and construction loans; and two also concentrated on commercial real estate.

Table 1.4 Causes of failure among state member banks supervised by the Federal Reserve

Institution	Structure			C		Assets							Management					E	Liquidity		
	1 STT	2 BHC	3 NEW	4 ILL	5 FGR	6 CON	7 RHM	8 ADC	9 CRE	10 DOW	11 WBM	12 IRC	13 UCA	14 RIC	15 IRS	16 VLR	17 MIR	18 NCF	19 BRD	20 FHLB Adv
MLRs																				
Failed in 2009																				
County Bank	CA			X		X	X	X	X		X	X	X					X	X	FHLB
Riverside Bank of the Gulf Coast	FL			X		X		X	X									X	X	
Failed in 2008																				
First Georgia Community Bank	GA	X		X	X	X		X			X	X	X		X				X	FHLB
Number of MLRs: 3	3	1		3	1	3	1	3	2	0	2	2	2	0	1	0	0	2	3	2

Key: **Structure:** (1) STT = S-ate; (2) BHC = Bank holding company; (3) NEW = bank less than 10 years old.

Capital: (4) ILL = Inadequate loan loss reserves.

Assets: (5) FGR = Rapid growth; (6) CON = Concentrated lending; (7) RHM = Risky home mortgage loans and mortgage-backed securities; (8) ADC = acquisition, development, and construction loans; (9) CRE = commercial real estate. **Management:** (10) DOW = Dominant owner; (11) WBM = Weak board or management; (12) IRC = Inadequate risk controls; (13) UCA = Weak underwriting/credit administration. (14) RIC = Risky incentive compensation; (15) IRS = Inadequate response to supervisory concerns. (16) VLR = Violated laws/regulations.

Earnings: (17) Misuse of interest reserves.

Liquidity: (18) Non core funds; (19) Brokered deposits; (20) FHLB advances.

Table 1.5 Federal Reserve supervision of banks failing with material losses

MLRs	1 Year open	2 Change	3 Date failed	4 Assets $m	5 Est. loss $m	6 PCA failed	7 Supervision slow and ineffective	8 Bank allowed to ignore	9 Guidelines ignored	10 Enforce actions
Failed in 2009[a]										
County Bank	1997		2/09	1,692	136	X	X	X	X	0:2
Riverside Bank of the Gulf Coast	1997		2/09	537	202	X	X	X	X	0:2
Total for 2009[a]										
Failed in 2008										
First Georgia Community Bank	1997		12/08	229	72	X	X	X	X	3:1
Total				**2,458**	**410** **16.7%**	**3**	**3**	**3**	**3**	**3:5**
MLRs Pending										
Michigan Heritage Bank	1997		4/09	161	68					1
Community Bank of West Georgia	1997		6/09	200	85					1
Neighborhood Community Bank	2000		6/09	210	67					
Bank First	n.a.	2005	7/09	246	90					

Community First Bank	n.a.		8/09	200	44
Community Bank of NV	1995	2002	8/09	1,500	767
Capital South Bank	n.a.		8/09	589	146
Irwin Union B&T	1928		9/09	2,701	622	1
Total Material Losses: 11				**8,165**	**2,299**
					28.2%

Note: [a] Data published by December 20, 2009.

Key: (1) Year opened; (2) Year of change of control or supervision; (3) Month/year closed; (4) Size (assets); (5) Estimated loss; (6) PCA was followed but failed; (7) Supervisory follow up/enforcement was slow and/or ineffective; (8) Bankers were allowed to ignore supervisory concerns; (9) Supervisory rules or guidelines were not followed; (10) Number of informal enforcement actions: number of formal enforcement actions.

Fast growth was perceived as less frequent a problem than among FDIC-supervised banks. Management and boards were judged to be weak—unable to control risks—conducting inadequate underwriting and credit administration, although not dominated by individuals. There was no mention of violations of laws or regulations, or inadequate accounting, or overstatement of earnings. Like the FDIC reviews, the Fed MLRs perceived liquidity to be a problem with heavy reliance on volatile sources of funds, such as brokered deposits, and also on FHLB advances.

3.2   Federal Reserve supervision

The IG assessments placed much of the blame for the failures on the sudden real estate bust and economic downturn, whose possibilities supervisors did not consider when they compared institutions' exposures to those of their peers. Nevertheless, as shown in table 1.5, all three MLRs considered that supervisors had not been sufficiently aggressive in addressing the failed banks' weaknesses, and that supervisors ignored their own rules and guidelines, especially in allowing these banks to ignore supervisory warnings. Enforcement actions were issued late (too late) in the process of failing bank deterioration.

The IG considered that PCA mandates had been followed, despite the fact supervisors did not use the discretion they had under PCA in Sections 131 and 132 of FDICIA to reign in unsafe and unsound practices and avoid losses to the Deposit Insurance Fund (DIF).

4.   Treasury Department Reviews of OCC-Supervised Banks

By mid-December 2009, the Treasury Department's IG had published seven MLRs of OCC-supervised banks that had failed in the period 2007 through March 2009.

4.1   Causes of failure

The findings show similarities with those of the FDIC's and Federal Reserve's IGs. Table 1.6 shows that capital and earnings were typically overstated by inaccurate accounting and inadequate loan loss reserves (called allowances for loan and lease losses or ALL), and in two instances by misuse of interest reserves. Asset portfolios had been increasing rapidly and were heavily concentrated—in commercial real estate in five of the cases.[10] Incentive compensation schemes were faulted in three instances.

Table 1.6 Causes of failure among national banks supervised by the OCC

Institution	Structure				C	Assets	Management								E		L
MLRs	1	2	3	4	5	6	7	8	9	10	11	12	13	14	15	16	17
Reviews of Banks that Failed in 2009[a]	STT	BHC	NEW	ILL	FGR	CONW	DOW	WBM	UCA	WRM	RIC	IRS	VLR	LVE	ACC	MIR	NCF
Omni National Bank		X		X	X	CRE	X	X	X	X		X	X	X	X	X	BD
Team Bank	KS	2		X	X	MBSCRE	X	X	X	X	X			X	X		BDFHLB
Ocala Bank	FL	1		X	X	RHMADCCRE	X	X	X	X	?	X	X	X			BDFHLB
National Commerce Bank	IL	1				GSE											
First National Bank	NV	2		X	X	RHMCRE	X	X	X	X	X	X	X	X	X		BD
Heritage Bank	CA	2		X	X	FdFCRE	X	X	X	X		X	X	X	X	X	

(Continued)

Table 1.6   Continued

Institution	Structure	C	Assets	Management							E	L
Failed in 2008												
ANB Financial	AK	1	X X	A D C C R E	X X X X	X X						B D F H L B
Number MLRs: 7		6	6	5 6 6 6	3 4 5 6						2	5 B D 3 F H L B

Note: ᵃ Data published by December 20, 2009.
Key: **Structure:** 1. STT = State; 2. BHC = Bank Holding Company; 3. NEW = Bank less than 10 years old. **Capital:** 4. ILL = Inadequate loan loss reserves (allowance for loan and lease losses). **Assets:** 5. FGR = Fast growth rate; 6. CON = Concentrated lending in—MBS = Mortgage-backed securities, RHM = Risky home mortgage loans, ADC = Acquisition, development, and construction loans, CRE = Commercial real estate lending, GSE = government sponsored enterprise securities, or FdF = federal funds. **Management:** 7. DOM = Dominant owner/manager; 8. WBM = Weak board or management; 9. Weak underwriting and credit administration; 10. Weak risk management; 11. RIC = Risky incentive compensation; 12. IRS = Inadequate response to supervisory concerns. 13. VLR = Violated laws/regulations. **Earnings:** 14. = Low and/or volatile earnings; 15. ACC = Accounting errors/violations; 16. Misused interest reserves. **Liquidity:** 17. Reliance on Non Core Funding, such as BD = Brokered Deposits; and 20. FHLB Advances = Federal home loan bank advances.

Management was typically dominated by one individual, had inadequate control over risks, maintained weak underwriting and credit administration policies and practices, and was found to be unresponsive to supervisory criticism in four of the failures. Liquidity was threatened by reliance on volatile sources of funding—frequently brokered deposits, which were sometimes supplemented by FHLB advances.

4.2   Assessment of OCC supervision

Table 1.7 shows that OCC's failed MLR banks were estimated to have cost the DIF $1.5 billion. The MLRs considered that supervisors in all but one case (Omni Bank) identified the weaknesses in each of the failed banks and reported them to the bank's board and management as matters requiring

Table 1.7 OCC supervision of banks failing with material losses

MLRs failed in 2009	1 Year open	2	3 Date failed	4 Assets $m	5 Est. loss $m	6 Failed to follow up	7 Slow not effective	8 Weak work papers	9 Failed to enforce laws/regs	10 Enforcement actions
Omni National Bank	1992	2000	3/09	937	288	MissX	X	X	X	0:1
Team Bank	1885	1997	3/09	670	98	X	X	X	X	0:1
Ocala Bank	1986	1997	1/09	224	100	X	X	X	X	0:2
National Commerce	1956	1984	1/09	431	92			X	X	0:0
First National Bank	1937	2001	7/09	3.4bn	706	X	X	X	X	0:3
Heritage Bank	2005		7/09	254	33		X	X	X	0:1
Total: 6				**5,916**	**1,317**	**4**	**5**	**6**	**5**	**0:8**
Failed in 2008										
ANB Financial	1954	2003	5/08	2.1bn	214	X	X	X	X	0:2
Total **Number: 7**				**8,016**	**1,531** **19.1%**	**5**	**6**	**7**	**6**	**0:10**

Key: (1) Year opened; (2) Year of change of control or supervisor; (3) Month/year closed; (4) Size (assets); (5) Estimated loss; (6) Supervisors failed to follow up; (7) Enforcement was slow and/or ineffective; (8) Weak examiner work papers; (9) Supervisors failed to enforce laws or regulations; (10) Informal: formal enforcement actions.

attention (MRAs), which were the OCC's preferred supervisory tool. OCC undertook no informal enforcement actions against banks that later failed with material losses to the DIF. (In Omni's case red flags were missed from 2003 through 2007 by an examiner-in-charge who was responsible for the bank throughout the period.) Unfortunately, the banks typically ignored these warnings and supervisors failed to follow them up and so were slow and ineffective in their oversight. Not only were there no informal enforcement actions against these failed banks, but formal actions were typically delayed until the bank was about to be closed. The IG criticized the agency for delaying formal action against Omni Bank, but OCC management rejected the criticism and maintained that it needed the time it took to justify and document the need for formal action. The IG in turn disagreed with the OCC and instead took into consideration that prompt corrective action was delayed by six months as a result.

With regard to Omni Bank, the MLR (Department of the Treasury, Office of the Insopector General, Audit Report OIG-10-016, p. 23) noted that for several years the OCC's examiner missed "excessive growth, a risky product and clientele, geographic expansion," which had long been recognized by the agency as red flags. Neither did he note that the bank was replacing foreclosed loans with larger loans to hide the losses. Nevertheless, OCC management disagreed with the IG that more timely enforcement action had been needed for Omni Bank, which had relied on appreciation for repayment of its loans and submitted inaccurate call reports.[11] The PCA actions the agency took were judged to be correct based on the false call reports. Even then they were delayed for six months by a disagreement with the external auditor. Formal enforcement action was delayed to obtain legal support for its actions until October 2008, just days before the bank was closed, even though a new examiner had recommended it in February.

It is perhaps ominous for the hopes of supervisory improvement in the future that John Dugan, Comptroller of the Currency, when responding to the MLR for Omni Bank, rejected the IG's criticism of the agency's delay in taking enforcement action (Department of the Treasury, Office of the Inspector General, Audit Report OIG-10-016, p. 59). "Again, I agree that it is absolutely critical that enforcement actions are timely. I do not agree, however, that the facts of this case support a conclusion that the OCC process used to issue the consent order, in response to the 2008 examination findings, was slow and requires review."

5.   Treasury Department's MLRs of OTS-Supervised Banks

The Treasury Department's Office of the IG had, by mid December 2009, published seven MLRs for thrifts that have failed since the beginning of 2007.

These have been expensive failures, with estimated losses of $13 billion to the DIF. The three most expensive failures were California thrifts, including IndyMac and Downey Savings. The failed thrifts typically belonged to a holding company and grew rapidly in the years before they failed. Table 1.8 reports that management and boards were universally judged to be weak, unable to control risk or ensure good underwriting and credit administration policies and practices. They were unresponsive to supervisory concerns expressed to them in reports of examination. Incentive compensation schemes were judged to have contributed to three of the thrifts' problems. Assets were heavily concentrated, especially on risky types of residential mortgages, which were intended to be converted into mortgage-backed securities until this market collapsed. Lending for commercial real estate and acquisition and development were less of a problem than for the banks (except for one MLR thrift).

Capital and earnings were overstated in a number of ways that ranged from overvaluing assets, accounting violations, holding insufficient reserves against losses, misusing interest reserves, and backdating capital contributions from the holding company (Department of Treasury, OIG, 2009). Such actions thwarted PCA by allowing thrifts to be treated as well-capitalized, free from regulatory restraint and able to garner brokered deposits, on which they were heavily dependent, without the otherwise necessary FDIC waiver, almost until they failed. FHLB advances were important to three of the failed thrifts.

5.1   OTS supervision

The OIG considered that examiners spotted failed thrifts' problems in six of the seven cases, as shown in Table 1.9. Management was warned but allowed to ignore the warnings. In one case, however the examiner who was in charge for four years missed the red flags and failed to point them out to management. Supervisors failed to enforce laws or regulations or failed to follow agency guidance according to five of the MLRs. OTS did utilize informal enforcement actions, but again, they reserved formal action until the thrift was about to be closed. The MLR for IndyMac criticized OTS's handling of the failed bank and stated that it should have taken PCA earlier. It noted (Department of the Treasury, FSB OIG-09-032, p. 15), "OTS's West Region officials and examiners believed their supervision was adequate. We disagree."

In the case of American Sterling Bank, the MLR noted (Department of the Treasury, OIG-10-011, p. 2) "the thrift's inaccurate financial reporting delayed OTS from taking required PCA as the thrift's capital was depleted. Prompt corrective action was thwarted across the supervisory board, but

Table 1.8 Causes of failure among federal thrifts supervised by the OTS

Institution	Structure		C		Assets			Management						E			L
	1	2	3	4	5	6	7	8	9	10	11	12	13	14	15	16	17
MLRs	ST	THC	NEW	ILL	FGR	CONC	DOW	WBM	UCA	WRM	RIC	IRS	VLR	LVE	ACC	MIR	NCF
Failed in 2009																	
American Sterling	MO	X	C	X	X	MBS	X	X	X	X	X	X		X	X	X	BD, FHLB
Suburban Federal	MD		C	X	X		X	X	X	X	X	X	X		X		
Failed in 2008																	
Downey Savings	CA	X		X	X	RES MBS		X	X	X	X	X		X	X	X	BD
PFF Bank and Trust	CA	X 2		X	X	ADC CRE		X	X	X		X					

		(1)	(2)	(3)	(4)	(5)	(6) CON	(7)	(8)	(9)	(10)	(11)	(12)	(13)	(14)	(15)	(16)	(17)
Ameribank	WV	X₁	C	X	X	X	X	FES	X	X	X	X	X	X	X	X		BD FHLB
IndyMac	CA	X₁	C	X	X	X	X	RESMBS	X	X	X	X	X	X	X			BD FHLB
Failed in 2007																		
NetBank	GA	X₁	C	X		X	X	MBS	X	X	X	X	X		X	X		INT
No. MLRs: 7		6	5	7	3	7	7		7	2	3	7	2	5	6	2		

Key: **Structure:** (1) STT = State; (2) THC = Thrift Holding Company; (3) NEW = Less than 10 years old or changed.

Capital: (4) ILL = Inadequate loan loss reserves.

Assets: (5) FGR = Fast growth rate; (6.) CON = Concentrated lending in MBS = Mortgage-Backed Securities, RHM = Risky Home Mortgage loans, ADC = Acquisition, Development, Construction loans, CRE = Commercial Real Estate lending, GSE = government sponsored enterprise securities, FdF = federal funds.

Management: (7) DOM = Dominant Owner/Manager; (8) WBM = Weak Board or Management; (9) UCA = Weak underwriting and credit administration; (10) WRM = Weak Risk Management; (11) RIC = Risky Incentive Compensation; (12) IRS = Inadequate Response to Supervisory concerns; (13) VLR = Violated laws/regulations.

Earnings: (14) = Low and/or Volatile Earnings; (15) ACC = Accounting errors/violations; (16) Misused interest reserves.

Liquidity: (17) Reliance on Non Core Funding, such as BD = Brokered Deposits, INT = internet deposits, FHLB = FHLB advances.

Table 1.9 OTS supervision of thrifts failing with material losses

MLRs Failed in 2009[a]	1 Year Open	2 Change	3 Date Failed	4 Assets $m	5 Est. Loss $m	6 Failed to follow up	7 Slow, not effective	8 Bank allowed to ignore	9 Weak Work Papers	10 Failed to enforce Laws/reg	11 Actions
American Sterling	1907	1999 2006	4/09	181	42	Late seeing	X	Not told to change		X	0:3
Suburban Federal	1954	2003/4	1/09	360	126	X	X	X			1:1
Total for 2009a: 2				**541**	**168**						
Failed in 2008											
Downey Savings	1957	1994	11/08	42.8b	1.4b	X	X	X	X	X	1:2
PFF Bank and Trust	1892	1996	11/08	3.7b	730	X	X	X	X	X	6:1
Ameribank	1997	2003	9/08	115	33	X	X	X	X	X	1:2
IndyMac	2000		7/08	32.0b	10.7b	X	X	X		X	1:1
Total: 4											
Failed in 2007											
NetBank	1988	1996	9/07	25b	108	X	X	X		X	0:1
Total/Number		**2001**		**104.2bn**	**13.14bn**	**6**	**6**	**6**	**3**	**5**	**10:11**

Note: [a] Data published by December 20, 2009.

Key: 1. Year opened; 2. Year of change of control or supervisor; 3. Month/year closed; 4. Size (assets); 5. Estimated loss; 6. Supervisors failed to follow up; 7. Supervision was slow and/or ineffective; 8. Bank was allowed to ignore supervisory concerns; 9. Work papers were insufficient; 10. Supervisors failed to enforce laws or regulations or to follow agency guidance; 11. Enforcement actions—informal: formal.

this exercise was particularly egregious at OTS, where senior officers permitted/required capital contributions from the holding company to be back-dated to allow the deteriorating thrift to be falsely regarded as well-capitalized. The OIG report (Department of the Treasury, OIG -09-037, p. 15 explained the significance of the back-dating for IndyMac as follows:

> The impact of OTS's approval to record the capital contribution in the quarter ending March 31, 2008, was that IndyMac was able to maintain its "well-capitalized" status, and avoid the requirement in law to obtain a waiver from FDIC to accept brokered deposits. It also solved another problem in that the independent auditor had advised IndyMac management that without IndyMac's acceptance of several proposed adjustments relating to the thrift's capitalization, the independent auditor would not have signed-off on the interim review. IndyMac needed the signed interim review in order to file a complete quarterly report (10Q), as required, with the Securities and Exchange Commission on May 15, 2008.

On page 19 of the report the OIG explained the significance of back-dating to another of five thrifts—unnamed because they were still operating—that had been found to have backdated capital contributions.

> The CFO also stated that the potential ramifications of filing the June 30 TFR as adequately capitalized, combined with the significant losses and elevated volume of classified assets, could create a liquidity crisis and materially impact the thrift's future viability. The CFO told the examiners that it was imperative that the thrift's well-capitalized status be maintained in order to have access to the broker deposit market for liquidity purposes.

6. Conclusions

Newspapers have focused on risky home mortgages and the collapse of the mortgage-backed securities markets as a major cause of bank and thrift failures. But MLRs for banks supervised by the FDIC, the Fed, and the OCC point to other aspects of the real estate markets as generating failures—lending for acquisition, construction, and real estate development and for commercial real estate, especially in fast growing bank portfolios. Fast growth, especially in the real estate markets, has long been internationally seen as a red flag (Lindgren, Garcia, and Saal, 1996).

Clearly the regulators did not perceive—or if they perceived, did not act on their perception—that the U.S. banking sector as a whole was over exposed to the real estate markets. Supervision by peer comparison—universally practiced by the supervisory agencies—contributed to missing this macro red flag. If everyone was doing something—ACD or CRE lending, funding by brokered deposits or FHLB advances—supervisors judged it to be acceptable. Only if an institutions stood out as undertaking a lot more (or possibly in some cases less) of it, was it seen as a cause for concern. Supervision by peer comparison needs to be rethought if supervision is, in future, to consider the banking sector as a whole instead of focusing on individual institutions.

A surprising number of new FDIC-supervised banks failed. Agencies typically monitored de novo banks more closely than older banks for three years, although the FDIC recently extended this more intensive oversight to seven years. But a number of the MLR banks had been opened almost ten years previously. Is seven years of extensive oversight sufficient?

Bankers have always had incentives to make themselves appear stronger than they really are, but PCA gave them a specific target to aim at in order to retain their well-capitalized designation and so avoid PCA's staggered restrictions for increasingly inadequate levels of measured capital. It is well known that capital is a lagging indicator that can delay supervisory action beyond the point that it is needed.[12] For this reason, Congress gave supervisors discretion to act in FDICIA, and these powers are embodied in Sections 38 and 39 of the FDI Act. But supervisors did not use them to reign in the abuses they observed at the MLR institutions.

Institutions knew how to manipulate their capital levels to avoid triggering the PCA provisions of FDICIA. FDI supervisors allowed them to do so by ignoring their discretionary powers to call troubled institutions to order. MLRs typically found that supervisors abided by PCA's mandatory rules; only rarely did an IG point out that supervisors had ignored their discretionary powers to reign in excessively risky or deceptive activities. Instead of using them, supervisors argued that they could not act because institutions appeared to be profitable and well-capitalized. OTS supervisors even connived to keep capital appearing at well-capitalized levels by allowing, even requiring, capital contributions from the holding company to be backdated. In addition, the OCC avoided using informal action against errant institutions, preferring instead to advise a bank's board and management of any changes that needed to be made.

The European Union (EU) has been attracted to the concept of PCA and is considering adopting it (Garcia, Lastra, and Nieto, 2009). Before it does so, it should draw lessons from the failure of PCA in the United States. It should design its own PCA scheme appropriately. Importantly supervisors' incentives need to be changed, both in the EU and the United States so that they better reflect the public interest and they need to be held to account for their actions as Kane (1996, 1998) has long argued.

* The author is a consultant in financial services. An earlier version of this paper was presented at the International Business, Economics, and Finance Association/Western Economic Association Meetings in Vancouver in July 2009. The author thanks George Blackford, Andrew Campbell, Robert Eisenbeis, George Kaufman, Raymond LaBrosse, Joseph Mason, and Maria Nieto for comments on an earlier draft of this paper, but remains responsible for any errors.

Notes

1. Currently, the OCC supervises national banks. Banks chartered by the states are overseen by their state regulator, while state banks that are members of the Federal Reserve System are also supervised by the Fed. State nonmember banks and savings banks report to the FDIC. The OTS supervises federal and most state-chartered savings associations.

2. The paper does not examine supervisory red flags overlooked by the Fed in its oversight of financial holding companies, the Securities and Exchange Commission (SEC), or the Commodity Futures Exchange Commission (CFTC), nor the problems in the insurance industry exacerbated, perhaps, by the absence of a federal insurance supervisor.

3. See, for example, Paletta (2009).

4. See, for example, Milbank (2009).

5. See http://www.fdicoig.gov/MLR.shtml.

6. A bank may lend to fund construction and also to allow the borrower to pay the interest that falls due during the period before the project earns revenue. Such an interest reserve may be misused to obscure problems in the construction project—problems that the bank should recognize by classifying the loan as nonperforming. For example, auditors wrote (FDIC OIG, 2009, AUD-09-008, p. 16–17) that interest reserves at Silver State Bank "allowed borrowers to fund their interest payments through a borrowing line with the bank. . . . SSB was masking the borrowers' inability to meet their repayment obligations and was allowing borrowers to draw on the reserves until they were depleted even if the intended real estate development project had ceased. In addition, the interest reserve loans were being modified and extended to bring potentially delinquent borrowers current."

7. This provision is captured in Section 2000, Part 337.6 on *Brokered Deposits* in the FDIC's *Rules and Regulations*.

8. See 365-2 of FDIC *Rules and Regulations* Interagency Guidelines for RE Lending Policies.

9. MLRs are pending for Michigan Heritage Bank, Community Bank of West Georgia, Neighborhood Community Bank (GA), First Bank (SD), Community First Bank (OR), Community Bank of Nevada, Capital South Bank (AL), and Irwin Union Bank and Trust (IN).

10. National Commerce Bank failed by concentrating on what it thought were safe government-sponsored-entity (GSE) securities.

11. The bank's failure imposed not only a $288m loss to the DIF but also a $1 million loss to the FDIC's Transaction Account Guarantee Program.
12. The MLR for Westsound Bank noted in the Executive Summary (p. 3), "PCA did not require action until the institution was at serious risk of failure."

References

Carnell, Richard S. (1993). "The Culture of Ad Hoc Discretion," in *FDICIA One Year Later*, ed. G. Kaufman and R. Litan (Washington, DC, The Brookings Institution), 113–121.

Department of the Treasury, Office of the Inspector General (2009). *Audit Report: Safety and Soundness: OTS Involvement with Backdated Capital Contributions by Thrifts*. OIG-09-037, May 21.

—— (2009). *Safety and Soundness: Material Loss Review of Omni National Bank*. OIG-10-016, December 9, at www.ustreas.gov/inspector-general/audit-reports/2010/OIG10017%20(Omni%20MLR).pdf, accessed December 21, 2009.

—— (2009). *Safety and Soundness: Material Loss Review of American Sterling Bank*, OIG-10-011, December 9, at www.ustreas.gov/inspector-general/audit-reports/2010/OIG10011%20(American%20Sterling%20MLR).pdf (accessed December 21, 2009).

—— (2009). *Safety and Soundness: Material Loss Review of IndyMac Bank, FSB*, OIG-09-032, at www.ustreas.gov/inspector-general/audit-reports/2009/oig09032.pdf (accessed December 21 2009).

De Young, Robert, and Hekkar Hasan (1997). "The Performance of De Novo Commercial Banks," Office of the Comptroller of the Currency, E&PA Working Paper 97-3, February.

Eisenbeis, Robert A., and Larry D. Wall (2002). "The Major Supervisory Initiatives Post FDICIA: Are They Based on the Goals of PCA? Should They Be?" In *Prompt Corrective Action in Banking: 10 Years Later*, edited by George G. Kaufman (Greenwich, CT, JAI Press), pp. 109–42.

FDIC, Division of Supervision and Consumer Protection. *Risk Management Manual*.

——. *Formal and Informal Action Procedures Manual* at www.fdic.gov.

——. (1998). *The FDIC and RTC Experience: Managing the Crisis* (Washington, DC, Federal Deposit Insurance Corporation).

FDIC, Office of Inspector General (2004). *Observations from FDIC OIG Material Loss Reviews Conducted 1993 through 2003*, Report No. 04-004, January 22, 2004, at www.fdic.gov/reports04/04-004.pdf (accessed November 22, 2009).

—— (2009). Material Loss Review of Silver Falls Bank, Silverton, Oregon, Report No. AUD-09-023, September.

—— (2009). Material Loss Review of Haven Bank and Trust, Duluth, GA, Report No. AUD-09-017, August.

—— (2009). Material Loss Review of MagnetBank, Salt Lake City, UT, Report No. AUD-09-021, August.

———— (2009). Material Loss Review of Silver State Bank, Hendersen, NV, Report No. AUD-09-008. March.

———— (2003). *The Role of Prompt Corrective Action as Part of the Enforcement Process*, OIG Report No. 03-038, September 12.

———— (2006). *Guidance on Concentration on Commercial Real Estates Lending: Sound Risk Management Practices*, Financial Institution Letter, 104-2006, December 12.

Fisher, Richard W. (2009). "Comments on the Current Financial Crisis," Remarks before the 2009 Global Supply Chain Conference, Fort Worth, TX, March 4.

Garcia, Gillian G. H., Rosa M. Lastra, and Maria J. Nieto (2009). "Bankruptcy and Reorganization Procedures for Cross-Border Banks in the EU: Towards an Integrated Approach to the Reform of the EU Safety Net," *Journal of Financial Regulation and Compliance* 17, no. 3, pp. 240–276.

Kane, Edward J. (1998). "Financial Reform as a as a Market-Constrained Political Process," Boston College Working Paper.

———— (1996). "The Opportunity Cost of Capital Forbearance during the Final Years of the FSLIC Mess," *Quarterly Review of Economics and Finance* 36, no.3. (Fall).

Kaufman, George G. (2004). "FDIC Losses in Bank Failures: Has FDICIA Made a Difference?" Federal Reserve Bank of Chicago *Economic Perspectives*, Third Quarter, pp. 13–25.

———— (2002). *Prompt Corrective Action in Banking: 10 Years Later*. Vol. 14. *Research in Financial Services: Private and Public Policy* (Stamford, CT, JAI Press).

Lindgren, Carl Johan, Gillian Garcia, and Matthew Saal (1996). *Bank Soundness and Macroeconomic Policy* (Washington, DC, International Monetary Fund).

Milbank, Dana (2009). "Bankers Make Turkeys out of Taxpayers," *Washington Post*, November 25, p. A2.

Paletta, Damian (2009). "Agencies in a Brawl for Control over Banks," *The Wall Street Journal*, Friday, December 18, pp. A1 and A22.

Yom, Chiwon, (2003). "Recently Chartered Banks' Vulnerability to Real Estate Crisis," FDIC Banking Review.

2

Too Much Right Can Make a Wrong: Setting the Stage for the US Financial Crisis

*Richard J. Rosen**

Abstract

The financial crisis that started in 2007 exposed a number of flaws in the financial system. Many of these flaws were associated with financial instruments that were issued by the shadow banking system, especially securitized assets. The volume and complexity of securitized assets grew rapidly during the run-up to the financial crisis that began in 2007. This chapter discusses how the financial crisis can be viewed as a possible but logical outcome of a system where investors are overconfident, busy, and investing other peoples' money and intermediaries are set up to take advantage of investors' tendencies. The investor-intermediary risk cycle in this crisis is common to other crises. However, there are a number of factors that may have made the 2007 crisis more severe. Among them are the length of the precrisis period, the shift from financial intermediaries to the shadow banking system, the increasing interconnectedness among financial firms, and the increased leverage at some financial firms.

Introduction

The financial crisis that began in 2007 may change the way firms and individuals borrow and save. The period leading up to the crisis was one where there was a rapidly expanding array of products that facilitated funds getting from savers to borrowers. At least, in part because of these

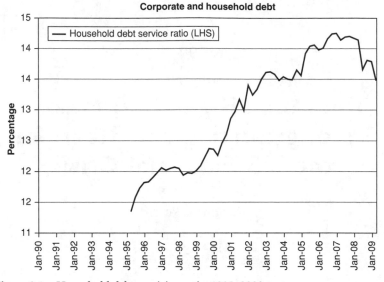

Figure 2.1   Household debt servicing ratio, 1995–2008

products, it became easy to borrow, leading to an expansion of debt (fig. 2.1 shows the growth in consumer indebtedness). In retrospect, it appears that many borrowers were given loans they should not have been or were given loans at interest rates that were too low to reflect the riskiness of the loan. The financial crisis brought a swift halt to this. In this paper, I describe the changes that preceded the crisis, then examine why they occurred and how they may have contributed to the crisis.

Much of the evolution of financial markets and institutions in recent years resulted in the movement of financing away from traditional bank lending (see, e.g., Adrian and Shin, 2009; Brunnermeier, 2009). Many of the new alternatives for borrowers and investors came, directly or indirectly, from what is sometimes called the shadow banking system (SBS).[1] The SBS is the term used for financial institutions that provide alternatives to traditional bank financing.[2] These firms can intermediate between borrowers and lenders, much as banks do. However, they offer a more complex array of products than just simple loans, and they are often subject to less intensive regulation.

As part of the move from bank financing to the SBS, one way that financial markets changed dramatically from the mid-1980s through the onset of the financial crisis in 2007 was in the rise of structured finance. While there is no single definition of structured finance, here I focus mainly on securitization (most market participants consider credit derivatives and other structured risk transfer products as part of structured finance, see, e.g., Davis, 2005). Securitization is the issuance of bonds backed by the payments on a pool of assets. It allows banks and other lenders to originate assets without the need to hold them on their balance sheets for an extended period of time. The initial securitizations involved pools of home mortgages, with the bonds issued called mortgage-backed securities (MBS). MBS were soon followed by so-called asset-backed securities (ABS), which were bonds backed by the payments on pools of loans such as automobile and credit card loans. In the last twenty years, the types of assets that were part of securitizations expanded to include large corporate loans and mortgages as well as more obscure assets (there was a securitization backed by the royalties on recordings by David Bowie). There have also been securitizations that are backed by the payments on pools of securitized bonds from different deals (collateralized debt obligations, or CDOs). The ability of lenders to easily sell loans into securitizations made the "originate-to-distribute" (OTD) business model possible. Instead of making a loan and holding it on its balance sheet until maturity, a lender could make (originate) a loan, then immediately sell it.

The ability of lenders to use the OTD model is frequently cited as one of the factors that contributed to the financial crisis. One argument goes as follows (Diamond and Rajan, 2009). A glut of foreign savings with a desire for safe securities led to an increase in demand for bonds such as highly rated MBS (and ABS) securities. The demand for these securities gave banks an incentive to create them by originating and selling loans. Problems crept into valuations, but rising home prices covered up these problems and allowed lenders to keep originating and selling new loans. When home prices started falling, losses became apparent. Since many holders of MBS, including banks and derivative conduits such as structured investment vehicles (SIVs)[3], were either leveraged (Adrian and Shin, 2008) or held longer-term assets along with short-term liabilities (Brunnermeier, 2009; Diamond and Rajan, 2009), the home price declines led to questions about the institutions viability. This, in turn, might have sparked a run on these institutions (Gorton and Metrick, 2009). Hidden in this line of thinking is why, as noted above, mispricing crept into valuations. In other words, why did the problems that followed once housing prices started to fall seem to surprise so many market participants? I explore why several tendencies of investors, and the ability of intermediaries to take advantage of these tendencies, may have made seemingly surprising deviations of prices from fundamentals more likely.

The SBS facilitated innovations such as the advances in securitization, but many of the innovations shifted the responsibility for screening and monitoring borrowers from lenders to investors in securitized bonds.

Traditionally, much intermediated finance was done by banks.[4] A bank would make a loan that would be financed with a combination of equity capital and deposits. The bank, because it kept the loan on its balance sheet, would have an incentive to screen potential borrowers to make sure they were creditworthy and to monitor the loan to maximize the chance it got repaid. Many of the new products facilitated by the SBS shifted some of this responsibility from banks to investors. This introduced two possible problems. First, investors were at least one step further removed from the actual lending decisions, making their ability to screen and monitor more difficult. Second, many of the investors in securities made available by the SBS were, in fact, agents for other investors, leading to potential incentive problems. I discuss how these two potential problems, especially following a long period of stability and growth in the financial system, can make a crisis more likely.

Why would the financially sophisticated investors that participate in structured finance markets be willing to purchase extremely complicated securities? The strong performance of structured finance in general gave three incentives for investors to purchase structured securities such as securitized bonds. First, behavioral finance has identified a number of circumstances where overconfidence affected investor decision making (see, e.g., Malmendier and Tate, 2005). The high returns on structured securities in the run-up to the crisis may have led investors to believe the securities were better than they actually were. Second, the credit ratings on these securities had proved reliable in the (recent) past (see, e.g., Moody's, 2006). It may have been rational for busy investors to rely on the recent track record of the securities and the rating agencies rather than to carefully examine each security they planned to purchase. Finally, many of these investors were investing for others (such as mutual fund managers acting on behalf of their fund investors), and this gave them an incentive to reach for yield and to follow the herd (see, e.g., Scharfstein and Stein, 1990, on herd behavior in Wall Street).

The factors that attracted investors to structured securities such as MBS could also explain some of the evolution of the securitization market over time. As noted above, securitizations became more complex over time. This is consistent with the intermediaries involved in issuing structure securities taking advantage of overconfidence and (rational) inattention, since overconfident investors are likely to believe they can evaluate the more complicated securities and inattentive investors are unlikely to notice as securities become gradually more complicated as long as credit rating agencies continue to give them strong ratings.

An important question in thinking about how to reform the financial system is whether the conditions and actions that led up to the crisis are quantitatively different from other incidents that did not lead to a worldwide crisis. The pattern in the years leading up to the crisis was that investors successfully invested in new securities, often ones promising them extra returns. The successful investments led to new investments and an increased reliance on simple guideposts. The investors were pushed toward similar but riskier investments by issuers or advisors. Finally, there was a reckoning as many of the risky securities saw a sharp decline in value. This investor-intermediary risk cycle fits not only the most recent crisis, but a number of prior examples such as the Asian currency crises in the late 1990s. Thus, the current crisis may have been more extreme than prior incidents, but a number of the factors that led to it were also present in previous incidents.

The remainder of the chapter is organized as follows. The next section gives some background on the U.S. financial system and its evolution. There is a particular focus on lending and the role of the SBS. In Section 2, I discuss why investors would buy securities that do not have a positive expected return. After that, I explore whether the run-up to the 2007 crisis was fundamentally different from anything in the past. Finally, Section 4 offers some concluding comments.

1.   Background

This section gives some background on how the evolution of financial institutions and markets in the United States set the stage for the financial crisis. I start with a basic comparison of intermediated versus market-based financing and then discuss the specifics for the United States. Understanding the rise of the SBS means understanding both the financial system structure and the incentives of the participants in the financial system. The structure and incentives in 2006 arose in part because of choices made in the last major crisis in the 1930s.

The traditional role of banks is transforming deposits into loans. Depositors and other bank liability holders generally value liquidity, so most bank liabilities are short term. Borrowers, on the other hand, often want longer-term loans. This mismatch between the desired maturities of savers and borrowers leaves a role for financial intermediaries such as banks. Banks are able to manage balance sheets with many assets and liabilities of different maturities. This allows them to transform short-term liabilities into long-term loans (and small deposits into large loans). A value added from having banks do asset transformation is that they are set up to screen potential borrowers and then to monitor the borrowers they eventually lend to.

In contrast to the traditional role of banks, the traditional role of other financial market participants such as investment banks and securities dealers is to help the sale of securities in markets. In this role, investment banks and securities dealers serve as brokers, holding securities for at most a short time period as part of the sale or underwriting process. In their traditional roles, investment banks and securities dealers help facilitate market-based finance. Market-based finance can have lower overhead costs than intermediated finance and can give borrowers access to a wider pool of potential investors.

Countries differ in the relative importance of bank-oriented and market-based finance. The United States has historically had a strong market-based finance sector. This is largely a function of laws and regulations that helped strengthen an independent investment banking sector.

The most important law that affected the structure of the financial sector in the United States in the period leading up to the financial crisis is the Glass-Steagall Act in 1933. Glass-Steagall, a response to the financial crisis that led into the Great Depression in the 1930s, effectively separated commercial banking from investment banking.[5] So, in the late 1950s, commercial banks made loans and took deposits while investment banks underwrote publicly issued securities. While the separation between commercial and investment banks was not complete, for the most part, each type of firm completed in its own type of market.[6] The Glass-Steagall separation of commercial and investment banks meant that the United States had a strong independent investment banking sector.

The separation of commercial and investment banking in the United States also resulted in investment banks that, in the 1950s, were not structured to compete with banks in the loan market. Realizing this, investment banks worked at innovations that would allow them to compete with banks. In part, the rise of the SBS in the United States can be viewed as an effort by nonbank financial firms to break down the Glass-Steagall barriers by stealing away banks' best customers.

Investment banks started to invade banks' territory by getting firms to move from bank loans to market-based debt. In the 1960s, investment banks got many large firms to replace loans with commercial paper (CP).[7] CP is short-term debt issued by nonfinancial companies and it substituted directly for bank loans. To make CP attractive to investors, the borrowers typically had a backup guarantee of repayment, which often came from banks. Investment banks liked CP because it generated fees for them, and investors liked it because it was a high-quality liquid security, but these features were not the only reasons for its success. One factor that contributed to the expansion of CP markets was regulatory arbitrage, by which I mean activities designed to get around regulations (or laws) while allowing parties to perform substantially the same activity. One big difference between the CP and loans is that a bank loan is reflected on the balance sheet of the bank. Banks are subject to capital requirements and reserve requirements. Capital requirements mean that a bank has to raise some costly equity capital to finance the loan (8% of the loan amount under the Basel 1 capital guidelines) while reserve requirements mean that the bank has to hold a percentage of some deposits in cash (meaning that it may have to raise more than $1 of deposits for each $1 it wants to lend). Both of these requirements impose costs on banks that can be avoided—or arbitraged—if a firm funds in the CP market rather than by using a bank loan.

Later, investment banks pioneered high-yield bonds. Typically, the only firms that could issue public debt (bonds) were those with an investment-grade rating (BBB or better) from the credit rating agencies. But starting in the 1980s, investment banks were able to market high-yield, or noninvestment grade, debt. High-yield bonds served as a substitute for bank loans. Again, regulatory arbitrage may have been one of the factors that contributed to the start of the high-yield bond market. One characteristic of both the CP market and the high-yield bond market is that intermediated debt (bank loans) was replaced by market-based (nonintermediated) debt.

The private securitization market, which started in 1977, but did not expand rapidly until the late 1980s, was a different sort of innovation than CP and high-yield debt because securitization is a form of intermediation. In addition, participants include both traditional banks and investment banks. Securitization was one of the first activities where investment banks competed with commercial banks as intermediaries.

The first securitizations in the United States preceded the private securitization market. Starting in 1970, banks and other lenders put together pools of home mortgages that were then guaranteed by the government agency known as Government National Mortgage Association (GNMA, also known as Ginnie Mae). The broad structure of these securitizations, except for the GNMA guarantee, was similar to most of the deals that followed.

The lenders sold their loans to intermediaries sponsored by commercial and investment banks (see Rosen, 2007, for a fuller description of the securitization process). For legal reasons, the loans were owned by so-called special purpose vehicles (SPV; sometimes these are called special purpose entities) rather than by the sponsoring institution. An SPV would collect some loans into a pool, and then issue MBS. The bondholders were repaid based on the payments on the loans in the pool. The initial GNMA securitizations passed through all payments (less fees). As an example, assume an issuer had collected 1,000 mortgages, each worth $100,000 with a 30-year maturity and a fixed interest rate of 6.50% in an SPV. This $100 million pool of mortgages could be used to back 10,000 bonds, each worth $10,000 with a 30-year term and a fixed coupon rate of 6.00%. Each bond would share the same coupon rate and other features, and importantly, each would have a similar claim on all payments. MBS are structured so that interest payments on the mortgages are at least sufficient to cover the interest payments due on the bonds (plus the fees of the intermediaries). Principal payments (either scheduled payments or prepayments) on the mortgages are used to pay down the principal on the bonds. The role of GNMA was to guarantee principal repayment. This leaves bondholders exposed to interest rate risk and the risk that the mortgage loans would be repaid early.[8]

The next step in the evolution of the securitization market was the entry of the government-sponsored entities (GSEs), the Federal National Mortgage Association (known as Fannie Mae) and the Federal Home Loan Mortgage Corporation (known as Freddie Mac).[9] Freddie Mac issued its first MBS in 1971 and was later joined by Fannie Mae. As with the GNMA, the GSEs guaranteed payments on the mortgages in the pool backing its MBS.

The private securitization market started in 1977 when Bank of America issued an MBS without guarantees from Ginnie Mae or the GSEs.[10] More private-label MBS followed, at first mostly sponsored by investment banks. The market did not grow appreciably, however, until a law was passed in 1984 that allowed regulated financial institutions such as banks to own MBS. Then, in 1985, the ABS market started with securities backed by computer leases and automobile loans. Private-label MBS (those without guarantees from Ginnie Mae or the GSEs) and ABS have a basic structure much like the GNMA-guaranteed MBS, but with some important differences. The firm putting together a private-label MBS or ABS deal sets up an SPV to purchase a pool of securities, then issues bonds with payments that are based on the payments on the loans in the underlying pool. However, since private-label MBS and ABS do not have government or GSE guarantees, they are structured with built in protections, something I discuss below. The private-label MBS and ABS markets grew rapidly in the following years, as figure 2.2 shows.

Securitization changes what banks do from screening, monitoring, and funding loans to originating loans after an initial screening, then selling the loans. This new process, known as the OTD model, can lead to an agency problem as it reduces the incentives of banks to carefully screen and monitor the loans they are planning to sell (e.g., Keys et al., 2010). This is why most of the early securitizations involved large pools of small, somewhat homogenous loans such as mortgages and automobile loans. Banks rarely monitored these kinds of loans as long as the borrowers were

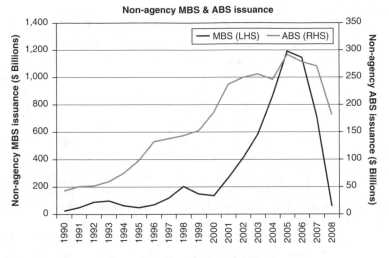

Figure 2.2   Issuance of securitized bonds, 1990–2008

current on payments. So, reducing the incentives to monitor was not a big issue. In addition, the banks that sold loans into a pool were able to give aggregate statistics on the loan pool, giving investors in the MBS a good idea of the overall default and prepayment characteristics of the pool. In addition to any contractual prohibitions against fraud, the desire to be able to sell future loans gave banks an incentive to report the information they learned from screening the loans.

Another feature common in private-label MBS and ABS is tranching. Starting in 1983, the securities offered in a securitization were split into different classes, or tranches. Many investors were willing to sacrifice some return for very safe, predictable payment streams while others were willing to accept more risk to get high yields. Bonds issued in a tranched deal generally differed in payment priority, and therefore risk. For example, a deal could have two classes of bonds, senior and junior. The interest payments on the underlying assets would be used to pay interest on both classes of bonds. Principal payments, whether scheduled or prepayments, would first be used to repay the principal of the senior bonds. Once these bonds were repaid, principal payments would be used to repay the junior bonds. Thus, the senior notes would have a shorter and more predictable maturity and be safer since initial principal losses would be borne by the junior bonds. Many securitizations had a large number of tranches, leading to complicated payment dynamics if a large number of the underlying loans defaulted.

Most private-label MBS and ABS also use overcollateralization and excess spread to provide a default buffer for all bondholders. Overcollateralization refers to the difference between the principal balance on the loans in the pool and the principal balance on the outstanding MBS or ABS; excess spread is the difference between the interest payments coming in (loan payments minus any fees) and the weighted average payments going to bondholders. They are related in that excess spread can be used to build up overcollateralization. The first use of excess spread is to cover default losses. If any excess spread is left, it can be used to build up a cushion against future losses. As noted above, the tranche structure of a securitization can be extremely complicated as the payment and default risk are split up in different ways. One measure of a bond's place in the seniority structure is its level of subordination. The level of subordination is the share of claims in a deal that are junior to the bond's claim. A higher level of subordination means that there would have to be a larger share of defaults before the bond suffered a principal loss.

One objective of tranching is to get one or more class of bonds that are rated AAA by a credit rating agency. The intermediaries involved in issuing these bonds (henceforth, the issuers) often wanted to issue as large a percent of the bonds with a AAA rating as they could. There was a complicated dance between issuers and the credit rating agencies about the level of subordination of the AAA bonds. One of the ways in which the credit rating agencies were accused of working with issuers during the boom was in structuring the tranches in a securitization so that the issuer had an attractive set of bonds to sell (Kane, 2008).

As the securitization market expanded and demand for securitized bonds increased, issuers started to include different types of assets in the pools backing the securitizations. Collateralized loan obligations (CLOs) are securities that are backed by the payments on a pool of commercial loans. CLOs differ from earlier ABS in part because the loans in the pool are large. Absent securitization, banks typically monitor even performing commercial loans. The need to monitor increases the agency problems with these loans, but market participants believed that the structure of the securitizations and reputational issues were enough to get the lenders to monitor them.

CLOs were followed by CDOs. The pool of assets backing CDO bonds varied, but in the mid-2000s often included bonds from other securitizations and commercial loans including commercial real estate loans. There were also CDOs that included bonds from other CDOs (these were often referred to as CDO-squared). Most CDOs were very difficult to value because of their complexity.

The expansion of securitization rested on three pillars. One pillar was regulatory arbitrage (see, e.g., Kohler, 1998). As noted earlier, there are regulatory costs for keeping a loan on a bank balance sheet. The OTD model allowed banks to make loans without the need to have as much costly capital. In addition, under the risk-based capital guidelines, banks that want to hold the exposure to a certain class of loans can reduce their risk-weighted assets by holding securitized bonds rather than whole loans.

The second pillar that facilitated the expansion of securitization was valuation. Technological advances made it easier to analyze large amounts of data in an attempt to price MBS and ABS bonds. Related to this was the willingness of credit rating agencies to rate the bonds. Together, these made investors comfortable purchasing what were often very complex securities. It is this second pillar that has crumbled during the recent crisis. As the rapid decline in value of some MBS and ABS bonds during the crisis shows, there were significant problems in the valuations and ratings. In the next section, I return to the question of why investors would purchase bonds that were difficult to price.

The third pillar is the ability to distribute risk inherent in securitization. Tranching allows issuers to divide the risk in the underlying assets in an almost unlimited way. They can design bonds with a broad variety of payment and risk characteristics. In theory, this allows investors to buy bonds with the characteristics that most appeal to them. Of course, as noted below, banks ended up holding much of the risk from structured securities (Shin, 2009).

Underlying the move to securitization, in particular, and the SBS, in general, was an attempt by financial firms to capture business from their rivals. Investment banks attempted to break down the Glass-Steagall barriers by innovating around them with products such as CP, high-yield bonds, and securitization. At the same time, banks were attempting to get into the underwriting field, formerly the province of investment banks. While some of these innovations offered potential improvements (such as securitization allowing risks to be divided), innovation was also aimed at regulatory arbitrage. In 1999, in an effort to level the playing field between banks and investment banks (and, coincidentally, reduce incentives for regulatory arbitrage), the United States implemented the Gramm-Leach-Bliley Act. Gramm-Leach-Bliley allowed commercial and investment banking in the same financial firm. This meant that the largest financial firms had both lending and investment banking arms, changing their incentives to innovate (Boot and Thakor, 1997).

The evolution of the financial industry and the rise of the SBS may have been motivated by efforts of industry players to capture revenue, but it drastically changed how firms profited from financial intermediation. As the lending process moved away from bank loans to either market-based alternatives such as CP or intermediation-based alternatives such as securitization, revenues for banks moved from interest-based to fee-based.

This only accelerated once commercial and investment banks could merge. The move to fee-based earnings reduced the incentives for banks to worry about the long run, and in particular, to worry about the risk of the loans or securities they were selling. This risk was shifted to the buyers. As long as there was someone to buy them, the banks had an incentive to sell them. This leaves the issue of what motivated the purchasers.

2.   Why Would Investors Buy "Bad" Securities?

Many of the structured finance securities described in the last section were quite popular in the period leading up to the financial crisis. Between 2002 and 2005, the value of mortgages that were issued to subprime borrowers and were then securitized more than tripled (fig. 2.3). This reflected a general increase in the share of MBS that were issued without a government or GSE guarantee (fig. 2.4). When housing prices started to fall in 2006 and 2007, it was the most recent vintage of securities (those issued closest to the crisis) that did the worst (Demyanyk and Van Hemert, 2008). Why did investors continue flocking into these markets until sometime in 2006? One possibility is that the investors were right *ex ante*, but the crisis was just extremely bad luck. This hypothesis cannot be rejected, but given what is known today about the quality of some of the assets in structured securities, bad luck does not seem to be a complete explanation. In this section, I consider some alternative hypotheses.

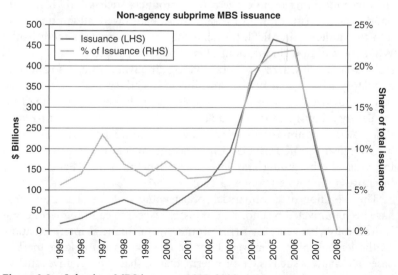

Figure 2.3   Subprime MBS issuance, 1995–2008

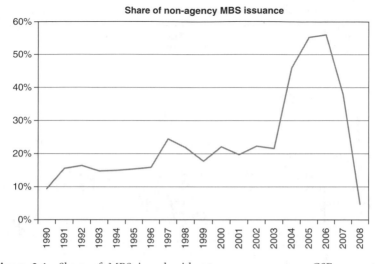

Figure 2.4   Share of MBS issued without a government or GSE guarantee, 1995–2008

One advantage of structured securities over alternative investments was their yield. ABS and MBS typically had higher yields than corporate bonds with equivalent ratings (fig. 2.5 gives yield spreads for some ABS).[11] While some of the yield spread was because structured securities had higher risk than similarly rated corporate bonds, the popularity of many of these securities during the mid-2000s suggests that investors acted as if the difference in yields meant that structured security markets were imperfect, in that the yield spread at least partially reflected money left on the table by others.

In the remainder of this section, I discuss some reasons why investors may have purchased securities that, at least in retrospect, seem to be bad investments. The first set of reasons can explain why "rational" investors can believe that markets leave money on the table by letting one security have a higher yield than another security with equivalent risk. The last reason can explain why investors may purchase a security that they believe has a worse risk-return tradeoff than alternative investments. In the background of these arguments is the role of the credit rating agencies.

2.1   Overconfidence and inattention

When making decisions, investors have access to several tools to help them evaluate a potential investment. There are also third-party evaluations

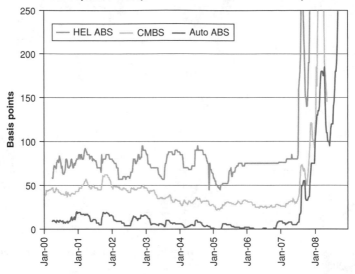

Figure 2.5   Yield spreads for selected ABS, 2000–2008

available, including that by the dealer selling a security. Still, for many of the complex securities, there is no consensus valuation, or even valuation method (see, e.g., Prince, 2006). This excess of material and lack of consensus on valuation complicates the decision of whether to buy a security at a given price. [12]

Given the complexity of structured securities, how should an investor, who may want to hold hundreds of different securities, evaluate each security? The literature on behavioral finance offers a number of psychology-based reasons why investors may not act as pure profit maximizers. One aspect of behavior evident from prior work is that investors tend to be *overly optimistic* or *overconfident* (I will generally use overconfidence to cover both overoptimism and overconfidence).[13] That is, some investors tend to overestimate their performance or overestimate the precision of their beliefs. There is also evidence of confirmation bias, the tendency to interpret evidence in a way that is consistent with prior beliefs. Confirmation bias leads individuals to put more weight on evidence that confirms their prior beliefs than on evidence that contradicts the beliefs. These aspects of investor behavior may have played a role in the evolution of structured finance and in setting the conditions for the financial crisis that started in 2007.

In addition to any biases, there is reason to believe that busy investors may take shortcuts, collecting and evaluating only information that they think will have a material effect on the profitability of an investment. Several studies have explored whether so-called *rational inattention* can be used to explain macroeconomic phenomena (see, e.g. Sims, 2003, and Reis, 2006).[14] The models in these studies show how capacity constraints for information or costly information processing may mean that individuals do not continuously update their knowledge. This can lead prices to deviate from their fundamental values. A form of rational inattention, especially when combined with overoptimism and overconfidence, may have helped set the stage for the financial crisis.

How should an investor make the decision to purchase a structured security? One way is to carefully analyze the prospectus and to make projections about future asset prices and default rates. This is extremely time consuming, and as noted above, there may be no consensus valuation method. An alternative is to spend less time on analysis, but instead to rely on some other party's valuation. For example, the investor could base investment decisions on the credit ratings provided by the Nationally Recognized Statistical Rating Organizations (NRSRO), primarily Moody's Investor Service, Standard and Poor's, and Fitch Ratings. These credit rating agencies have a long track record of evaluating securities. To be an NRSRO, a credit rating agency must be recognized by users as "an issuer of credible and reliable ratings" (SEC, 2003, p. 9). As I discuss below, whether the credit ratings of the NRSROs should be considered credible and reliable is controversial (see, e.g., Partnoy, 1999). Still, there is reason to believe that investors relied more on ratings over time, at least prior to the recent financial crisis, perhaps because of the rating agencies' reputations (see, e.g., Covitz and Harrison, 2003). The track records of the rating agencies may have led investors to pay less attention to the complicated details of each deal and instead to use the ratings assigned by the credit rating agencies as a starting point (and possible ending place) for any analysis. In essence, the credit rating of a security may serve as an anchor around which the investor can interpret any additional evidence.[15]

Consider a busy investor trying to decide whether to invest in a subprime MBS in 2004. The investor may want the extra yield offered by the MBS, but not be certain of how to value the security. She may look into the details of subprime mortgage defaults, which were relatively stable and low for over five years prior to 2004, and evaluate prepayment risk. The implied losses on the MBS bonds based on outside assessments of mortgage default and prepayment rates at that point would imply that the subprime MBS bond yields provide adequate compensation for the risk. This is a reasonable amount of work, and still suggests that the MBS are a good buy. Given the anchor provided by the credit rating, her analysis may be enough to overcome any belief that there rarely is money left on the table by the market.[16] This may happen even if the investor is aware of the debate surrounding the accuracy of credit ratings.

The point at which an investor stops her analysis may depend on how she rates her ability to price securities relative to others in the market. The more confident she is, the more willing she might be to believe that the market is mispricing the security. This may mean that more confident investors stop their analysis earlier than their less confident brethren. An overconfident investor can believe that a high yield on the security is money left on the table. If she considers herself better at analysis than the average investor, she may believe she can estimate default risk better than others. This means that for the securities she chooses to purchase, the overconfident investor incorrectly believes the high yields exist because other investors wrongly, in the mind of the overconfident investor, overestimate default risk. Also, if an over-confident investor believes she can make more precise estimates of the possible return paths of a security than other investors, she can place a lower price on true risk than other investors (since true risk is greater than her perception of risk). Thus, overconfidence can sway an investor toward structured securities because of their high yield relative to their credit rating. Enough overconfident investors can drive yields below a level commensurate with their risk, even if the yield stays high compared to alternative (traditional) securities.

Rational inattention may explain why an investor would shift from doing her own analysis of a particular type of security to relying on a credit rating. The investor has access to two public signals: the payments on the security and the credit rating. During the 2000–2006 period, most struc-tured securities based on pools of mortgages or other assets had very low defaults.[17] Thus, these securities were performing at least as well as their credit rating implied. After doing a detailed analysis once (or more) and finding that the credit rating provided a floor for the risk, the investor may decide that the credit rating is reliable enough to allow her to purchase the securities without doing a full analysis. A busy investor allocates her time toward decisions where she believes it is best used. When the securities are performing and there is no external signal to suggest an increase in the expected default rate in the underlying assets, she can choose to be inattentive to the detailed information and rely instead on the credit rating because her initial analysis suggests the information from the rating is a good enough signal to allow her to avoid costly information acquisition.[18] This is especially true for very safe securities, which rarely provide negative signals to investors. There is evidence that investors in AAA securitization were less informed about the quality of the securities than investors in lower-rated securities (Adelino, 2009).

An investor may not bother to do a detailed analysis even for new securities as long as they seem to her to be close in structure to securities she is already comfortable with, since the cost of the analysis may not be worth the expected improvement in valuation. Confirmation bias would likely push the investor toward believing that a reliance on credit rating was a good decision, reducing her perceived need to do a detailed analysis of new securities. Similarly, confirmation bias also suggests that even some noise in the signals, such as the early news about the housing bubble, may not be enough to shake an investor's belief that things are going well. Thus, it may not be until well after there are risk signs that an investor starts to pay careful attention to the details about a particular class of securities. An investor more confident about her ability to evaluate securities is likely to need a bigger change in securities or signals to prompt careful attention.

The above argument suggests that investors may react to a strong track record for a particular type and rating of structured security (or any other investment) by spending less time investigating the details of the investment and, if they are overconfident, becoming more certain that they can analyze the securities better than other investors. These possibilities give issuers an opening to slightly change the structure of the securities they issue so as to increase risk but maintain the same credit rating. This is important because issuers have a strong incentive to add risk because they get fees for arranging securitization deals, and to arrange deals, the issuer needs underlying assets.[19] It is easier to get assets if the issuer can broaden the quality range that the SPV will buy.

The evolution of deals suggests that, over time, SPV pools got riskier and this led to riskier securitized bonds. Take, for example, subprime MBS. One measure of risk of a subprime mortgage is whether the mortgage was written with full documentation of income, assets, and employment as opposed to those written without full documentation (so-called low-doc or no-doc mortgages). Not surprisingly, low-doc loans were more likely to default than full-doc loans. Consistent with a move toward riskier securities, the share of low-doc loans in subprime security pools increased from 2000 to 2006 (no-doc loans made up less than one percent of all subprime loans in pools during the period). In general, there is evidence that "the quality of [subprime] loans deteriorated for six consecutive years before the crisis and that securitizers were, to some extent, aware of it" (Demyanyk and Van Hemert, 2008).[20] The fact that subprime lending and the share of private-label MBS (which was mostly subprime MBS) both increased during this period, especially from 2002 to 2005 (as shown in figures 2.2 and 2.3 earlier), is a sign that investors did not stop purchasing subprime MBS as they got riskier. Thus, the evolution of subprime MBS is consistent with overconfidence, confirmation bias, and rational inattention given the anchor of credit ratings.[21]

One can tell similar stories for the structured finance market as a whole. The new securities that were introduced as the market evolved were often somewhat riskier innovations on prior securities. For example, subprime MBS were similar to prime MBS but slightly riskier because subprime mortgage default rates were historically higher and more variable than prime mortgage default rates. CLOs looked like other ABS such as those based on pools of automobile loans in the sense that both were based on the payments on pools of loans. But, because CLOs included a small number of large loans that required monitoring rather than a large number of small loans that were not monitored unless payments were missed, there were bigger moral hazard problems than in other ABS. Securities like CDOs based on pools of MBS and ABS securities were yet more complicated. Investors may have been lulled into a false sense of security by the high yields offered, the strong performance of structured securities in general, and the credit ratings. Thus, overconfident and inattentive investors could be been led into riskier securities without requiring compensating yield increases. That is, the fact that a structured security offered a higher yield than an equivalently rated corporate bond may have attracted investors, but the excess yield may not have been enough to compensate for the additional, but somewhat hidden, extra risk.[22]

One feature running through this entire argument is the role of credit ratings. The argument relies on the premise that a credit rating does not reflect the true risk of a security, and that this problem was magnified for later vintages of structured securities. This suggests that the credit rating agencies did not do a good job. But that suggestion depends on what credit rating agencies thought their job was. The role of the credit rating agencies was controversial, even before the financial crisis. There has long been a debate about how well credit ratings anticipate future defaults, as evidenced by their failure to accurately anticipate the default of bonds issued by firms such as Washington Public Power System and Enron (Partnoy, 1999; Hill, 2009). It has been argued that credit rating changes lag changes in risk (Altman and Rijken, 2004). Some believe that these problems at least partially stem from conflicting incentives that can lead the credit rating agencies to sacrifice ratings accuracy in an effort to satisfy other concerns (Mason and Rosner, 2007; Partnoy, 2006). The credit rating agencies get most of their revenues from issuers, and this could give them a reason to please issuers at the expense of ratings accuracy. These incentives may be especially severe in structured finance, which was a rapidly growing market from 2002 to 2006, providing over half of Moody's revenues at its peak (Mason and Rosner, 2007). Moreover, ratings agencies know that issuers can shop around for ratings, which may increase the incentives to bend ratings to issuers' desires (Fons, 2008). This is likely to be a bigger problem for structured securities than for traditional corporate bonds, because one big issue in rating structured securities is setting up the tranche structure. It is claimed that choosing the tranche structure often can be an iterative process where the rating agencies give feedback to the issuer, who then can modify the proposed structure (Mason and Rosner, 2007). There is a lot of room for subtle changes in risk through small changes in subordination.[23] A conclusion from this line of reasoning would be that credit rating agencies, by working with or for issuers, abetted an increase in risk for structured securities that was not apparent to many investors (Kane, 2008).[24]

An alternative for why credit ratings may not have fully reflected the risk of structured securities and why the differences between actual risk and credit rating agency estimates may have increased over time is based on the models the agencies use to estimate risk. Whether or not it was due to conflicts of interest, there is evidence that credit ratings agencies did not account for the predictable risk of some structured securities, and that this problem was strongest right before the financial crisis in 2007 (Mason and Rosner, 2007; Ashcraft et al., 2009). Structured securities were often very complicated and hard to price. This was especially true when the pools of assets were divided into a large number of tranches. Additionally, the estimated value of some securities was very sensitive to the assumptions on asset default. The models use by credit ratings agencies may have missed many of the subtleties because they use simplifying assumptions for tractability. The risk estimates were also based largely on historical data. This was an issue for many securities because recent history generally did not include a major downturn. Also, because of changes in lending patterns, some of the history was probably not relevant to current pools of assets. As evidence of the last point, consider subprime mortgages. The typical subprime mortgage borrower in 2005 was probably much riskier than the typical subprime mortgage borrower in 2001. So, using default rates on 2001 subprime mortgages to predict default rates on 2005 mortgages would likely underestimate true risk. An analysis based on old default rates would mean that an AAA rating in 2005 implied a higher risk than the same rating in 2001. While investors could have learned some of the details about rating agency models, it is likely that few of them spent the time to do this. An open question is the extent to which issuers exploited this quirk in the rating agencies' models (and in investors' learning habits).

To sum up, overconfidence and inattention may have contributed to the expansion of the SBS and to the severity of the financial crisis. Whatever their motivations for purchase, early investors did well. The strong performance of the economy as a whole, and housing, in particular, during the 2001–2006 period meant that very few structured securities defaulted. This strong performance reinforced the opinions of investors and may have led them to rely more on credit ratings (that is, become less attentive). Given the issues with credit rating agencies, this all meant there was room for issuers to produce riskier securities at a given credit rating, something they did.

2.2   Other people's money

Another reason for the evolution of the structured security market may be that many purchasers used other people's money. In Section 1, I discuss the differences between direct and intermediated finance. But within intermediated finance, there are differences in the number of steps between savers and borrowers. In traditional bank financing, a saver deposits with a bank, which then makes loans. However, the process for structured securities and other investments can be much more complicated. The chain from a saver to the ultimate borrower can be long (see Shin, 2009, for some examples). These long chains can increase agency problems.

Consider the simple case of an individual investing in a bond mutual fund (see fig. 2.6). The mutual fund manager, acting as an agent for the individual, uses the investment to purchase securities, including perhaps structured securities. The structured securities are put together by an issuer

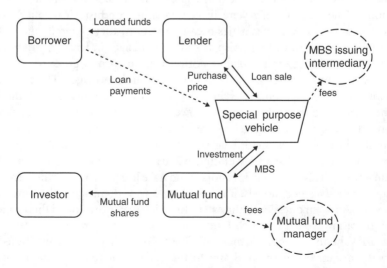

Figure 2.6   Intermediation chain for the purchase of securities through a mutual fund

who buys the underlying assets from lenders such as banks. The banks lend to the borrowers. How should the mutual fund manager choose what to invest in? The fund manager is likely aware that investors tend to put more money in funds that outperform their peers (see, e.g., Sirri and Tufano, 1998). The fund flows may not be predictive of future returns, and there is some thought that these investors are "dumb money" (Frazzini and Lamont, 2008). In order to increase her compensation, the fund manager needs to attract investors. This gives her an incentive to report high returns both relative to her peers and overall.[25] Structured securities offer a good way to do this. Thus, even if a fund manager believes that the yields on structured securities are insufficient to compensate for their risk, she may still (rationally) invest in them.

A fund manager's choice of whether to invest in structured securities will depend on the risk of the securities and the fund manager's discount rate, but it can also depend on what other fund managers do. There is evidence of return persistence among mutual funds that perform worse than their peers (Hendricks et al, 1993). To avoid being categorized as a poor performer, a fund manager would want to avoid having her fund perform poorly when other similar funds were performing well. This gives her an incentive to follow the herd (see Scharfstein and Stein, 1990, on herd behavior). So, if enough fund managers start investing in structured securities to get new investors, other managers will have an incentive to follow them.

Combining the incentives to chase yield to attract new customers and the incentives to herd with overconfidence only reinforces the attractiveness of structured securities. It also gives issuers more reason to be innovative. Securities with high yields where risk is concentrated are likely to be attractive to those investing money for others. High yields are popular with the ultimate investors, and concentrated risk means it is unlikely that the agent investing for others will look bad (although when things get bad, they can be very bad). These characteristics are consistent with the evolution of structured finance and the SBS.

One theme running through the argument so far is that smart issuers innovated to take advantage of investors. One potential criticism of this story is that most of the losses from the financial crisis that started in 2007 were borne by banks and other financial firms. One estimate is that financial firms would suffer roughly one-half of potential losses from subprime mortgages (Greenlaw et al., 2008). Not all of these losses were from structured securities, but there is abundant evidence that investment banks and commercial banks had major losses on structured securities in 2007 and 2008.[26] Some of these came from their role as issuers. When the payments on a pool of assets are divided into tranches, there can be tranches that are difficult to sell. In order to keep the fees coming, issuers sometimes keep bonds from the tranches that are less attractive to the market.[27] Investment and commercial banks also suffered significant losses from proprietary trading. This may have been a function of overconfidence on the part of traders. But it also may have reflected a culture of risk taking, perhaps related to compensation schemes (Diamond and Rajan, 2009). There is a saying in banking that some trades are good because "I.B.G.-Y.B.G." (I'll be gone and you'll be gone).[28] That is, the traders will get their bonuses if the trade works and, if not, there would be no negative bonus. So, people in different parts of a financial firm can have different incentives. The firm can be both intermediating the sale of risky securities and buying them at the same time.

As a side note, for the overall argument here to hold, it is not necessary that all investors were overconfident, inattentive, or agents for others. There may have been investors that made decisions about whether to purchase structured securities based on a purely profit maximizing basis. However, the rapid increases in the sale of these securities and the losses investors took on them suggest that the profit-maximizing investors may not have been setting the prices for the securities. Why did these investors not short the securities to benefit from any mispricing caused by overconfident and inattentive investors? One possible reason is that it may not be optimal for investors with limited capital to try to bet against non–profit-maximizing investors (see, e.g., DeLong et al., 1990).

3.   How this Crisis Was Different

The early 2000s, the period leading up to the crisis in 2007, was characterized by significant financial innovation with, by and large, investor acceptance of (if not enthusiasm for) the new instruments. As I described above, one feature of the innovation was the production of more complex securities that often have significant risk. However, this risk may not have been fully priced into the securities. Above, I argue that investor overconfidence and agency problems contributed to this by giving issuers an incentive to produce more complex securities. In this section, I first provide several examples to show that this pattern is not an isolated incident. Then, I explore some possible reasons why the 2007 crisis was especially severe.

The pattern in the recent crisis mirrors that in prior incidents. A particular investment or class of investments has realized returns that are higher than many other investment opportunities. Investors flock to this apparently hot market. As investors crowd in, the investment opportunities change. In particular, the investments get riskier. Investors, perhaps because of overconfidence and inattention resulting from strong recent performance, increase their exposure to the risky securities. These incidents can end with investors suffering large losses. This investor-intermediary risk cycle is apparent in other crises and bubbles. One example is the investment in emerging market countries in the period ending with the currency crises in 1997 and 1998. Focusing on Asia, many countries were relaxing regulations on financial markets and capital accounts in the early 1990s. In part because of this, capital flows into these countries increased dramatically. Net private capital flows in the five Asian countries that later suffered from a currency crises (Indonesia, Malaysia, the Philippines, South Korea, and Thailand) went from $11 billion in 1989 (near the 1971–1989 maximum of $13 billion) to $61 billion in 1995 and $63 billion in 1996.[29] During this period, these countries offered high realized returns for investors. As evidence of this, the Dow Jones South Asia Index returned about three percentage points more per year than the S&P 500 from the start of 1992 through the end of 1996. However, the increases in capital flows occurred following economic growth and appear not to have increased growth (Chan-Lau and Chen, 1998). One could argue that investors were chasing high returns. Over time, it is likely that investments became riskier on average.[30] Nonetheless, capital continued to flow in. There is some evidence that investment banks used the desire of investors to enter markets such as these as an opportunity to sell high-margin products.[31] In the end, the investments in emerging market economies caused large losses for investors when the economies weakened and the countries' currencies lost significant value. A similar pattern happened in what were then called less-developed countries (LDC) in the 1970s. Famously, when asked about the riskiness of investing in LDC debt, Walter Wriston, the then-chairman of Citicorp, said that countries do not go bankrupt. Of course, later, some LDC countries defaulted on their debt. The rise of the technology bubble in the 1990s also had investors moving into risky securities following a period of strong performance on existing securities, in this case, technology stocks.

The evolution of investments from those that are safe and easy to understand to those that are risky and hard to understand is present for individual firms as well. In the 1990s, Bankers Trust (BT) entered into a number of interest rate swap agreements with Gibson Greetings, a mid-size company specializing in greeting cards and related products. The evolution of the swaps shows a pattern similar to the evolution of MBS ten years later (the history here follows Overdahl and Schachter, 1995). Companies can use swaps to hedge interest rate risk, and the first swap Gibson Greetings entered into with BT was designed to do that. The initial swap, in late 1991, was a plain vanilla swap where the net payment by BT to Gibson would increase proportionally to any decrease in the

London interbank offer rate (LIBOR). Given the realized change in the LIBOR, by July 1992, Gibson was ahead $260,000 on the swap. After BT and Gibson settled the plain vanilla swap, BT convinced Gibson to enter a series of swaps, where each swap was typically riskier and more complex than the prior one.[32] The riskier swaps were essentially more leveraged bets on the path of interest rates. It is possible that overconfidence and inattention led Gibson to agree to the risky swaps, since there appeared to be little business reason to enter into them (that is, they provided little clear hedging of Gibson's risks). Initially, the realized path of interest rates meant that Gibson made money on the swaps. This may have led Gibson to believe that they were able to understand and make money from their swap contracts. Over time, this overconfidence may have led Gibson to pay less attention to the details of each subsequent swap. But, when interest rates started rising in 1994, Gibson began losing money on its swaps. They announced a first quarter loss in 1994 from the swaps of $16.7 million, more than 60 times as large as the gain on the first plain vanilla swap. This fits the broad pattern of the investor-intermediary risk cycle that led to the 2007 financial crisis: initial success may have fed overconfidence and inattention to details for the investor (Gibson Greetings). This, in turn, encouraged the issuer (BT) to offer investments that were riskier and harder to evaluate, but more profitable for the issuer. The overconfident investor may not fully examine the risks, leading to big losses when conditions changed.[33]

The above examples show patterns of investor and financial institution behavior similar to those in the run-up to the 2007 crisis. However, while some of the earlier situations led to localized crises, none led to anything near the magnitude of the 2007 crisis. There are a number of factors that may have made the 2007 crisis more severe. Among them are the length of the precrisis period, the shift from financial intermediaries to the SBS, the increasing interconnectedness among financial firms, and the increased leverage at some financial firms.

The evolution of products offered during the run-up to a crisis suggests that the longer the run-up period, the riskier are the products eventually offered. Overconfidence, inattention, and potential agency problems give issuers more scope to issue risky products when investors as investors have a longer track record of successful investments. Thus, one potential explanation for the magnitude of the 2007 crisis was that, for whatever reason, there was a longer than usual period of higher returns on the affected asset class, in this case securitizations and other structured securities.

There are also structural reasons why the 2007 crisis may have been particularly severe. As the OTD model increased in popularity, more intermediation moved from banks to the SPVs underlying securitizations. This introduced screening problems, as inattentive investors may have allowed issuers to include lower quality loans into securitization pools. Adding to this problem, one difference between the intermediation done in banks and that done using structured securities is the length of the intermediation chain (Shin, 2009). For the most part, in traditional bank financing, the bank balance sheet sits directly between savers and borrowers. With securitization, there is at least one more link in the intermedia-tion chain as the SPV stands between a lender and the ultimate investor. As discussed above (and in Shin, 2009), the chain can be much more complex. Each link in the chain introduces potential agency problems and the possibility of overconfident or inattentive decision makers. This increases the scope for bad assets to be funded, specifically those that are riskier than investors think they are. This can happen by a breakdown in screening or through innovations such as CDOs that are so opaque as to be nearly impossible to evaluate.[34] As discussed in the previous section, these problems become more severe during sustained good times. It should also be clear that the problems become more severe the longer the intermediation chain. This suggests that while securitization in particular and long intermediation chains in general may have some advantages in broadening the potential investor base and spreading risk (and avoiding regulatory costs), they bring with them the problem that misaligned incentives get worse during boom periods.

There are also some other differences between the current crisis and previous ones. In recent years, banks and other financial institutions have become more intertwined, in part because of securities issued in the SBS (Gorton, 2008). This means that damage to one institution can spread to others more easily than in past years. In addition, the leverage of interme-diaries was much higher in the mid-2000s than in earlier periods (in part because investment banks had higher leverage than commercial banks). Once there is a precipitating event, high leverage causes market partici-pants to worry about the solvency of banks. Since both commercial and investment banks are largely financed with short-term debt (Diamond and Rajan, 2009), the event can lead to a run, much as some argue the losses on subprime mortgages did in 2007 (e.g., Gorton, 2008). While the broad structure of the financial industry is not new, its intertwined nature and high leverage may have made the shocks in 2007 propagate more widely than prior shocks did.

The evidence suggests that the investor-intermediary risk cycle that was at the root of the run-up to the financial crisis that started in 2007 was common to other crises, but that there were aggravating factors that may have made the 2007 crisis more severe than earlier crises. This suggests the need to address both the risk cycle and the aggravating factors when considering reforms to the financial system.

4. Concluding Comments

The financial crisis that started in 2007 exposed a number of flaws in the financial system. Many of these flaws were associated with financial instruments that were issued by the SBS. The growth of the SBS as an alternative to traditional banking products had been going on for a number of years, but accelerated rapidly with the expansion of securitization in recent years. In particular, the expansion of securitization included many new, intrinsically riskier securities. I explore how natural tendencies of investors may have allowed issuers of securitized bonds (and other SBS products) to increase the risk of these securities without many investors realizing it.

Paradoxically, the good news of the years up to 2006 may have led to the bad news that started in 2007. The strong performance of structured securities such as securitized bonds fed into the natural overconfidence of some investors. The performance reinforced the decisions of these investors to buy structured securities. It also may have led investors to rely more on credit ratings, since the high credit ratings many bonds received seemed to be confirmed by their performance. Busy investors may have become more willing to trust the ratings since that would allow them to focus their scarce attention elsewhere. The strong performance in the early part of the 2000s also put pressure on investors that were using other peoples' money to show high returns. This could have led these investors to reach for the high yields offered by structured securities even if they thought that the high yield was insufficient to compensate for the risk of the securities.

A mix of overconfidence, inattention, and desire for high yields on the part of investors gives the intermediaries in the SBS an incentive to create securities that had high yields but a lot of possibly hidden risk. Beyond that, since many investors were relying on credit ratings, it would be more valuable to the intermediaries if they could issue securities that had more risk for a given level of credit rating. It appears now that the intermediaries were able to do this.

The financial crisis can be viewed as a possible but logical outcome of a system where investors are overconfident, busy, and investing other peoples' money and where intermediaries are set up to take advantage of investors' tendencies. There are other examples of similar behavior by investors and intermediaries, although the consequences in the earlier cases were less severe than in the current financial crisis. Thus, when thinking about how to reform the financial system, one question is whether to attempt to break this investor-intermediary risk cycle or attempt to minimize its impact. Many of the current regulatory reform proposals take on one or the other of these options.

The proposals to break the investor-intermediary risk cycle include credit rating agency reform and reducing the role of the SBS. Credit rating agency reform is intended to make credit ratings more accurate by reducing agency problems at the rating agencies. More accurate ratings would reduce the costs for investors of being inattentive to the details of debt securities. Of course, believing that ratings accuracy has increased may lead more investors to rely on ratings rather than on their own research, so the impact of ratings agency reform may be limited. Reducing the role of the SBS may mitigate the effects of agency problems by shortening the intermediation chain (Shin, 2009). While this would be useful, it may be difficult to accomplish in the long run. Among the reasons for the rise of the SBS were innovations that increased efficiency and arbitraged around regulatory restrictions. The incentives to increase efficiency and evade regulation will remain.

The 2007 crisis was made worse because some financial firms were highly levered and interconnected (Gorton, 2008). Proposals that reduce leverage and interconnectedness, or at least reduce the impact of shocks to banks, may reduce the multiplier impact of a financial shock.

Finally, the argument that the investor-intermediary risk cycle combined with shifts in screening and monitoring caused by the movement from banks to SBS made a financial crisis more likely does not absolve other agents from blame. In this chapter, I have not focused on whether regulators contributed to the problems that led to the recent crisis. Sub-optimal actions by regulators (and other parties) could have exacerbated the problems caused by a shift to the SBS. In addition, the highly levered structure of financial intermediaries combined with the maturity mismatch of their balance sheets may have contributed to magnifying the effect of the shock to underlying assets (Diamond and Rajan, 2009).

*The author is an Economic Advisor and Senior Economist at the Federal Reserve Bank of Chicago. This paper is a revised and extended version of "Investor behavior in the period before the 2007–2008 financial crisis," in *Managing Systemic Risk* ed. J. R. LaBrosse, R. Olivares-Caminal, and D. Singh (Cheltenham: Edward Elgar, 2011 [forthcoming]). I would like to thank Crystal Cun for research assistance and the participants at presentations at the Federal Reserve Bank of Chicago and the FUNCAS conference "Crisis y Regulación Financiera" for comments. The views in this chapter are those of the author and may not represent the views of the Federal Reserve Bank of Chicago or the Federal Reserve System.

Notes

1. The SBS is a slightly more expansive definition of nonbank alternatives than, for example, the securitized banking sector referred to by Gorton and Metrick (2009) and the market-based financial intermediation in Shleifer and Vishny (2009).

2. The types of firms that are included as part of the SBS are investment banks, hedge funds, monoline insurance companies, the government-sponsored entities (GSEs), and a number of specialized entities that are set up to issue derivative financial securities. Banks can be part of the SBS to the extent that they participate in financing that is different from traditional lending. I discuss the purchase of securities created in the SBS below.

3. SIVs held long-term assets but issued primarily short-term liabilities (such as commercial paper) to purchase the assets. This exposed them to the risk that they would not be able to roll over their liabilities.

4. I am using the term "banks" to refer to all kinds of depository institutions.

5. The Bank Holding Company Act of 1954 separated commercial banking and insurance.

6. There were exceptions, for example, banks could underwrite government securities and privately placed (as opposed to publicly traded and registered) debt.

7. The CP market has been around for a long time in the United States and elsewhere. Interestingly, Goldman Sachs got its start issuing CP in 1869.

8. For some pools of loans, interest payments were not guaranteed, leaving bondholders exposed to the risk of missed interest payments as well.

9. The GSEs are government-charted private companies. Their guarantees were not explicitly backed by the U.S. government, but when the GSEs got into financial trouble, the government stepped in to help them (technically, by taking them into conservatorship in late 2008).

10. Private-sector securitizations backed by mortgages are sometimes referred to as mortgage asset-backed securities.

11. Evidence for the extra yield for subprime MBS is more anecdotal. See, for example, Subprime Securities Market Began as 'Group of 5' Over Chinese," Mark Pittman, Bloomberg News, December 17, 2007, which notes that there were times when AAA-rated securities based on home loans offered yields averaging a full percentage point higher than ten-year Treasuries.

12. "The only entity that really understood the true value and risk in a mortgage-backed security or a CDO was the mortgage broker who originated the loans that made up the underlying assets," explains Niket Patankar, CEO of the hedge fund advisory company Adventity. "And that person was long gone from the picture by the time they were sold as part of a CDO." From "Navigating subprime securities," Katie Benner, *Fortune Magazine*, August 2007.

13. There are a number of studies of overconfidence in financial markets. Evidence of overconfidence is found in stock trading and financial markets (Daniel et al., 1998; Odean, 1998; Barber and Odean, 2001), managerial decision making (Ben-David et al., 2007; Malmendier and Tate, 2005), and home

purchases (Agarwal, 2007). See Malmendier and Tate (2008) for a review of some of the psychology literature on overconfidence and Rabin and Schrag (1999) for a discussion of confirmation bias. See also the chapters in the *Encyclopedia of Social Psychology* (2007) on belief perseverance, beliefs, and confirmation bias.

14. There is also empirical evidence of inattention (whether rational or not) in financial markets. For example, there is evidence that investors respond less to earnings announcements (and possibly other news announcements) that are made on Fridays (DellaVigna and Pollet, 2009). In addition, investors tend to be net buyers of stocks that are in the news more (Barber and Odean, 2008).

15. Anchoring refers to a bias in how individuals assess probabilities. People tend to anchor on certain pieces of information, effectively ignoring or under-weighting other data (e.g., Tversky and Kahneman, 1974).

16. Investors who dug deeply enough to believe that the yield spreads for some of the MBS and ABS were insufficient to cover the risks of the structured securities would not have purchased them. Clearly, the growth in structured securities markets suggests that there are relatively few investors like this (or that these investors were agents for others as discussed in the section on other people's money).

17. Each year from 2003 to 2005, the rate of default on both investment grade and high-yield structured securities was lower than in the prior year (Moody's, 2006). By 2005, the default rate was at an all-time low.

18. Brunnermeier and Oehmke (2009) argue that there can be information overload with complex securities, implying there is a limit to the ability of an investor to analyze information. When this happens, how information is released is crucial, perhaps more than how much information is released. The credit rating can serve as an anchor, as I argue, for investors' analyzing the overload of information.

19. There is evidence that firms try to take advantage of investor overconfidence and inattention (e.g., DellaVigna and Pollet, 2009; Daniel et al., 2002).

20. Note that this view, while held by many, is not universal. See Bhardwaj and Sengupta (2009).

21. In addition, some investors may have understood what was happening, but overconfidently believed they could sell the overpriced subprime MBS to others. In theory, such beliefs can support a deviation of prices from fundamentals (Scheinkman and Xiong, 2003).

22. Of course, the risk differences were not that hidden. The historical default rate on structured securities of a particular rating was much higher than the historical default rate on corporate bonds of the same rating, as data published by the ratings agencies showed.

23. An increase in average subordination does not necessarily mean that risk goes down. There is evidence that while the subordination on AAA-rated subprime MBS went up from 2001 to 2007, the pool of underlying assets increased in risk enough so that the MBS issued in later years were riskier than those issued in earlier years (Ashcraft et al., 2009).

24. Investors could have known about the incentive problems with credit ratings, but there is evidence that, in general, investors do not discount enough for the effects of the incentives of interested parties such as the ratings agencies (Daniel et al., 2002).

25. Mutual fund flows tend to be negatively correlated across categories of fund (Goetzmann et al., 2001).

26. See the many stories on hedge fund and other losses at Bear Stearns, Lehman Brothers, and other financial firms.

27. See, for example, "Wall Street's Money Machine Breaks Down," in *Fortune* magazine, November 12, 2007.

28. See the quote in note 12 and "What's Really Wrong with Wall Street Pay" in the Economix section of the *New York Times*, September 18, 2009.

29. This data is from the World Economic Outlook Database provided by the International Monetary Fund, and the figures are in 1995 U.S. dollars.

30. In the decade before the crises, investment efficiency fell, the share of bank credit to GDP rose, and the share of short-term external debt to foreign exchange reserves rose in the affected Asian countries (Bustelo et al., 1999). This made the economies of these countries riskier.

31. "Hot Ticket: Emerging Market Derivative; For Banks, Profit Margins 20 Times Those of Plain Vanilla" (Jill Hamburg and Michael Smith, *American Banker*, August 22, 1996) discusses the sale of derivatives on emerging market currencies.

32. The swaps moved from plain vanilla to "ratio swap" to "periodic floor" to "spread lock" to "Treasury-linked" to "knock-out call" to "wedding band."

33. Gibson's actions may have been influence by the fact that the managers of Gibson Greetings were agents for the shareholders, and this agency problem may have led them to choose investments that generally gave high returns. At least one of the riskier swaps was setup such that, given the expected paths of interest rates, the vast majority of the time, BT would pay $600,000 to Gibson with Gibson paying a much larger amount to BT a much smaller percentage of the time. One could argue that this was optimal for Gibson's managers if shareholders did not understand where the extra $600,000 came from.

34. Some CDOs seem to have been purchased by investors who may not have known which securities were in the pool backing the bonds (e.g., "The Challenge of CDO Squared," *Risk*, March 2005).

References

Adelino, Manuel, 2009, "Do Investors Rely Only on Ratings? The Case of Mortgage-Backed Securities," working paper.

Adrian, Tobias, and Hyun Song Shin, 2008, "Liquidity, Monetary Policy, and Financial Cycles," *Current Issues in Economics and Finance*, 14(1).

———, 2009, "Money, Liquidity, and Monetary Policy," *American Economic Review Papers and Proceedings* 99(2): 600–605.

Agarwal, Sumit, 2007, "The Impact of Homeowners' Housing Wealth Misestimation and Consumption and Savings Decisions," *Real Estate Economics* 35(2): 135–54.

Altman, Edward I., and Herbert A. Rijken, 2004, "How Ratings Agencies Achieve Rating Stability," *Journal of Banking and Finance*, 28(11): 2679–2714.

Ashcraft, Adam, Paul Goldsmith-Pinkham, and James Vickery, 2009, "MBS ratings and the mortgage credit boom," working paper.

Barber, Brad M., and Odean, Terrance, 2001, "Boys Will Be Boys: Gender, Overconfidence, and Common Stock Investment," *Quarterly Journal of Economics*, 116, 261–93.

————, 2008, "All that Glitters: The Effect of Attention and News on the Buying Behavior of Individual and Institutional Investors," *Review of Financial Studies*, 22, 785–818.

Kathleen D. Vohs (eds.), 2007, *Encyclopedia of Social Psychology*, 1st edition, Thousand Oaks, CA: Sage.

Ben-David, I., J. R. Graham, and C. R. Harvey, 2007. "Managerial Overconfidence and Corporate Policies," NBER Working Paper.

Bhardwaj, Geetesh, and Rajdeep Sengupta, 2009, "Where's the Smoking Gun? A Study of Underwriting Standards for US Subprime Mortgages," Federal Reserve Bank of St. Louis Working Paper 2008-036B.

Boot, Arnoud W. A., and Anjan V Thakor, 1997, "Banking Scope and Financial Innovation," *Review of Financial Studies*, 10(4): 1099–1131.

Brunnermeier, Markus K., 2009, "Deciphering the Liquidity and Credit Crunch 2007—08," *Journal of Economic Perspectives*, 23(1): 77–100.

Brunnermeier, Markus K., and Martin Oehmke, 2009, "Complexity in Financial Markets," working paper.

Bustelo, Pablo, Clara García, and Iliana Olivié, 1999, "Global and Domestic Factors of Financial Crises in Emerging Economies: Lessons from the East Asian Episodes (1997–1999)," working paper.

Chan-Lau, Jorge A., and Zhaohui Chen, 1998, "Financial Crisis and Credit Crunch as a Result of Inefficient Financial Intermediation—with Reference to the Asian Financial Crisis," working paper.

Covitz, Daniel M., and Paul Harrison, 2003, "Testing Conflicts of Interest at Bond Ratings Agencies with Market Anticipation: Evidence that Reputation Incentives Dominate," working paper.

Daniel, Kent D., David A. Hirshleifer, and Avanidhar Subrahmanyam, 1998, "Investor Psychology and Security Market Under- and Overreactions," *Journal of Finance,* 53(6): 1839–85.

Daniel, Kent D., David A. Hirshleifer, and Siew Hong Teoh, 2002, "Investor Psychology in Capital Markets: Evidence and Policy Implications," *Journal of Monetary Economics*, 49, 139–209.

Davis, Henry A., 2005, "The Definition of Structured Finance: Results from a Survey," *The Journal of Structured Finance*, 11(3), 5–10.

DellaVigna, Stefano, and Joshua M. Pollet, 2009, "Investor Inattention and Friday Earnings Announcements," *Journal of Finance*, 64, 709–49.

DeLong, J. B., A. M. Shleifer, L. H. Summers, and R. J. Waldmann, 1990, "Noise Trader Risk in Financial Markets," *Journal of Political Economy* 98, 703–38.

Demyanyk, Yuliya, and Otto Van Hemert, 2008, "Understanding the Subprime Mortgage Crisis," *The Review of Financial Studies*, December 2008.

Diamond, Douglas W., and Raghuram G. Rajan, 2009, "The Credit Crisis: Conjectures About Causes and Remedies," working paper.

Fons, Jerome S., 2008, "Rating Competition and Structured Finance," *Journal of Structured Finance*, 14(3): 7–15.

Frazzini, Andrea, and Owen A. Lamont, 2008, "Dumb Money: Mutual Fund Flows and the Cross-Section of Stock Returns," *Journal of Financial Economics* 88(2): 299–322.

Goetzmann, William N., Massimo Massa, and K. Geert Rouwenhorst, 2001, "Behavioral Factors in Mutual Fund Flows," working paper.

Gorton, Gary, 2008, "The Panic of 2007," in *Maintaining Stability in a Changing Financial System*, Proceedings of the 2008 Jackson Hole Conference, Federal Reserve Bank of Kansas City, 2008.

Gorton, Gary, and Andrew Metrick, 2009, "Securitized Banking and the Run on Repo," working paper.

Greenlaw, D., J. Hatzius, A. Kashyap, and H. S. Shin, 2008, "Leveraged Losses: Lessons from the Mortgage Market Meltdown," US Monetary Policy Forum Report 2, http://www.chicagogsb.edu/usmpf/docs/usmpf2008confdraft.pdf.

Hendricks, Darryll, Jayendu S. Patel, and Richard J. Zeckhauser, 1993, "Hot Hands in Mutual Funds: The Persistence of Performance, 1974–87," *Journal of Finance* 48, 93–130.

Hill, Claire A., 2009, "Why Did Anyone Listen to the Rating Agencies After Enron?" *Journal of Business and Technology Law*, 4(2), 283–94.

Kane, Edward J., 2008, "Who Should Bear Responsibility for Mistakes Made in Assigning Credit Ratings to Securitized Debt?" working paper, 2008.

Keys, Benjamin J., Tanmoy K. Mukherjee, Amit Seru, and Vikrant Vig, 2010, "Did Securitization Lead to Lax Screening? Evidence from Subprime Loans," *Quarterly Journal of Economics*, 125(1): 307–62.

Kohler, K. E., 1998, "Collateralised Loan Obligations: A Powerful New Portfolio Management Tool For Banks," *The Securitization Conduit*, 1(2): 6–15.

Malmendier, Ulrike, and Geoffrey Tate, 2005, "CEO Overconfidence and Corporate Investment," *The Journal of Finance*, 60(6): 2661–700.

———, 2008, "Who Makes Acquisitions? CEO Overconfidence and the Market's Reaction," *Journal of Financial Economics*, 89(1) (July 2008): 20–43.

Mason, Joseph R., and Josh Rosner, 2007, "Where Did the Risk Go? How Misapplied Bond Ratings Cause Mortgage Backed Securities and Collateralized Debt Obligation Market Disruptions," working paper.

Moody's, 2006, "Default & Loss Rates of Structured Finance Securities: 1993–2005," April 2006.

Odean, Terrance, 1998, "Volume, Volatility, Price, and Profit When All Traders Are above Average," *Journal of Finance*, 53(6), 1887–934.

Overdahl, James, and Barry Schachter, 1995, "Derivatives Regulation and Financial Management: Lessons from Gibson Greetings," *Financial Management* 24(1); 68–78.

Partnoy, Frank, 1999, "The Siskel and Ebert of Financial Markets?: Two Thumbs Down for the Credit Rating Agencies," Washington University Law Quarterly 77(3): 620–712.

———, 2006, "How and Why Credit Rating Agencies are Not Like Other Gatekeepers," Financial Gatekeepers: Can They Protect Investors?, ed. Yasuyuki Fuchita and Robert E. Litan, Brookings Institution Press and the Nomura Institute of Capital Markets Research.

Prince, Jeffrey T., 2006, "A General Review of CDO Valuation Methods," The Journal of Structured Finance, 12 (2): 14–21.

Rabin, Matt, and Joel L. Schrag, 1999, "First Impressions Matter: A Model of Confirmatory Bias," Quarterly Journal of Economics, 114(1): 37–82.

Reis, Ricardo, 2006, "Inattentive Producers," Review of Economic Studies, 73(3), 793–821.

Rosen, Richard J., 2007, "The Role of Securitization in Mortgage Lending," Chicago Fed Letter, Federal Reserve Bank of Chicago, November 2007.

Scharfstein, David S., and Jeremy C. Stein, 1990, "Herd Behavior and Investment," American Economic Review, 80(3): 465–79.

Scheinkman, J. A., and W. Xiong, 2003, "Overconfidence and Speculative Bubbles," Journal of Political Economy, 111(6): 1183–219.

Securities and Exchange Commission (SEC), 2003, "Report on the Role and Function of Credit Rating Agencies in the Operation of the Securities Markets," January 2003.

Shin, Hyun Song, 2009, "Financial Intermediation and the Post-Crisis Financial System," working paper.

Shleifer, Andrei, and Robert Vishny, 2009, "Unstable Banking," working paper.

Sims, Christopher A., 2003, "Implications of Rational Inattention," Journal of Monetary Economics, 50(3): 665–90.

Sirri, Erik R., and Peter Tufano, 1998, "Costly Search and Mutual Fund Flows," Journal of Finance, 53, 1589–622.

Tversky, Amos, and Daniel Kahneman, 1974, "Judgment under Uncertainty: Heuristics and Biases," Science, New Series, 185(4157), 1124–131.

3

The U.K. Banking Crisis

*Philip Molyneux**

Abstract

As in many other countries, the banking market in the U.K. has undergone radical transformation since the onset of the mid-2007 credit crisis. What was once a profitable, innovative, and dynamic industry has virtually collapsed and now major banks are state owned, the government has had to inject massive funds to support lending, and a crisis has ensued. The collapse of global real estate markets prompted by the U.S. sub-prime crisis, is usually put down as the main causes of the crisis. Also, excessive risk-taking by banks and inappropriate governance structures have been highlighted as other major factors that led to the meltdown. Of course, the environment that led up to these problems had been created over the last 25 years and was mainly driven by domestic deregulation as well as various other forces that changed the supply-and-demand characteristics of the financial services industry. In this context, this chapter aims to review the structural features of the U.K. banking industry, including an analysis of the credit crisis and how it unravelled. We then review the recent performance of U.K. banks and illustrate that up to 2006–2007, they were among Europe's best-performing financial firms. However, the returns of major U.K. banks collapsed in 2008 (e.g., RBS made a loss of minus 43%!). Finally we focus on the regulatory environment, with particular attention on recent changes and their impact on the sector.

Introduction to U.K. banking

In contrast to other large European countries, the U.K. has a relatively small number of banks. As table 3.1 illustrates, the total number of authorised

Table 3.1 Number of banks and building societies, 1985–2008

	1985	1986	1987	1988	1989	1990	1991	1992	1993	1994	1995	1996	1997	1998	1999	2000	2001	2002	2003	2004	2005	2006	2007	2008
Authorised institutions	605	595	588	567	551	548	530	518	508	486	481	478	466	468	449	420	409	385	380	356	346	335	335	338
UK incorporated	290	291	298	313	295	289	275	263	253	232	224	220	212	214	202	190	188	184	185	174	171	159	160	158
MBBG members	40	47	52	51	50	47	45	41	39	37	37	40	41	44	43	41	42	41	42	35	32	30	28	24
Building Socities	167	151	138	131	126	117	110	105	101	96	94	88	82	71	69	67	65	65	63	63	63	60	59	55

banking institutions has fallen from around 600 in 1985 to 338 by the end of 2008. The table also shows the decline in the number of mutual building societies over the same period.

The decline in the total number of banks is attributable to foreign banks, which already had U.K. operations, acquiring relatively small U.K. investment banks as well as consolidation in the domestic retail banking market.

Table 3.2 shows that during the second part of the 1990s the decline in the number of foreign banks has been greater than that for U.K. incorporated banks, although mergers and acquisitions between U.K. incorporated banks resulted in a fall in their number from 202 in 1999 to 158 by the end of 2008. During the second half of the 1990s, a decline in the number of non-European banks (particularly Japanese banks) was counteracted by the increased presence of European institutions, whose number increased from 79 to 105 between 1993 and 1999; the number of European banks subsequently fell to 98 by 2008. Table 3.2 illustrates these trends and shows that the total number of foreign banks operating in the U.K. fell from 257 to 183 between 1995 and 2008. The recent crisis in U.K. banking is expected to result in further consolidation in the sector.

The table illustrates the number of banks and subsidiaries of the main U.K. retail banks—otherwise known as the Major British Banking Groups (MBBG). These banks dominate sterling denominated banking business in the U.K. Up until the end of 2007 the MBBG included Abbey National, Alliance & Leicester, Barclays, Bradford and Bingley, HBOS, HSBC Bank, Lloyds TSB, Northern Rock, and the Royal Bank of Scotland. Four of these were mutual building societies that converted to bank status—Abbey National (converted in 1989), Alliance and Leicester (1997), Bradford and Bingley (2000), and Northern Rock (1997). HBOS was formed by the merger of Halifax (that converted into plc and bank status in June 1997) and the Bank of Scotland in September 2001.

Since mid-2007 the MBBG have experienced turmoil resulting from the credit crisis and there have been significant developments adversely affecting their activities. Northern Rock was the first casualty of the crisis, revealing on 13 September 2007 that it had received emergency financial support from the Bank of England, having been unable to refinance itself in the interbank markets. Over the next few days £1bn was withdrawn from the bank's high street branches, in what was the first bank run in the U.K. for over a century. To stop the panic, on 17 September 2007 the U.K. government announced a full guarantee of depositors' savings. Later in the same month, Lloyds TSB announced that it was to acquire HBOS for £12bn, creating a merged entity with a market share of around one-third in the U.K. savings and mortgage markets. The U.K. competition authorities viewed that the aim of preventing the collapse of HBOS overrode

Table 3.2 Number of banks in the United Kingdom

	1995	1996	1997	1998	1999	2000	2001	2002	2003	2004	2005	2006	2007	2008
Number of authorised Institutions	481	478	466	468	449	420	409	385	380	356	346	335	335	341
of which:														
U.K. incorporated	224	220	212	214	202	190	188	184	185	174	171	159	160	158
European authorised institutions	102	103	105	105	109	103	97	89	92	89	87	93	93	98
Incorporated outside the European Economic Area	155	155	149	149	138	127	124	112	103	93	88	83	82	85
MBBG members & their banking sector subsidiaries (a) (included above)	37	40	41	44	43	41	42	41	42	35	32	30	28	24
BBA member banks (included above) (b)	307	306	311	337	327	302	295	265	244	236	218	206	199	203

Note: Lists of authorised institutions are published by the Bank of England.

(a) Major British Banking Groups (MBBGs) in 1999 included the following: Abbey National Group, Alliance & Leicester Group, Barclays Group, Bradford and Bingley plc (from 2000), The HBOS Group, HSBC Bank Group, Lloyds TSB Group, Northern Rock Group (from 1999), and the Royal Bank of Scotland Group.

(b) As at end-March.

Source: Adapted from *Banking Business. An Abstract of Banking Statistics* (2008), vol. 25, table 1.04; (2005) vol. 22, table 1.04, p. 6; (1999) vol. 16, table 1.04, p. 6; and (1996) vol. 13, table 6.01, p. 6 (British Bankers Association: London).

antitrust concerns that would otherwise stem from the merger of two large high-street retail banks. On 29 September 2008 the U.K. government announced that it was acquiring the mortgage-lending arm of Bradford and Bingley, and selling the still-viable depositor base and branch network to the Spanish Santander banking group.

Up until the onset of the mid-2007 credit crisis the investment banking industry was dominated by major U.S. and European banks including Goldman Sachs, Morgan Stanley, Merrill Lynch, Lehman Brothers, Bearn Stearns, Citigroup, Deutsche Bank, UBS, and Credit Suisse. Also, the main U.K. banks had (more modest) investment banking subsidiaries (e.g., Barclays Capital). This industry has dramatically changed since the crisis. In particular, the face of the US investment banks has been transformed. In March 2008, Bear Stearns became the largest casualty of the "credit crunch" to that date when the failing investment bank was purchased by J. P. Morgan Chase for a nominal amount ($2 per share or $236 million). The following September witnessed further turmoil with the demise of Lehman Brothers and the sale of Merrill Lynch to Bank of America. The two remaining large investment banks, Goldman Sachs and Morgan Stanley, converted into commercial banks (so they could raise more retail / core deposit funding). So by mid-2009 the major U.S. investment banks had either collapsed, merged or converted into traditional commercial banks. Nevertheless, of those banks still in existence, the main "players" remain pretty much the same although some Europeans appear to have strengthened their relative position (including Barclays Capital).

There are few independent U.K. merchant banks as most have been acquired by overseas investment and commercial banks. Table 3.3 illustrates the importance of London as an investment banking centre as banks based in the city play a dominant role in the markets in foreign equities trading, foreign exchange trading, over-the-counter derivatives, and international bonds issuance.

1.   U.K. Banks and the Credit Crisis[1]

As we have already noted, turmoil in the banking system since mid-2007 has impacted severely on the U.K.'s economic prospects. What was once a profitable, dynamic and innovative banking sector has been publicly humiliated, its bankers have been derided, and lending activity has almost stalled. This section briefly highlights the key crisis events that unfurled between mid-2007 and mid-2009, impacting on the U.K. banking sector.

The U.S. sub-prime crisis that "broke" in the summer of 2007 raised international concerns about banks' exposure to real estate lending and also the value of securities backed by property assets. All banks with

Table 3.3 London's share of investment banking and other international financial services (%)

Trends in UK's share (%)	1992	1995	1998	2001	2004	2005	2006	2007	2007 ($bn)	% change (2001–2007)
Cross-border bank lending	16	17	20	19	20	20	20	21	65,673	197
Foreign equities turnover	64	61	65	56	44	43	50	46	4,261	132
Foreign exchange daily turnover	27	30	33	31	31	32	32	34	13,594	170
Exchange-traded derivatives turnover	12	12	11	7	7	6	7	6	970	35
Over-the-counter derivatives daily turnover	—	27	36	36	43	—	—	43	10,614	293
Marine insurance net premium income	24	21	14	18	19	21	24	—	4.75	125
Fund management (as a source of funds)	—	—	8	8	8	7	8	—	49,425	65
Hedge funds assets	—	—	—	9	19	20	21	—	3605	620
Private equity	—	—	—	6	24	22	14	—	515	750
IPOs	—	—	—	—	23	27	25	18	50	—
Securitisation	—	—	—	—	4	4	6	6	237	451

Note also the major share in other banking areas such as cross-border lending (both commercial and investment banks undertake this type of business).
Source: International Financial Markets 2008, City of London Corporation.

significant real estate exposure came under scrutiny by analysts and (more importantly) depositors and investors (see Berger et al., 2009).

The crisis that occurred at Northern Rock in early September 2007 was the first bank run in the U.K. for over a century. To stem depositor panic, as noted above, the U.K. government announced a full guarantee of depositors' savings. Underlying causes of the Northern Rock failure included overaggressive growth in mortgage lending, and overdependence on short-term wholesale funding. To further strengthen depositor confidence, on 1 October 2007 the U.K. authorities strengthened its deposit guarantee scheme, by eliminating a provision whereby deposits between £2,000 and £35,000 were only 90% guaranteed (a factor that had contributed to the loss of depositor confidence in Northern Rock).

On 6 December 2007, worries about the possibility of a major slowdown in the U.K. economy led the Bank of England to implement a base rate cut down to 5.5%. This was the first of series of cuts that saw the base rate reduced to a historically unprecedented 0.5% by March 2009. On 12 December 2007, the Bank of England also participated in a coordinated international effort to increase liquidity in the interbank markets (as banks were not lending to one another in wholesale short-term money markets) by increasing the size of its next two auctions of short-term funds, in December 2007 and January 2008, from £2.85bn to £11.35bn each (the Bank of England was injecting more short-term money into the banking system, hoping this would boost bank liquidity and encourage them to lend).

Concerns about global financial sector instability continued into 2008 and on 21 January 2008 several global stock market indexes, including the U.K.'s FTSE 100, plummeted, amid continuing concerns over the scale of losses emanating from U.S. sub-prime lending and the potential for a global recession. The U.S. Federal Reserve cut their federal funds rate by 0.7% and the U.K. authorities also responded with a 0.25% cut in the base rate on 7 February 2008.

On 17 February 2008 the U.K. government finally exhausted its attempts to find a private sector buyer for Northern Rock, and announced the remedy of full-scale nationalization. A few days later, on 21 February 2008, the U.K. Banking (Special Provisions) Act was introduced providing new provisions for faster intervention and resolution of bank failures, in recognition that authorities' powers to intervene had been inadequate as the crisis at Northern Rock first broke and escalated. The new powers allowed for the authorities (namely, the Bank of England) to intervene and help sort out problems at a troubled bank at a stage before corporate bankruptcy procedures were triggered. Permissible types of intervention would include transfer of assets and liabilities to a third-party bank, transfer of assets to a "bridge bank," temporary nationalization, or liquidation.

In an attempt to inject more liquidity into a floundering U.K. banking system, on 21 April the Bank of England introduced a Special Liquidity Scheme (that had been announced in March), to allow banks to swap temporarily high-quality, illiquid mortgage-backed, and other securities for Treasury Bills. Swaps would be available on demand throughout the following six months. The swaps were initially for a period of one year, but were renewable for periods of up to three years. An estimated £50bn in liquid assets would be made available through the scheme. The banks would receive liquid assets of lower value than the illiquid securities being exchanged. The swaps were available only for assets existing at the end of 2007. U.K. banks and building societies had borrowed £185bn from this scheme by February 2009.

While the monetary authorities continued with their efforts to inject liquidity into the banking system, the potential for write-offs of non-performing assets to erode the capitalization of the U.K.'s largest banks was a growing concern and in late April, Royal Bank of Scotland (RBS) announced plans to raise £12bn in capital via a rights issue. This followed an announcement of a £5.9bn write-down on its investment portfolio, at the time the largest such announcement by any U.K. bank. Over the next few months, several other U.K. banks announced plans to raise new capital although these were not always too successful. For instance, on 18 July 2008 Barclays announced that only 18% of the shares in a £4.5bn rights issue had been taken up, with the rest acquired by an investment group including the Qatar Investment Authority.

In July 2008, HBOS attempted to raise £4bn through a rights issue, but only 8% was taken up, the remainder reverting to the underwriters. The inability of U.K. banks to convince their current shareholders to invest in rights issues provided a clear signal that further serious difficulties lay ahead. Growing concerns about the stalling of the housing market prompted a U.K. government announcement on 2 September of a temporary (one-year) rise in stamp duty (a tax on property purchases) exemption from £125,000 to £175,000.

September 2008 or "meltdown month" experienced the most momentous events global banking systems have experienced in over 70 years. Two major U.S. government sponsored organizations, Fannie Mae and Freddie Mac (responsible for the securitization of around 50% of U.S. mortgages) had been placed in "conservatorship" (effective government ownership). Following crisis meetings held over the weekend of 12–14 September, Lehman Brothers, the fourth largest U.S. investment bank, filed for bankruptcy. The Lehman collapse triggered a spectacular sequence of events that brought the global financial system to the brink of catastrophe, including the failure of AIG (the largest U.S. insurance firm) and Washington

Mutual (the largest U.S. savings and loan institution) as well as various bank bailouts in Europe (Fortis, Dexia, Hypo Real Estate). In the U.K., Lloyds TSB announced its acquisition of the troubled HBOS for £12bn (with strong government encouragement). And at the end of September, the UK government announced that it was acquiring the mortgage-lending arm of Bradford and Bingley, and selling the still-viable depositor base and branch network to the Spanish Santander banking group.

The main features of the U.K. government's immediate response to the crisis has been policy actions aimed at boosting capital and liquidity positions of U.K. banks and also providing various guarantees aimed at encouraging lending activity. On 8 October 2008, the U.K. government announced that it would do the following: .

- Allocate £50bn for recapitalization of ailing banks. The mechanism would be government purchase of (nonvoting) preference shares;
- Provide an extension of the Special Liquidity Scheme, making available on demand Treasury Bills to the value of at least £200bn, to be swapped for illiquid high-quality securitized assets;
- Treasury guarantees would be provided on commercial terms for up to £250bn of wholesale funding.

Two days previously, on 6 October 2008, the U.K. government had lifted the ceiling on the deposit guarantee scheme from £35,000 to £50,000. Although this fell short of the guarantees of all deposits that had recently been announced by the Irish and German governments, the impression of an implicit 100% guarantee was conveyed by the announcement on 8 October that the deposits of all U.K. residents in Icesave, the internet banking branch of the failed Icelandic bank Landsbanki, would be guaranteed by the Treasury.

On 13 October 2008, capital injections were announced for RBS (£20bn), and Lloyds TSB and HBOS (£17bn combined), increasing the government stakes in their ownership to around 60% and 40%, respectively. In return for government capital injections, the U.K. banks were required to make commitments to lend at competitive rates to homeowners and small businesses, reschedule mortgage payments for homeowners facing difficulties, and exercise restraint over executive compensation. Meanwhile Barclays announced that it planned to raise £6.5bn by private means, avoiding the need for partial nationalization.

On 3 November 2008, the U.K. government set-up a new "arms-length" company, U.K. Financial Investments Limited (UKFI), to manage the banks in public ownership, Northern Rock and Bradford and Bingley. A large fiscal stimulus was announced on 24 November 2008, including a temporary reduction in the rate of Value Added Tax (VAT) from 17.5% to 15%, until the end of 2009. Renewed efforts to restore confidence became essential when official statistics published in January 2009 showed the U.K. economy to be in recession for the first time since the early 1990s. On 14 January, the U.K. government announced that it would guarantee up to £20bn of loans to small- and medium-sized firms. On 19 January, a comprehensive plan was announced to restore confidence to the U.K. financial markets. Building on the measures implemented in October 2008, the principal features included

- Extension of the drawdown window for new debt under the Credit Guarantee Scheme (CGS), intended to reduce the risks on interbank lending;
- a new facility for asset backed securities to be used as collateral for banks seeking to raise additional funds to support mortgage lending;
- extension of the maturity date for the Bank of England's Discount Window Facility, providing liquidity by allowing banks to swap illiquid assets for Treasury Bills. This provision replaced the Special Liquidity Scheme;
- a new Bank of England facility for purchasing high quality assets. The Treasury will authorise initial purchases of up to £50bn, financed by the issue of Treasury Bills; and
- subject to Treasury assessment on a case-by-case basis, certain bank assets were to be eligible for inclusion in a new capital and asset protection scheme.

On 21 February 2009, the Banking Act 2009 established a permanent Special Resolution Regime (SRR), providing the authorities with tools to deal with banks facing financial difficulties. Details of recourse to the capital and asset protection scheme by RBS and the Lloyds Banking Group (formerly Lloyds TSB and HBOS) were unveiled shortly afterwards. Having posted recorded losses of £24bn, RBS would participate in respect of £325bn of assets, in exchange for a fee of £6.5bn. RBS will bear first losses of up to £19.5bn, and make new lending commitments totalling £25bn for 2009. The Treasury also agreed to purchase £13bn of capital, and granted an option for a further £6bn. Exercise of this option would leave 95% of RBS in public ownership. Lloyds announced subsequently that it had agreed to participate in respect of £260bn of assets, increasing its public ownership stake from 43% to 65%.

The U.K. base rate reached 0.5% on 5 March 2009. With its interest rate ammunition virtually exhausted, the Bank of England announced the implementation of quantitative easing, a new form of monetary stimulus.

They assigned £75bn for the direct purchase of assets (predominantly gilts) from the banking system, with the banks' accounts at the central bank to be credited directly with newly created money.

On 18 March 2009 the FSA published the Turner Review of bank regulation. Recommendations included extension of coverage of bank regulation based on economic substance rather than legal form; improved capital provisioning; enhanced liquidity regulation and supervision; improved supervision of credit rating agencies; codes covering remuneration to limit incentives for excessive risk-taking; centralized clearance of trades in credit default swaps (CDS) to reduce counterparty risk; and improved regulation of cross-border banking.

The first failure of a U.K. financial institution in 2009 occurred on 30 March when the Treasury announced its acquisition of around £1.5bn of nonperforming mortgages and commercial property loans from Dunfermline Building Society. The rest of the Dunfermline's loans portfolio, and its deposits and branch network, were taken over by Nationwide Building Society.

In July 2009 the Walker Review that focused on corporate governance in U.K. banks and other financial firms was published. The report highlights that weak corporate governance structures were likely to have been responsible for excessive risk-taking by banks and therefore were a cause of the crisis. Stronger oversight of the composition and role of boards is recommended, especially covering executive remuneration, risk management, and other strategic issues. Institutional investors are also asked to play a more active role in the governance of banks and other financial institutions.

One can see that a lot has happened since the onset of the crisis in mid-2007, and the implications of these dramatic changes are just becoming slowly apparent. What is clear is that we have a dramatically different UK banking system than we had just a few years ago. By mid-2009, two of the country's largest banks, Royal Bank of Scotland (70%) and Lloyds Group (43%), are in state ownership while Northern Rock remains 100% state owned. Even those banks not under state ownership have benefited directly or indirectly from the massive capital and liquidity provision granted by the government via the Bank of England. There is ongoing debate about how the government should divest their bank holdings as the Financial Times reports in Box 3.1 show.

The established tri-partite regulatory structure where the Bank of England undertook monetary policy, the Financial Services Authority (FSA) regulated the banks, and the Treasury acted on behalf of the government seems to be less than a success. Various proposals suggest a reorganization of the current regulatory structure—the most common being to reduce the

Box 3.1   Privatisation of UK banks post crisis?

Rapid mass privatization, anyone? Of the various ways of ridding the British government of its unwanted bank stakes, the quickest would be to distribute shares to the adult public. For a struggling government, this might seem like a vote winner—after all, every household in the UK has £3,000 invested in the Royal Bank of Scotland and Lloyds Banking Group alone. Predictably, the Treasury officials playing fund manager over at UK Financial Investments, the body managing the 70 per cent and 43 per cent stakes in RBS and Lloyds respectively, mention the idea nowhere in the exit strategy paper released on Monday.

This is hardly surprising, not just because "shock therapy" has fallen out of fashion in recent years, blamed for corruption, disorderly markets, undercapitalised industries and even higher adult mortality rates in some post-communist societies. It is a non-starter because all non-cash methods of privatisation have zero appeal to Alistair Darling, Chancellor of the Exchequer. Distributing free vouchers exchangeable into shares in RBS and Lloyds might be a politician's dream, but it would not help repay the £37bn debt amassed in the October recapitalisation of the two banks. The political gains would also be short lived: households receiving the windfall would have to hand it back in higher taxes.

UKFI's exit strategy will therefore depend on a mixture of institutional placements, secondary offerings and issuance of structured instruments such as exchangeable bonds. UKFI is also open to what it calls reactive options, such as strategic sales through mergers or acquisitions, private stake sales and share repurchases by RBS and Lloyds (if they can ever afford them). UKFI sees itself probably using a welter of different methods to offload its investments. That is less dramatic than rapid mass privatisation. But taxpayers have had as much excitement as they can take from the banks for quite some time.

Source: Financial Times, July 13, 2009.

role of the FSA and bolster that of the Bank of England—is needed if the financial system is to be overseen appropriately. Only time will tell how these issues work out. The U.K.'s National Audit Office reported in December 2009 that the official bank bailout cost stood at £850bn. In contrast, the Labour government's pre-budget report (of the same month) reckoned that once all bank assets acquired in the crisis were sold, the rescue scheme would end up costing just £8bn, barely 0.5% of GDP.

2.   Performance of U.K. Banks

Up until mid-2007, U.K. banks had been among Europe's best performing financial firms. This was because U.K. banks benefited from the buoyant domestic economy and also managed to maintain relatively high interest margins (the difference between interest revenue and interest cost) although these have fallen since 1997. In addition, costs have been reduced and provisioning (the amount of funds set aside to cover loans that are not repaid) has fallen dramatically. Also the lack of foreign competition in the retail banking market has been argued by some as another reason why profitability has been substantial. Taking these factors together, this resulted in substantial banking sector profitability up until year-end 2007 and a collapse in 2008.

Table 3.4 shows the trend in domestic business net interest margins for a handful of U.K. banks up to 2008. One can see that some of the main banks have been able to sustain margins around the 2–3% level. While interest income, as a proportion of total income, declined during the second half of the 1980s and the recession years of the early 1990s, it increased from 1993 onward exceeding 60% between 1996 and 1998, but fell gradually from then to 2006. Table 3.5 shows a broader measure of interest margins—net interest income as a proportion of total assets—for banking systems overall in the U.K., Europe, the U.S., and Japan. It can be seen that U.K. banks have managed to generate higher levels of margins than their counterparts in Europe and Japan, although U.S. bank margins are typically higher. This is one of the main factors explaining why U.S. banks have been, on average, the most profitable in the Western world up until 2007!

As already mentioned, banks have increasingly relied on noninterest income as a source of total income. This is shown for major U.K. banks up until 2006 in table 3.6—thereafter this source of income has collapsed and has been replaced by interest income. Note also that the MBBG posted negative net income in 2008, reflecting the massive losses posted as a result of the credit crisis.

On the cost side, the main U.K. banks have been, on average, successful at reducing their cost-to-income ratios, from around 65% in 1994 to 54% in 1999. These costs increased to around 60% by 2004 (presumably associated with the expenditures incurred from mergers and acquisitions activity and other restructuring), but then fell to just under 54% by 2007. The credit crisis effects can be clearly seen in table 3.6 when cost-to-income levels increased to 109% forcing the MBBG to post losses for 2008. Staff costs as a proportion of total income have also declined to around 27% of gross income by 2006 but increased thereafter. In addition, the net costs of provisioning fell since 1992, acting as a strong boost to overall profitability although these have increased gradually from 2000 onwards and

Table 3.4 Net interest margins—U.K. retail banks, 1990–2008

Bank	1990	1995	1996	1997	1998	1999	2000	2001	2002	2003	2004	2005	2006	2007	2008
Barclays	3.9	4.2	4.3	4.5	4.4	4.5	4.2	3.8	3.6	3.6	2.6	3.2	2.9	3.1	2.6
HBOS	n.a	n.a	n.a	n.a	n.a	n.a	n.a	2	1.9	1.8	1.8	1.8	1.8	1.6	1.6
HSBC Bank	n.a	n.a	n.a	n.a	2.5	2.7	2.7	2.8	2.3	2.2	2.1	2.1	2.0	2.1	2.0
Lloyds TSB	n.a	3.6	3.5	3.7	3.8	4	3.6	3.5	3.3	3.0	2.8	3.1	2.4	2.5	2.7
Royal Bank of Scotland	3.1	2.4	2.3	2.2	2.3	3.1	3.0	3.2	3.1	3.0	2.8	2.6	2.5	2.3	2.1

Notes: (a) Net interest margins 5 net interest income as a % of average interest earning assets

(b) n.a 5 not applicable.

Source: (a) Adapted from *Banking Business. An Abstract of Banking Statistics* (2009), vol. 26, table 3.06; (2005), vol. 22, table 3.08, p. 37; and (1999), vol. 16, table 3.07, p. 35 (British Bankers Association: London) and own estimates.

Table 3.5   Net interest income / total assets—U.K., European, U.S., and Japanese banks, 1995–2007

						Net Interest Income / Total Assets						
	1995	1996	1997	1998	1999	2000	2001	2002	2003	2004	2005	2006	2007
United Kingdom	2.2	2.07	1.99	2.01	1.96	1.66	1.68	1.82	2.24	2.44	1.39	2.28	2.33
Euro Zone	1.79	1.67	1.52	1.44	1.39	1.34	1.35	2.13	2.04	2.00	1.83	1.79	1.75
European Union	1.84	1.73	1.58	1.51	1.45	1.38	1.4	2.70	2.62	2.52	2.36	2.36	2.36
United States	3.44	3.46	3.37	3.25	3.26	3.28	3.34	3.44	3.28	3.19	3.23	3.66	3.11
Japan	1.44	1.39	1.31	1.37	1.42	1.27	1.37	1.83	1.76	1.74	1.73	1.73	1.66

Notes: (a) Before 1 May 2004, European Union countries included Austria, Belgium, Denmark, Finland, France, Germany, Greece, Ireland, Italy, Luxembourg, Netherlands, Portugal, Spain, Sweden, and the United Kingdom. After that the European Union membership expanded to include Cyprus, Czech Republic, Estonia, Hungary, Latvia, Lithuania, Malta, Poland, Slovakia and Slovenia. (b) Euro Zone countries include Austria, Belgium, Finland, France, Germany, Greece, Ireland, Italy, Luxembourg, Netherlands, Portugal, and Spain. (c) Slovenia is not included in the 2007 result for consistency.

Source: The figures from 1995 to 2001 are from *European Commission (2002)*, The Monitoring of Structural Changes and Trends in the Internal Market for Financial Services, Study Contract ETD/2001/B5-3001'A/63, November 2002, Annex Table 84. The figures from 2002 to 2007 are calculated from Bankscope.

Table 3.6 Income of major British banking groups, 1985–2008 (% of gross income)

	1985	1986	1987	1988	1989	1990	1991	1992	1993	1994	1995	1996	1997	1998	1999	2000	2001	2002	2003	2004	2005	2006	2007	2008
Net interest income	65.5	63.7	62.7	63.8	62.5	61.4	59.7	57.8	55.5	57.2	57.3	60.8	61.3	60.7	59.3	56.8	55.9	55.1	51.3	43	42.1	41.3	46	64.3
Non-interest income (net)	34.5	36.3	37.3	36.2	37.6	38.7	40.3	42.2	44.5	42.8	42.7	39.2	38.7	39.3	40.7	43.2	44.1	44.9	48.7	57	57.9	58.7	54	35.5
Net income	34.6	34.8	35.5	34.8	35.2	34	33.8	34.1	36.8	35.9	36.3	37.9	39	43.5	45.4	44.5	40.9	37.4	40.8	36.5	38.9	42	46	–9.4

then rocketed to record levels in 2008. These trends for the MBBGs are shown in table 3.7.

As already noted, with relatively high margins, lower costs, and buoyant economic conditions to increase loan demand, these have fed through into a sustained increase in the profitability of U.K. banks from 1992 to 1999, with after-tax returns hovering between 20% and 25% from 2000 to 2007 and then collapsing into major losses in 2008, as shown in table 3.8. The relatively high level of profitability experienced in 2006 and 2007 was the end to the U.K. banking boom. For instance, Barclays posted a return-on-equity (ROE) of 20.5% in 2007, and this fell to 14.6% in 2008; Lloyds Group reported an ROE of 34% in 2007, and this fell to 8% in 2008; and most spectacularly, RBS's ROE declined from 18.6% in 2007 to minus 43.7% in 2008 (hence the government bailout!). U.K. bank profitability has rebounded since then, although the heady days of the mid-2000s appear a long way off.

3. Changing Regulatory Environment

The regulatory environment in the U.K. banking and financial services industry has changed dramatically since the mid-1980s. In general, new legislation has covered four main areas. First, a range of regulatory changes have been sought to reduce demarcation lines between different types of financial service firms (especially between banks and building societies) as well as commercial and investment banking business. Second, the U.K. has also implemented various pieces of EU legislation into domestic banking law facilitating the introduction of the single banking licence and harmonising prudential regulation for both commercial banks and investment firms. Third, legislation laid down in the Financial Services and Markets Act 2001 to put in place the transfer of regulatory responsibility for the whole financial system to a "super regulator"—the Financial Services Authority—in the light of the Labour Government's announcement to make the Bank of England independent for monetary policy purposes.

Changes governing the regulatory treatment of the building society sector have had a major impact on the competitive environment in the retail banking sector. Ironically, reforms that have been put in place to improve the competitive stance of the mutual sector vis-à-vis commercial banks have led to a systematic decline of the former. This is because most of the largest building societies, as outlined above, embraced demutualisation, leading to a shift of assets from the mutual to the commercial banking sector. While the mutual sector has declined in relative importance those societies that converted still mainly undertake mortgage business—their balance sheet structures have not changed dramatically. Having said this, however, the Cruickshank Report in 2000 noted that the mortgage sector was one of the most competitive segments of the U.K. banking sector. This it attributed partially to these conversions but more importantly to new insurance company entrants (such as Standard Life Bank) that offered highly competitive mortgage products. The same report also noted that competitive conditions in the U.K. mortgage market compare favourably with those of North America, France, and Germany.

Another area where the change in legislation has had a big impact is in the restructuring of the domestic merchant banking industry. Prior to the 1986 "Big Bang" reforms, investment banking and securities business was dominated by U.K. owned banks—mainly partnerships operating in the city. Independent U.K. firms like Morgan Grenfell, Kleinwort Benson, S. G. Warburg, and so on dominated domestic business. The "Big Bang" reforms allowed commercial banks to be members of the London Stock Exchange and the legal separation between stockbroking and jobbing firms (those operating on the floor of the exchange) was abandoned. This led to a frenzy of domestic and foreign commercial banks (as well as the main U.S. investment banks) acquiring domestic securities firms. The merger and acquisition frenzy faltered, to a certain extent, after the 1987 stock market crash—although Deutsche Bank acquired Morgan Grenfell in 1989. It commenced again post the U.K. recession, particularly from 1995 onwards, and by 2005 there were hardly any significant independent U.K. merchant banks. Investment banking and securities business in the U.K. are now dominated by the major U.S. "bulge bracket" firms (Goldman Sachs, Morgan Stanley, Merrill Lynch, and Citigroup's Global Corporate and Investment Banking Group) as well as by various Swiss (Credit Suisse First Boston and UBS Investment Bank) and German banks (Deutsche Bank).

The gradual structural deregulation relating to commercial banking, investment banking, securities business, and insurance now means that financial firms have the choice of being universal operators. The linkage between banks and markets has accelerated and financial innovation has exploded, particularly in structured products and securitized instruments linked to real estate (Frame and White, 2009). In the domestic banking market all of the commercial banks and building societies offer a full range of financial services to their customers. Even relatively new operators like Tesco (the supermarket chain) offer banking, insurance, and various investment services. The decision by the government to create a single financial services regulator (the Financial Services Authority) is another clear reflection of the ongoing universalization of the U.K. banking industry.

Many of the above mentioned regulatory initiatives sought to create a more competitive and innovative banking and financial system. Domestic banks became engaged in noninterest business on a bigger scale and competed with other domestic financial firms, as well as foreign banks and even new nonbanking firms that had moved into financial service provision. An area for excess competition was the real estate lending market where a boom in mortgages fed a property price bubble. When the bubble burst in the United States and sailed across the Atlantic in mid-2007, U.K. banks were overexposed to the property market, real estate prices fell, and (together with gridlock in interbank lending markets) the system collapsed. The U.K. regulatory response to the crisis has been rapid and aimed to reestablish stability in a crisis situation. The U.K. authorities have injected capital (via nationalisation), liquidity (via various schemes where banks could pledge unsellable assets in return for sellable treasury bills and other instruments), and various guarantees have been given to get bank lending moving. Banks' response to these initiatives has been sluggish—they remain reluctant to lend, have become much more risk averse and still have significant bad assets (particularly commercial real estate assets) on their balance sheets. Of the main U.K. banks, HSBC and Barclays have probably fared best—mainly because they have a larger proportion of their business outside the U.K. compared to their main rivals!

4. Conclusions

Up until mid-2007, the changing features of the U.K. banking system were mainly a consequence of the evolving market environment and also the result of various domestic regulatory reforms. Since the credit crisis hit in the summer of 2007, all has changed. It is estimated that the financial resources already committed by governments around the world in direct response to the credit crisis, amount to $7 trillion and the U.K. authorities have a big share! Short-term firefighting to try to prevent the crisis from evolving into a serious recession and deflationary spiral has been at the top of U.K. policy agenda as the crisis has developed.

U.K. banks have been transformed from highly profitable, well managed, and innovative institutions to pariahs—subject to constant public and private derision. There is extensive debate surrounding the longer-term implications of the crisis for the future architecture of the U.K. (and global) banking and financial system. In bank regulation, support has been expressed for a "return to basics" involving greater emphasis on simple leverage and liquidity ratios; more realistic risk assessment as the basis for risk-based capital regulation; greater transparency and the curtailment of opaque business models (e.g., complex securitisation and derivatives activity); and the development of effective early warning systems and other procedures for early intervention in cases of financial distress. Whatever changes take place, there is no doubt that the momentous events of the past

Table 3.7 Costs of major British banking groups, 1985–2008 (% of gross income)

	1985	1986	1987	1988	1989	1990	1991	1992	1993	1994	1995	1996	1997	1998	1999	2000	2001	2002	2003	2004	2005	2006	2007	2008
Operating expenses	65.4	65.2	64.5	65.2	64.8	66	66.2	65.9	63.2	64.1	63.7	62.1	61	56.5	54.6	55.5	59.1	62.6	59.2	63.5	61.1	58	54	109.4
Provisions (net)	11.7	11	30	6.1	31.6	19.3	25.7	27.3	19.7	8.1	7.4	5.6	5.3	7.1	6.6	6.6	7.9	9.8	9.2	7.5	8.2	9.2	11.8	39.7
Staff costs	39.1	39	37.6	38.3	37.6	37.7	31.1	36.3	34.8	35.9	35.7	33.6	32.4	29.3	28.7	27.6	29.1	28.4	27.5	25.3	25.3	26.4	29.3	35

Table 3.8 Profits of major British banking groups, 1985–2008 (% of gross income)

	1985	1986	1987	1988	1989	1990	1991	1992	1993	1994	1995	1996	1997	1998	1999	2000	2001	2002	2003	2004	2005	2006	2007	2008
Profits before tax	23	23.9	5.5	28.7	3.6	14.7	8.1	6.7	17.1	27.8	28.8	32.3	33.7	36.4	38.9	37.9	33	27.6	31.8	29.9	30.7	32.7	34.3	−49.1
Profits after tax	12.6	15.4	1.2	18.2	1.3	8	4.7	3	10.9	18.5	19	21	23.3	25.7	27.1	26.4	22.6	18.3	22.5	21.7	21.8	23.2	26.5	−44.2

24 months will resonate for many years to come, and that U.K. banks must anticipate significant restrictions on their future lending and securitization activities and risk-taking capabilities.

*The author is Professor in Banking and Finance and Head of Bangor Business School at Bangor University.

Note

1. Parts of this section are taken from Goddard, Molyneux, and Wilson (2009).

References

Berger, A. N, P. Molyneux, and J. O. S Wilson (2009). "Banking: An Overview," in *Oxford Handbook of Banking,* ed. A. N. Berger, P. Molyneux, and J. O. S. Wilson, Chapter 1. Oxford: Oxford University Press.

Competition in UK Banking: A Report to the Chancellor of the Exchequer (2000). The Cruickshank Review, available at the UK Governments Treasury website at: http://www.hm-treasury.gov.uk/documents/financial_services/banking/bankreview/fin_bank_reviewfinal.cfm (accessed July 8, 2010).

Frame, W. S., and L. J. White (2009). "Technological Change, Financial Innovation, and Diffusion in Banking," in *Oxford Handbook of Banking,* ed. A. N. Berger, P. Molyneux, and J. O. S. Wilson, Chapter 19. Oxford: Oxford University Press.

Goddard, J, P. Molyneux, and J. O. S. Wilson (2009). "Crisis in UK Banking: Lessons for Public Policy," *Public Money and Management* 29 (5 September): 277–284.

Turner Review (2009). A Regulatory Response to the Global Banking Crisis, March, London: Financial Services Authority. http://www.fsa.gov.uk/pubs/other/turner_review.pdf (accessed July 8, 2010).

Walker Review (2009). A Review of Corporate Governance in UK Banks and other Financial Industry Entities, July, London: HM Treasury.

4

The Sub-Prime Crisis, the Credit Crunch, and Bank "Failure": An Assessment of the U.K. Authorities' Response[†]

Maximilian J. B. Hall[*]

Abstract

On 8 October 2008 the U.K. government announced a far-reaching plan to restore financial stability, protect depositors, and reinvigorate the flow of credit to businesses and individuals in the U.K. The £400 billion bailout plan embraced three elements: a massive expansion in emergency liquidity support from the Bank of England; recapitalization of U.K. banks and building societies using taxpayers' money; and the provision of a government guarantee of new short- and medium-term debt issuance made by U.K.-incorporated banks and building societies. This action proved necessary in the wake of continuing and substantial weaknesses in many banks' share prices despite the temporary ban on short-selling imposed by the Financial Services Authority. It followed two revisions to domestic deposit protection arrangements, and the adoption of a piecemeal approach to failure resolution that saw the eventual nationalization of Northern Rock in February 2008, the nationalization of Bradford and Bingley in September 2008, and the brokering of takeover-rescues of Alliance and Leicester and HBOS by Banco Santander and Lloyds TSB, respectively, in July and September 2008, of the Cheshire and Derbyshire Building Societies by the Nationwide Building Society in September 2008, and of the Dunfermline Building Society by the Nationwide in March 2009. This metamorphosis in approach to failure resolution by the U.K. authorities in response to the sub-prime crisis and the credit crunch—nationalization by default to (part) nationalization as the preferred course of action, a policy continued under the second comprehensive bank bailout plan of January 2009—is duly analyzed in this article.

Introduction

Following the provision of a 100 percent guarantee to depositors and other creditors of Northern Rock in September 2007, a revision of deposit protection arrangements in October 2007, and a belated acceptance by the Bank of England (the Bank) of the need to dramatically expand the scale of its emergency liquidity support operations in the autumn of 2007 for both the market in general and Northern Rock in particular, domestic financial stability appeared to be restored. But, and not withstanding the eventual nationalization of Northern Rock in February 2008, the worsening of the credit crunch through 2008 and its impact on British banks' balance sheets served only to heighten investors' concerns about the health of the U.K. financial system. Stung by criticism from the House of Commons' Treasury Committee and others, the U.K. authorities duly drafted wide-ranging proposals to restore financial stability and prevent a recurrence of a Northern Rock–style fiasco, but, before they could enact the necessary legislative provisions, the U.K. banking industry's fortunes took a distinct turn for the worse. Unsurprisingly, the Alliance and Leicester, given its exposure to the U.K. housing market that was now in "meltdown" mode as lenders both withdrew loan products and raised the price of those remaining, was the first to suffer speculative attack. With the authorities' blessing, it was acquired by the Spanish bank Santander in July 2008 prior to reporting a 99 percent crash in pretax profits to just £2 million for the first half of 2008. The next to cause concern was HBOS, the U.K.'s largest mortgage lender, which announced, in July 2008, a 72 percent fall in pretax profits to £848 million for the first half of 2008. Following further sharp falls in its share price in the wake of a ratings downgrade, the bank was shepherded into the arms of Lloyds TSB under the terms of a £12.2 billion all-share takeover announced on 18 September 2008. And finally (if struggling building societies are ignored), Bradford and Bingley, the only surviving converted building society, also lost its independence following the nationalization of its loan book and the industry-financed sale of its deposits and branch network to Banco Santander on 29 September 2008. Such drastic action proved necessary in the wake of the bank's announcement of a pretax loss of £26.7 million for the first half of 2008, its subsequent downgrading by Moody's to just one notch above junk status, and its failure to find a "White Knight" amongst the U.K.'s five largest banks.

Whilst such ad hoc action temporarily calmed nerves, events surrounding the U.S. administration's attempt to enact the so-called ($700 billion) Paulson plan (i.e., the "Troubled Asset Relief Programme," or "TARP") further spooked markets on both sides of the Atlantic. Indeed, despite both the Upper and Lower houses of Congress voting in favor by the week ending 5 October 2008, stock markets went into free fall, with knock-on effects for a number of banks in Europe. This duly led to "beggar thy neighbour" blanket deposit guarantees being given to all or part of their national banking systems by the likes of Greece, Germany, and others following the lead taken by the Irish government, the British government content, at least for the time being, to increase the level of deposit protection from £35,000 to £50,000 on a per capita per bank basis. By now, however, it had become clear that a pan-European solution to financial/banking instability was needed, and that a more comprehensive solution, additional to the massive infusion of liquidity by central banks, was in order. Taxpayer-funded, recapitalization of sound but ailing banks, as practised by Scandinavian countries and Japan in the 1990s, seemed the only answer, in preference to a backdoor recapitalization through purchases of impaired assets at above-market prices (as feared under TARP in the United States). The evolution of official thinking, which ended up with the adoption of this approach, is duly examined in this article.

The paper is structured as follows. In Section 1, I briefly review the background to the collapse of Northern Rock, the events leading up to its eventual nationalization and the regulatory (and supervisory) response to the bank's demise as a private entity. In Section 2, I chart the authorities' handling of the troubled organizations Alliance and Leicester, HBOS, and Bradford and Bingley (plus some ailing building societies) before analyzing and explaining the nature of, and necessity for, the October 2008 and January 2009 bailout packages. Section 3 summarises and concludes.

1. The Northern Rock Crisis

1.1   A brief review of the events which led to its eventual nationalization

The events surrounding the collapse of Northern Rock—summarised in Table 4.1—are by now well known. The impact of the U.S. sub-prime crisis on the international wholesale money markets—and hence on Northern Rock, given its excessive reliance on such funding sources—that drove the bank into the arms of the Bank of England in September 2007 in search of an emergency liquidity lifeline and that subsequently led to a nationwide

Table 4.1   The Northern Rock crisis: Key events

14.9.07	Following assurances from the FSA that the bank is solvent, the Bank of England provides emergency funding, at a penalty rate, to Northern Rock because of the latter's acute funding difficulties.
17.9.07	HM Treasury announces a full guarantee of Northern Rock's existing deposits in an attempt to stem the deposit run on the bank and restore financial confidence. The guarantee is designed to last until the financial turmoil subsides.
1.10.07	The Chancellor of the Exchequer announces that the level of depositor protection available under the Financial Services Compensation Scheme is increased to 100 percent of £35,000 (previously, it was 100 percent of the first £2,000 plus 90 percent of the next £33,000), on a per institution, per customer basis.
19.10.07	The chairman of Northern Rock resigns.
16.11.07	The chief executive of Northern Rock resigns along with most of the Board.
21.1.08	The size of the Bank of England's loan to Northern Rock is revealed to have climbed to £28 billion.
24.1.08	House of Commons' Treasury Committee publishes its report on Northern Rock.
17.2.08	The Chancellor of the Exchequer announces that Northern Rock is to be nationalized, with a view to returning the bank to the private sector at some future date.
19.2.08	Emergency legislation allowing for the nationalization of Northern Rock is introduced to Parliament.
21.2.08	The bill to nationalize Northern Rock (and any other bank) receives the Royal Assent.

deposit run on the bank, have been well documented.[1] Likewise, the subsequent developments at the bank preceding its nationalization[2] in February 2008 have also been well chronicled.[3] While it is hoped to sell the bank back to the private sector at some future point, given recent events in the markets (see Section 1.2 below) and the continuing slowdown in the U.K. housing market, this is unlikely to happen in the short- to medium-term.

1.2   The regulatory response to the financial crisis and the Northern Rock fiasco

1.2.1   Actions taken by the Bank of England

Despite the intensifying liquidity crisis in the summer of 2007, the Bank initially refused to offer additional liquidity to the market other than through the "standing facility" under which banks can borrow (against eligible collateral), without limit, beyond their "target reserve balance" at a penalty of 100 basis points above the official Bank Rate, under the modifications to official money market operations introduced in 2006.[4] The Bank's reluctance to do more was based mainly on its fear that the moral hazard induced would damage long-term stability (see Hall, 2008).

The first sign of the Bank retracting from this principled approach came on 5 September when, in addition to accommodating the U.K. commercial banks' increased demand for target reserve balances, it announced that it would allow the banks to bid for an additional £4.4 billion of cash the following week, *without payment of a penalty*, if overnight rates remained high. The move was designed to narrow the gap between secured overnight rates and the official Bank Rate (5.75 percent), which had peaked at around 75 basis points, and to stimulate interbank lending by increasing the banks' liquidity cushion. Unlike the European Central Bank's (ECB) earlier move on 22 August (see Hall, 2008, table 1) it was not intended to influence the three months' rate that, the Bank argued, was beyond their control, comprising both liquidity and credit risk premia. In the event, the full £4.4 billion was taken up by the market on 13 September.

Having initially stood out from the crowd, the Bank was always "on a hiding to nothing" if unfolding events necessitated a change of tack. And, unfortunately for the Bank, just such a change was deemed necessary only two days after publication of a letter sent by the governor to the Treasury Select Committee outlining his reasons for reticence. For, on 14 September, following assurances given by the Financial Services Authority (FSA) that the bank remained solvent, the Bank provided emergency funding to Northern Rock. (Additional lending facilities were also made available on 9 October—see House of Commons, 2008a, p. 127, para. 341.) The move was taken to allow the bank to continue operating, to reassure depositors of the bank, and to prevent wider contagion should a bank run spread. Under the arrangements, the bank had access to an unlimited amount of funding (subject to the provision of "suitable" collateral, which could now include mortgages and mortgage-backed securities) for as long as the turmoil persisted,[5] although a (unrevealed) penalty rate was imposed.[6] By the end of December the scale of Northern Rock's indebtedness to the Bank had risen to over £25 billion, the U.K. taxpayers' total exposure had risen to over £55 billion (because of the extension in the Treasury's deposit guarantee—see Section 1.2.3 below) and there was no end to the bank's plight nor to the credit crunch (see Hall, 2009b, table 2) in sight.

Subsequent to this, on 19 September, the Bank announced that it would, after all, lend to banks for periods of up to three months and against a wider range of collateral than it had hitherto (to include, as in the Northern Rock case, mortgages, for example) under a new emergency facility. An initial £10 billion injection of cash, via public auction, was to be made the following week, with weekly auctions to follow thereafter until the market turmoil subsided.

In the event, however, there were no takers for the newly proffered funds at either the auction held on 26 September or in subsequent weeks.

Whether this reflected an underlying improvement in banks' liquidity positions, the costly nature of the funding, or a reluctance by borrowers to be stigmatized by taking advantage of it, nobody is too sure. But it is clear some small banks still faced funding problems in the wholesale markets at the time; and the market's appetite for the auction of three-month money announced on 12 December suggested that funds, at the right price, were still widely needed and that borrowers' fears of being stigmatized if they availed themselves of the special funding facilities might be waning. Indeed, this appears to be one of the positive outcomes of the coordinated central bank action announced on 12 December (see Hall, 2008, tables 1 and 2), together with a narrowing of the spreads between three-month interbank rates and policy rates.

Since the end of 2007, the Bank has been more receptive to the idea of expanding emergency liquidity support in the face of a worsening financial and economic outlook, both at home and abroad. Apart from a willingness to roll over and increase the size of auctions of three-months, sterling-denominated money, it provided £5 billion of three-day money in the wake of the uncertainty generated by the Fed-sanctioned rescue of Bear Stearns (17 March 2008); and, on 21 April 2008, it unveiled a new £50 billion—later extended to £200 billion—"Special Liquidity Scheme" under which it will swap Treasury bills for securities backed by mortgages made before 1 January 2008 or credit card debts. Since then, the Bank has offered substantial dollar-denominated funds to the market, both on an overnight basis and for longer periods, following currency swaps with the Fed, and has extended the range of collateral it is willing to accept in all of its deals. On 16 October 2008, the Bank also unveiled a revised set of "rules" for its money market operations, designed to operate in normal and crisis times. A new "operational standing facility" will allow banks to borrow against top-quality collateral, without the risk of being identified, for up to a month. A permanent "discount window facility" will also allow banks to swap illiquid assets for government securities, again without the risk of being identified, for up to one month (later increased to one year). The fees charged will depend on the size of the loan and quality of collateral offered. And, finally, as part of the Government's "bailout" package of January 2009—see Section 2.4—the Bank, from 2 February 2009, was authorized to purchase up to £50 billion of triple-A rated corporate debt under a new "Asset Purchase Facility," the amount subsequently being increased to £200 billion, although the bulk was spent on the purchase of government securities (i.e., gilts).

1.2.2 Actions taken by the FSA

Apart from endorsing the moves to reform the deposit protection, failure resolution and Tripartite Arrangements—see Section 1.2.3 and Sections

2.1 to 2.4 below—the FSA also published a discussion paper reviewing liquidity requirements for banks and building societies (FSA, 2007a), in the light of its earlier acknowledgement of flaws in its assessment regime (FSA, 2007b). A consultative paper on the subject, promised for mid-2008, was eventually published in December 2008 (see FSA, 2008a) with new rules being introduced in 2009 (see FSA, 2009a).

Further to this work, the FSA began monitoring all wholesale and retail banks and deposit-taking institutions more closely under a continuing, principles-based philosophy, while reviewing its risk-assessment and risk-mitigation practices. Its internal audit division also delivered a report on the lessons to be learnt from the Northern Rock affair, as promised in December 2007 (FSA, 2007c), although the Treasury Committee much preferred an independent inquiry (House of Commons, 2008a, p. 104, para. 268). The conclusions were subsequently made public in March 2008 (FSA, 2008b), precipitating the adoption of a "supervisory enhancement programme" by the FSA.[7] Finally, the new Chairman of the FSA, Lord Turner, revealed his review (the "Turner Review") of U.K. regulation in the light of the global banking crisis on 18 March 2009 (FSA, 2009b). (For further details, see Hall, 2009c.)

1.2.3   Actions taken by HM Treasury

As noted earlier, the Treasury first took action in September 2007 to amend the deposit protection arrangements—blanket protection was extended to all depositors until the financial turmoil subsides—and to put in train, with the other Tripartite Authorities, a wider review of such arrangements (HM Treasury, FSA, and Bank of England, 2007).[8] (Under the proposals announced by the FSA in November 2007 for adoption in April 2008, the Financial Services Compensation Scheme's annual capacity to pay out depositors was increased from £2.7 billion to £4.03 billion, to be funded through ex-ante contributions from financial intermediaries.) And, in response to instability in world banking markets, the de jure limit of protection afforded U.K. depositors was raised twice in October 2008, initially to £35,000[9] and then to £50,000.

Second, the Treasury was keen to reform the so-called Tripartite Arrangements (Bank of England, 1998) that relate to the arrangements put in place in October 1997 to deliver financial stability by ensuring close cooperation and coordination between the interested parties (the Bank, the Treasury, and the FSA), especially in the event of a financial crisis, following the Labour government's decision to strip the Bank of responsibility for banking supervision (Hall, 1997). The involvement of the Bank is necessary because of its continuing lender-of-last-resort function and its responsibility for "maintaining overall financial stability,"[10] while the FSA's presence is obviously required as the main regulatory/supervisory authority and the first port of call for any financial firm that gets into difficulties. Finally, the Treasury is primarily responsible for the international structure of regulation and the regulation that governs it, and has to be consulted if there is a perceived need for an official "support operation." Basically then, in the case of the liquidity lifeline thrown to Northern Rock, the FSA's role was to determine whether or not the bank was solvent, following an appeal for help from the bank; the Bank, as well as the FSA, had to determine whether its failure posed a systemic threat; and the Treasury, as keeper of the nation's purse strings, had to decide, following the receipt of advice from the former bodies, whether to authorize a support operation.

Although both the FSA and the Bank[11] were at pains not to criticize the working of the arrangements during their interrogations at the hands of the Treasury Select Committee, outside commentators took a different view. Moreover, the Treasury, in its evidence before the Committee (given on 25 October 2007), indicated that it would seek clarification, in a future draft, of its power to ultimately determine the outcome of Tripartite talks in a wider set of circumstances than it believes is currently covered by the agreements. (Should the Bank have bowed to FSA/Treasury pressure to provide additional liquidity earlier?) Additionally, like the Bank, it is keen that the central bank is involved more directly in the monitoring of individual banks' financial health, notwithstanding the FSA's broader remit in this area. Finally, the Treasury was also determined to reform bank failure resolution policies to reduce the impact of bank failure, should it happen. The formal Tripartite proposals for reform were revealed on 30 January 2008 in the shape of a consultation paper (HM Treasury, FSA, and Bank of England, 2008a); and two further consultation papers were subsequently issued in July 2008 (see HM Treasury, FSA, and Bank of England, 2008b and 2008c). The new Banking Bill was, in turn, introduced to Parliament on 7 October 2008 (House of Commons, 2008b), and the resultant Banking Act was adopted in February 2009 (see Appendix A).

2.   "Failure" Resolution Policy Post Northern Rock

2.1   Brokered takeover rescues

As a former building society, and hence an institution whose fortunes are inextricably linked to the state of the U.K. housing and property markets, with a funding model—roughly 50 percent wholesale and 50 percent retail—lying closest to that of Northern Rock, the Alliance and Leicester was always going to attract the attention of speculators and struggle to survive as an independent entity during the credit crunch. Along with

Bradford and Bingley, its shares suffered most in the wake of the near-collapse of Northern Rock, taking further hits following the announcement in February 2008 of £185 million of write-downs on Treasury investments for 2007. And then, in May 2008, a further £192 million of write-downs was revealed. Within two months, the bank, with the blessing of the FSA, had found a willing partner, the Spanish bank Banco Santander, which duly made a bid for the bank on 11 July 2008. Three days later, the Board formally accepted the offer, not surprising given that figures released at the end of the month revealed a 99 percent crash in pretax profits to just £2 million for the first half of 2008, following yet another £143 million of write-downs and £209 million of losses on toxic securities.

The next takeover-rescue brokered by the U.K. authorities was that of HBOS, the U.K.'s biggest mortgage lender, by Lloyds TSB. The first signs of trouble at the bank emerged in February 2008 when it announced sub-prime-related losses for 2007 of £227 million. These losses, however, were dwarfed by the £2.84 billion of first-quarter write-downs on complex debt securities announced at the end of April, which necessitated the instiga-tion of a £4 billion rights issue to repair damage to the bank's capital base. In the event, however, only 8.3 percent of its investors had taken up their allocations in the rights issue by 21 July, leaving the underwriters and sub-underwriters nursing hefty paper losses. And then, to make matters worse, a 72 percent fall in pretax profits to £848 million for the first half of 2008, following a £1.09 billion sub-prime-related write-down, was announced at the end of July. Desperate to avoid further carnage on the banking high street, the government duly waived, on national interest (i.e., financial stability) grounds, the competition rules to allow Lloyds TSB's £12.2 billion all-share takeover bid to proceed. The bid, announced on 18 September, was made in the light of a collapse in the bank's share price over the previous few days owing to ratings downgrades and investor concerns about the bank's excessive reliance on wholesale markets for its funding and on the U.K. property market for its profits, neither of which was desirable at that particular juncture. Despite HBOS's subsequent fall in share price, which led to the renegotiation of the takeover terms—0.605 of one Lloyds TSB share was now offered for one HBOS share rather than the original 0.833 agreed—the takeover was duly completed in January 2009, with the state taking a 43.4 percent stake in the combined entity under the industry bailout plan announced in October (see Section 2.3 below). Subsequent steep falls in the combined entity's share price, however, suggest that HBOS is proving more indigestible for Lloyd's TSB than originally envisaged, reopening the debate over whether nationaliza-tion of HBOS might have been the more sensible option, particularly in the light of the subsequent revelation that HBOS had received additional covert support of up to £25 billion from the Bank of England in the fourth quarter of 2008.[12]

The third takeover-rescue brokered by the authorities took place within the building society sector of the U.K.'s deposit-taking industry when the largest building society, the Nationwide, was cajoled into rescuing the struggling societies, the Derbyshire and the Cheshire. The announcement of takeover talks was made on 7 September 2008, and, with the blessing of the authorities, the deal was finalised before the end of the year. In this way it was hoped to preserve investor confidence in the building society movement—both societies were expected to report pretax losses for the first half of 2008—although further consolidation is inevitable.[13]

And the fourth and final takeover-rescue brokered by the authorities also involved the Nationwide when the Dunfermline Building Society, the largest in Scotland, was acquired by the former institution on 30 March 2009, having incurred losses on commercial real estate activities, sub-prime lending, and investments in mortgage-backed securities (MBS). Under the terms of the deal, involving activation of the "special resolution regime" for the first time (see Appendix A), the government paid the Nationwide £1.6 billion to assume all of the society's liabilities while retaining responsibility for over £900 million worth of the society's toxic loans/assets. The government expects to retrieve most of its "investment" through the eventual wind-down of the assets acquired and compensation from deposit-takers under the deposit sub-scheme of the Financial Services Compensation Scheme (FSCS).

2.2   Nationalization of Bradford and Bingley

As noted above, the Bradford and Bingley was the other converted building society to suffer from speculative attack on its share price in the wake of the near-collapse of Northern Rock, although, in this case, the eventual outcome was less favorable than for the Alliance and Leicester. Apart from its funding model, the other aspect of the bank's operations that particularly concerned investors was its over-dependence—they comprised over 85 percent of the mortgage book—on buy-to-let and "self-certified" mortgages, both of which contributed to rising arrears and repossessions as the U.K. housing market progressively deteriorated. Evidence of this first appeared with the announcement, in February 2008, of sub-prime-related losses of £226 million for 2007. Then, in June 2008, the bank announced that it would make losses of £8 million in the first four months of 2008 because of rising arrears on its mortgage book and a squeeze on its net interest margins. Accompanying this announcement was a statement that, because of dramatic changes in recent trading conditions, it had proved necessary to lower the rights issue price—from 82p. to 55p.—and to raise the amount of external funding sought from £300 million to £400 million, 23 percent to be provided by the U.S. private equity investor TPG Capital. Having destabilized the rights issue process, the bank's collapsing share price took a further hammering when, on 27 June 2008, the Board announced that it rebuffed entrepreneur Clive Cowdery's proposed rescue deal by his Resolution vehicle. A second downgrading of the bank's credit rating—from "A2" to "Baa1," the lowest rating of any U.K. bank—a few days later by Moody's led to TPG's withdrawal from the deal to inject £179 million into the ailing bank. This led the bank to revamp, for the third time in three weeks, its fund-raising efforts, duly raising the amount sought from the rights issue to £400 million to cover the £179 million shortfall. Under FSA pressure, the regulator being desperate to avoid another banking casualty, the bank's largest shareholders—Legal and General, M&G, Standard Life, and Insight Investments—reluctantly agreed to ride to the rescue, despite the bank's share price collapsing to 50p., 5p. below the rights issue price. In the next few days the share price continued to fall—to a low of 33p. on 8 July—as investors questioned the bank's long-term value, threatening heavy losses for the underwriters and sub-underwriters. The following month, the bank then revealed a first half loss of £26.7 million after making write-downs on its structured credit portfolio and suffering a £74.6 million credit impairment charge relating to rising arrears. A further downgrade, to just one notch above junk status, by Moody's at the end of September and a statement by the bank, just two days later, that it was to make further write-downs of up to £133.8 million, duly sealed the bank's fate. On 29 September 2008 the government announced that the bank was to be nationalized following the FSA's decision that the bank was no longer a viable deposit-taking institution and its failure to find a "White Knight" from the banking community.

Having learnt lessons from the earlier nationalization of Northern Rock and, given a determination to protect taxpayers' interests at all costs, the nationalization process was structured in such a way as to minimize potential costs for the public purse. The bank's £42 billion mortgage book was duly taken over by the state, to be wound down in due course, while the bank's 197 branches were sold to Banco Santander for £612 million. Intriguingly, however, the Chancellor secured the maximum protection for taxpayers from the unwinding of the mortgage book by forcing the U.K. banking sector to shoulder much of the risk. He did this by making the Treasury a more senior creditor than the FSCS, which was asked, on behalf of the banks, to pay £14 billion—funded by a short-term Bank of England loan later converted into a three-year government loan on which the banks must pay interest at one-year LIBOR plus 30 basis points—to Banco Santander to enable the Bradford and Bingley's insured deposits to be transferred to the Spanish bank. This means that any losses exceeding £3 billion or so, which are shouldered by equity investors and subordinated debt holders, will fall first upon the banks who will have to reimburse the FSCS via levies for any losses it incurs. Taxpayers will thus not take a hit unless losses exceed £17 billion or so, an unlikely scenario given that this would require arrears at the defunct bank to increase from the current 3 percent to something close to 10 percent.

2.3   Part-nationalisation under the October 2008 bailout plan

The October bailout plan, which reflected the government's attempt to move from a piecemeal approach to failure resolution (akin to "fire fighting") to a broadly based solution to a systemic crisis, embraced three elements (HM Treasury, 2008a). The first of these was a massive extension in the provision of emergency *liquidity* from the Bank of England.[14] At least £200 billion (double the amount previously intended) is now to be made available under the "Special Liquidity Scheme"; and, until markets stabilize, the Bank will continue to conduct regular auctions of three-months sterling-denominated funds and one-week dollar-denominated funds against a wider range of collateral.[15] The second element of the plan relates to the *recapitalization* of the banking industry. "Eligible institutions" (to include U.K.-incorporated banks and U.K. bank subsidiaries of foreign institutions that have a substantial business in the U.K. plus all building societies)[16] can approach the government for up to £25 billion of funding in aggregate in the form of preference shares, PIBS, or as assistance (e.g., through underwriting) to an ordinary equity fund-raising (at the institution's request).[17] In return for such assistance, recipient institutions will be bound by restrictions on dividend payouts and executive compensation and will be required to commit to lending to small businesses and home buyers. Finally, in order to try and reopen the market for medium-term funding for eligible institutions that agree to raise appropriate amounts of Tier 1 capital, the government will make available, for an interim period as agreed and on appropriate commercial terms,[18] a government guarantee of such institutions' new short- and medium-term debt issuance—in the form of senior unsecured debt instruments of varying terms of up to 36 months denominated in sterling, Euros, or U.S. dollars—to assist in refinancing maturing, wholesale funding obligations as they fall due. The government envisaged a take-up[19] of up to £250 billion under this guarantee scheme, the guarantees to be issued by a specifically designated, government-backed, English-incorporated company.

With respect to recapitalization, the initial government injections were announced on 13 October 2008. A total of £37 billion (£12 billion more than was initially envisaged) was injected into three of the largest banks, RBS, HBOS, and Lloyds TSB. The capital injections took the following forms: for RBS, a total of £20 billion was injected, comprising £15 billion of new equity and £5 billion of five-year preference shares, paying 12 percent per annum (this is better for taxpayers than the earlier proposal, envisaging investment in nonvoting preference shares only, as it allows them to benefit from any recovery in the banks' share price); for HBOS, a total of £11.5 billion was injected, £8.5 billion in new equity and £3.0 billion in preference shares; and, for Lloyds TSB, a total of £5.5 billion was injected, comprising £1 billion of preference shares and £4.5 billion of new equity. Assuming no "clawback" by existing shareholders at the open offer—the most likely scenario unless the restrictions on the payment of dividends were eased—this would give taxpayers a 57 percent (later confirmed at 57.9 percent but raised in January 2009 to 70 percent on conversion of the Treasury's preference share holdings into common equity) controlling stake in RBS and 43.5 percent (it turned out to be 43.4 percent) of the combined Lloyds TBS-HBOS entity (later named Lloyds Banking Group), with HBOS shareholders holding a 20 percent stake and Lloyds TSB shareholders a 36.5 percent stake.

In return for accepting public sector funds, the banks had to abide by a number of restrictions. First, they could not pay any dividends to ordinary shareholders until the preference shares were fully redeemed. Second, restrictions were placed on bonuses and executive remuneration. Third, lending to small businesses and home-owners must be maintained, at competitive prices, at 2007 levels (both the desirability and feasibility of this have been challenged in a number of quarters). Fourth, the government has a say in the appointment of new Board members. And, finally, the chief executive and chairman at both RBS and HBOS, were asked to "fall on their swords" and depart without payoffs. The government, in turn, promised to manage its investments at "arms length."[20]

Overall, the market's initial reaction to the announcement was positive—with the FTSE 100 rising by 8.3 percent on the day and CDS spreads on the large banks falling—but the share prices of the three banks affected fell further (by 14 percent in the case of Lloyds TSB, 27 percent in the case of HBOS, and 8 percent in the case of RBS) as investors pondered the likely impact of the restrictions imposed—not least that on the payment of dividends—leaving the government sitting on a paper loss of over £2 billion on its acquisitions (by 19 January 2009, this had risen to over £17 billion)! Moreover, medium-term sterling interbank rates barely moved. Longer term, external holders of sterling are likely to determine the extent to which the government can borrow to finance the bailout package,[21] the preferred domestic solution in the face of a deep recession.[22]

2.4   Extended nationalization under the January 2009 bailout plan

While the comprehensive bailout package of October 2008—and the subsequent £62 billion of covert central bank support—saved the British banking system literally from collapse, it failed to stimulate bank lending, as intended. As a result, a desperate attempt was made by the government in January 2009 to try to unblock lending channels as evidence emerged pointing to a serious contraction in the real economy and the withdrawal of foreign banks—Icelandic, Irish, EU, and North American—and others (e.g., GE Capital) from U.K. loan markets. The package, revealed on 19 January (HM Treasury, 2009a), comprised seven elements, and was supported by the FSA's decision to tweak the rules relating to banks' (i.e., those which benefited from the October 2008 bailout) use of internal models to generate regulatory capital charges—by switching from a "point-in-time" to a "through-the-cycle" assessment basis, the probability of loan default can now be averaged over the economic cycle rather than being based on the most recent, and hence more dismal, data—in order to increase the banks' capacity to lend in the downturn (FSA, 2009c).[23] The FSA has also indicated its willingness to treat a (post stress test) 4 percent core Tier-1 ratio (equivalent to a 6–7 percent tier-one ratio) as an "acceptable minimum," potentially providing further scope for an expansion in bank lending.

The detailed nature of the latest bailout package, which complemented the government's earlier introduction of a partial (50 percent) guarantee on up to £20 billion of working capital loans to SMEs, is duly analyzed immediately below before a wider assessment of the likely impact of the package and its chances of success is provided.

The first element of the bailout package involves the government, in return for a fee payable in cash or preference shares and verifiable commitments to support lending to "creditworthy" customers, insuring some of the risky assets currently held by U.K.-incorporated, authorized deposit-takers against extreme, unexpected losses (HM Treasury, 2009b). Banks, however, will still be liable for a proportion of any future losses on such assets beyond an agreed "first loss" amount before the insurance threshold is reached. And banks that have not yet written down such assets to reflect market prices will be asked to shoulder a higher proportion of possible future losses. The idea behind the scheme, which would be in place for at least five years and had earlier been adopted in the United States with respect to the bailouts of Citigroup and Bank of America, is to set a floor to the scale of losses that banks might incur on their *existing* loans and investments, thereby increasing certainty about bank solvency and enhancing financial stability. For the participating banks, this, in turn, should increase their willingness to lend as their need to hoard capital and liquidity against an uncertain future is correspondingly reduced. And, for the system as a whole, it should help defreeze the interbank markets, thereby increasing each bank's capacity and willingness to lend.

The main problems with the scheme, known as the "Asset Protection Scheme"—which was preferred to the creation of a "bad bank" (which would assume the illiquid toxic assets of the banks directly) because of the lack of up-front costs and the hope that merely offering to write the insurance would reduce the need for it as increased lending and economic activity are stimulated—lie in its practical application. For example, which assets should be insured, what premia should be charged, and where should the insurance threshold be drawn? The initial focus was to be on the banks' most toxic assets (e.g., collateralized debt obligations [CDOs] and MBS, which will continue to fall in value as long as house prices decline), as well as commercial property loans; and RBS was to be the "guinea pig." As for "price," this is the same problem that the U.S. authorities faced with their Troubled Asset Relief Programme, or "TARP," whose focus was switched from buying up toxic debt to bank recapitalization direct (Hall, 2009b); too high a premium and the banks will not play ball, probably accelerating their full nationalization, while too low a premium will saddle taxpayers with larger contingent liabilities. And, with respect to the establishment of the insurance threshold, again drawing it too low (i.e., forcing the banks to shoulder more of their unexpected losses) or too high will have the same effects as outlined immediately above for imposing too high/low a premium.[24]

The second strand of the "economy bailout" package, as the government prefers to call it, involves an extension of the time limit on the £250 billion Credit Guarantee Scheme for bank funding, announced as part of the October bailout package—see Section 2.3 above—from end-April 2009 to end-2009. The focus here is on keeping open this line of attack on the frozen interbank markets.

The third component relates to the introduction (that commenced in April 2009) of a new guarantee scheme for triple-A rated asset-backed securities—initially involving new mortgages, but later to include corporate and consumer debt—as called for in the "Crosby Report" (HM Treasury, 2008b). The intention here is to try and restart the securitization markets, thereby improving bank/building society and market liquidity and hence increasing bank lending capacity and reducing U.K. borrowers' cost of funds. Again, however, practical difficulties abound. How will the fees be determined? By auction, as suggested by Crosby? For how long should the scheme last? And how can market distortions be minimized (e.g., to limit the subsidization of poor-quality credits)?

Fourth, the government, as owner, is to force Northern Rock to slow the rate of contraction in its lending activities—it was announced on 23 February 2009 that the bank would now be expected to *increase* net mortgage lending by up to £14 billion over the next two years—thereby reversing the previous policy of trying to extract the fastest possible repayment of the bank's loan from the Bank of England.[25] Although serving to limit the contraction in housing-related loans in the U.K., and thereby limiting house price deflation, the policy volte-face does highlight the inherent contradiction in current government policy; on the one hand, it wants to limit the severity of this recession by slowing the pace of credit contraction in the economy, yet, on the other, it wishes to limit taxpayers' losses arising from its policy actions. Encouraging increased mortgage lending at a time when house prices are widely expected to fall by at least another 10 to 15 percent on average before the floor is reached is not going to improve bank solvency; nor should would-be homeowners be induced to enter the housing market currently with the prospect of negative equity looming for an uncertain period of time. Similarly, forcing, exhorting, or otherwise inducing banks to lend more to industry and individuals at a time of deepening recession, when output is plummeting and unemployment rising remorselessly, is again going to do little to boost individual banks' short-run profitability/solvency. Indeed, the danger is that adverse selection ensures that the banks end up with the credits that it least needs, as rising unemployment and falling demand create a new wave of "sub-prime" (i.e., uncreditworthy) personal and corporate borrowers, respectively. Moreover, it is not clear that stemming house price deflation, and hence slowing the pace of adjustment to a more sustainable level, nor indeed keeping Northern Rock going, either as a public or privately owned entity, is in the long-term interests of either taxpayers or the U.K. economy.

Fifth, the government promised to revise the terms of its October 2008 bailout of RBS in recognition of the fact that demanding a 12 percent coupon on the preference shares received—which must be redeemed before dividend payments to shareholders can resume—was too harsh (similar bailouts carried out subsequently elsewhere in the world set the coupon payments at a much lower level) (HM Treasury, 2009d). Accordingly, it proposed to swap its preference shares for common stock that would boost its stake in the bank from 58 percent to 70 percent, a move designed, in part, to stimulate the banks' lending activities by up to £6 billion.

Sixth, in order to ensure the availability of long-term bank liquidity, the period for which banks can swap illiquid assets for Treasury bills under the new Discount Window Facility was increased from one month to one year, for an incremental fee of 25 basis points.

Finally, the government gave the nod to the Bank of England to start lending directly to U.K. businesses, as the Fed had been doing in the United States for some months with respect to U.S. corporates, through the purchase of "high quality" (i.e., investment grade or better) private sector assets (including corporate bonds, commercial paper, and some ABS). Under a new "Asset Purchase Facility," the Bank would thus initially purchase, through a newly created subsidiary, up to £50 billion of commercial paper (Bank of England, 2009b), with the Treasury indemnifying the Bank against loss. The purchases, however, will be "funded" (i.e., "sterilised"), with the Treasury issuing Treasury bills to finance the purchases, thereby nullifying the impact of the purchases on the money supply. The door had been opened, however, for the Bank to move toward "quantitative easing" (i.e., unsterilized asset purchases, involving the "printing of money") should it prove necessary in the wake of its effective policy rate falling toward zero, a policy already prevalent in the United States and adopted long ago in Japan in the face of seven years of deflation and near-zero nominal policy rates (Hall, 1998). While the intention of the policy initiative was to widen large corporates' access to credit and reduce their costs of funding, the scale of potential losses that may ultimately fall upon taxpayers' shoulders is difficult to quantify. What seems "high quality" today may have lost its luster by tomorrow if the rate of economic contraction continues apace. And, before quantitative easing becomes a reality in the U.K.,[26] the Bank needs to identify in advance a clear exit strategy if runaway inflation down the road is to be avoided.

Such, then, was the nature of the government's latest plan for arresting economic decline and preserving financial stability. But what are we to make of it? Accepting the premise that economic recovery cannot occur before financial stability is restored and "normality" returns to lending channels,[27] was the latest package of measures sensible? As alluded to above, when discussing attempts to reinvigorate mortgage lending, real concerns surround the wisdom of trying to slow the pace of adjustment to a more sustainable economy where house prices are lower, consumers and businesses are less indebted, the services sector (including financial services) is less dominant relative to manufacturing, and the twin deficits—budgetary and the balance of payments—are more readily financeable. Of course, overnight "deleveraging" to achieve this more sustainable equilibrium would impose intolerable burdens on the real economy, and firms and individuals, but the extent to which this pain can be avoided, rather than simply deferred—to future generations—is not clear.[28] Already concerned with the impact of the government's fiscal stimuli, the markets are showing signs of alarm with the scale of the potential burden that bank/economy stabilization initiatives are creating for the public finances, whatever the treatment of contingent liabilities in the national accounts. (In a report released in December 2009, the National Audit Office put the total level of financial market support provided by the government at £850 billion.) And the government's economic forecasts delivered at the time of the Pre-Budget Report have already proved to be woefully optimistic, as widely argued at the time, compounding market fears about the sustainability of current policy. These fears extend to the possibility that, at some stage, a ratings downgrade for long-term U.K. sovereign debt will follow that meted out to Greece, Spain, and Portugal, thereby raising gilt funding costs and further deterring potential investors. Moreover, the rising cost of insuring against the possibility of a U.K. government default on its debts in the CDS market is evidence that some, at least, believe such a likelihood is certainly not negligible, raising the prospect—however remote—of the U.K. following the likes of Iceland, Hungary, Ukraine, Pakistan, and others to the doors of the IMF. As noted by many (including the IMF, see IMF, 2009a), and in defiance of government assertions to the contrary, the U.K. economy has always been one of the worst-placed industrialized nations to weather the current economic and financial storm because of the relative size of its housing bubble, the extent of its people's indebtedness, and the significance of the "City" and financial services more generally to domestic economic prosperity.[29] And the government's failure to better balance the books in the good times—a legacy of the prime minister's stint as Chancellor—left the public finances seriously exposed to the worsening economic and financial climate.[30]

As for the future direction of policy, and notwithstanding the renewed uncertainty created by the Dubai government's funding difficulties revealed in November 2009, the market appears to believe that the worst of the U.K. banking system's troubles are behind it.[31] RBS is already 84 percent owned by the state and Lloyds Banking Group appears to have successfully avoided entering the Asset Protection Scheme, thereby keeping the state's stake in the banking group at 43 percent. Reduced financial fragility, renewed investor appetite for bank stock, an improving outlook for the real economy and a determination by the two main political parties to address fiscal imbalances and the burgeoning public sector debt mountain (at least, once recovery is assured) will hopefully ensure no further policy initiatives are needed to restore stability to the U.K. banking sector.[32]

3. Summary and Conclusions

The metamorphosis in bailout philosophy, from nationalization by default to (part) nationalization by choice, within a period of just eight months is truly remarkable, even for a Labour government. That this has then spread around the globe, even into the heart of capitalism in the United States, is equally remarkable. While systemic problems undoubtedly demanded comprehensive and systematic solutions, the scale of the global "socialisation" of banking still came as a shock to most. The necessity for it, within a domestic context, has duly been analyzed in this article, as well as the various stages of the transformation process. It remains to be seen if enough has been done to stabilize the domestic banking system or if further public handouts, beyond those agreed to under the second comprehensive bailout package of January 2009—which raised the cumulative amount of public money at risk to nearly £1 trillion—will prove necessary, heralding yet further state inroads into the hitherto bastions of laissez-faire capitalism.

Appendix A: A Brief Summary of the Banking Act 2009*

- The centerpiece is a permanent "*special resolution regime*" (SRR) that provides the authorities with a range of tools to deal with banks in financial difficulties. It builds on and refines the temporary tools introduced by the Banking (Special Provisions) Act 2008, which was used to bring Northern Rock plc into temporary public ownership in February 2008, and to resolve Bradford and Bingley plc in September 2008 and the U.K. subsidiaries of two Icelandic banks in 2008.
- *Other measures* contained in the Act relate to improvement to the legal framework surrounding the operation of the Financial Services Compensation Scheme; enhancement of the operation of the regulatory frameworks preventing firms from failing; consumer protection; strengthening of the Bank of England; and new powers for the Treasury to lay regulations to deal with Investment Bank insolvency.
- With respect to the SRR, provisions relate to stabilization options (of which there are three), bank insolvency procedures, and bank administration procedures. Each of the three stabilization options is achieved through the exercise of one or more of the "stabilisation powers"—the transfer of shares or the transfer of property.
- The *objectives* of the SRR are as follows:
  - to protect and enhance the stability of the financial systems of the U.K. (including the continuity of banking services);
  - to protect and enhance public confidence in the stability of the banking systems of the U.K.;
  - to protect depositors;
  - to protect public funds; and

– to avoid interfering with property rights in contravention of a Convention right (within the meaning of the Human Rights Act 1980

The Authorities must have regard to these objectives when using, or considering using, their SRR powers, which are also covered by a Treasury "Code of Practice." A "Banking Liaison Panel" will also advise the Treasury on the likely impact of the SRR on banks, their customers, and financial markets.

- *Exercise of the Stabilization Powers*
  A stabilization power may only be exercised if the FSA is satisfied that the following conditions are met:
  – that the bank is failing, or is likely to fail, to satisfy the "threshold conditions" (within the meaning of section 41(1) of the Financial Services and Markets Act 2000, which relates to permission to carry on regulated activities); and
  – that, having regard to timing and other relevant circumstances, it is not reasonably likely that (ignoring the stabilization powers) action will be taken by or in respect of the bank that will enable the bank to satisfy the threshold conditions.

Before deciding whether the second condition is met, the FSA must consult with both the Bank of England and the Treasury.

The **Bank of England** may exercise a stabilization power *in respect of a bank transfer to a private sector purchaser or a bridge bank* only if it is satisfied that it is necessary to secure the public interest (i.e., in relation to financial system stability, public confidence in the stability of the banking system, and depositor protection).

Before determining whether this condition is met, and if so how to react, the Bank must consult with the FSA and the Treasury.

Alternatively, when the Treasury notifies the Bank that they have provided financial assistance in respect of a bank for the purpose of resolving or reducing a serious threat to the stability of the U.K. financial systems, the Bank may again exercise a stabilization power only if it is satisfied that the Treasury has recommended such action in order to protect the public interest and that, in the Bank's opinion, this is an appropriate way to provide that protection.

In respect of a bank transfer to temporary public ownership, the **Treasury** may only exercise a stabilization power if it is satisfied that one of the following conditions are met:
  – that the exercise of the power is necessary to resolve or reduce a serious threat to the U.K. financial system stability; or
  – that the exercise of the power is necessary to protect the public interest, where the Treasury has provided financial assistance in respect

of the bank for the purpose of resolving or reducing a serious threat to U.K. financial system stability.

Before determining whether either condition is met, the Treasury must consult with the FSA and the Bank of England.

(N.B. The above arrangements confirm that it is the FSA, sometimes following consultation with both the Bank and the Treasury, that actually "triggers" the use of a stabilization power under the SRR, although it is the Bank/Treasury which then assumes operational responsibility for the exercise of such powers, following consultation with the other authorities.)

- *The Stabilization Options*
  The three stabilization options comprise:
  – selling all or part of the bank's business to a commercial purchaser;
  – transferring all or part of the bank's business to a company which is wholly owned by the Bank (a "bridge bank"); and
  – taking the bank into temporary public ownership.

A.1   Bank insolvency arrangements

The main features of the bank insolvency arrangements are as follows:
- a bank enters the process by court order;
- the order appoints a bank liquidator;
- the bank liquidator aims to arrange for the bank's eligible depositors to have their accounts transferred or to receive their eligible compensation from the FSCS; and
- the bank then winds up the bank.
  - *The bank insolvency order*
    Application for such an order may be made to the court by the Bank of England, the FSA, or the Secretary of State on the following grounds:
    (A) that the bank is unable, or likely to become unable, to pay its debts;
    (B) that the winding up of the bank would be in the public interest; and
    (C) that the winding up of the bank would be fair.
    The Bank of England may apply for a bank insolvency order only if:
    – the FSA has informed the Bank that it is satisfied that the general conditions for the exercise of a stabilization power are met; and
    – the Bank is satisfied that the bank has eligible depositors and that Ground (A) or (C) applies.

The FSA may apply for a bank insolvency order only if:
- the Bank consents; and
- the FSA is satisfied that the general conditions for the exercise of a stabilization order are met, that the bank has eligible depositors and that Ground (A) or (C) applies.
- Finally, the Secretary of State may apply for a bank insolvency order only if satisfied that the bank has eligible depositors and that Ground (B) applies.

- *The bank insolvency process*
  A bank liquidator has two *objectives*:
  - to work with the FSCS so as to ensure that, as soon as is reasonably practicable, each eligible depositor has the relevant account transferred to another financial institution, or receives payment from (or on behalf of) the FSCS; and
  - to wind up the affairs of the bank, so as to achieve the best result for the bank's creditors as a whole.

  The first objective takes precedence over the second, although the bank liquidator is obliged to begin working toward both objectives immediately upon appointment.

  Following a bank insolvency order, a *liquidation committee* must be established, for the purpose of ensuring that the bank liquidator properly exercises the functions prescribed in the Act.

  This committee shall consist of three individuals, one nominated by each of the Bank, the FSA and the FSCS.

A.2   Bank administration arrangements

- The main features of the bank administration arrangements are that:
  - it is used where part of the business of a bank is sold to a commercial purchaser or to a bridge bank in accordance with the relevant provision of the Act;
  - the court appoints a bank administrator on the application of the Bank;
  - the bank administrator is able and required to ensure that the nonsold or nontransferred part of the bank (the "residual bank") provides services or facilities required to enable the commercial purchaser or the transferee (the "bridge bank") to operate effectively; and
  - in other respects, the process is the same as for normal administration under the Insolvency Act 1986, subject to specified modifications.

- A bank administrator has two *objectives*:
  - to provide support to the commercial purchaser or bridge bank; and
  - to engage in "normal" administration (i.e., to rescue the bank as a going concern or achieve a better result for the residual bank's creditors as a whole than would be likely if the residual bank were wound up without first being in bank administration).

  The first objective takes priority over the second objective although, upon appointment, a bank administrator is obliged to begin working toward securing both objectives immediately.
- An *application* for a bank administration order may be made to the court by the Bank of England, wherein a person to be appointed as the bank administrator must be nominated and the bank be given due notice of the application.

  The grounds for said application are:
  - that the Bank has made or intends to make a property transfer instrument in respect of the bank in accordance with the relevant sections of the Act relating to such transfers to a commercial purchaser or a bridge bank; and
  - that the Bank is satisfied that the residual bank is either unable to pay its debts or is likely to become unable to pay its debts as a result of the property transfer instrument that the Bank intends to make.

* Which received the Royal Assent on 12.2.09 and took effect on 21.2.09.
* The author is Professor of Banking and Financial Regulation in the Economics Department of Loughborough University. This chapter was presented at the 84th Annual Conference of the Western Economic Association International (Vancouver, July 2009). An earlier version of the chapter was published in the *Journal of Financial Regulation and Compliance* (see Hall, 2009a).

Notes

† An earlier version of this paper was published in the *Journal of Financial Regulation and Compliance* (see Hall, 2009a).

1. See, for example, Hall (2008) and Bank of England (2007). A review and assessment of both the House of Commons' Treasury Committee's report on Northern Rock (House of Commons, 2008a) and the Tripartite Authorities' proposals for reform is also provided in Hall (2009a).
2. The private sector battle for Northern Rock prior to the Government's decision to nationalise it is discussed in Hall (2009b) at footnote 8.
3. See, for example, Hall (2009b) and Bank of England (2008).

4. As noted in Hall, 2008, table 2, Barclays Bank twice accessed such funding in the Summer of 2007. Although borrowers in such situations are supposed to remain anonymous, its identity leaked out to the market causing Barclays furiously to deny that it was in need of an infusion of liquidity other than for technical reasons. Barclays' experience is likely to have caused other banks to think twice before taking advantage of the facility, even if it were profitable to do so.

5. Although some argued a six month limit may be operable under EU law on state aid (the Treasury was looking toward a solution being reached by February 2008), a further six months of "restructuring" (as opposed to "rescue") aid might have been possible.

6. The presumption is that a rate of at least 7 percent was initially charged as this would have been in excess of the penalty rate (6.75 percent) charged on drawings under the standing facility discussed earlier in the text. The size of "haircuts" being applied to the nonstandard collateral is also unknown.

7. The FSA's findings and details of the supervisory enhancement programme are reviewed in Hall (2009b) at footnote 26.

8. For a critique of previous arrangements under the FSCS, see Hall (2001 and 2002).

9. Under the U.K. Financial Services Compensation Fund, protection was previously limited to 100 percent of the first £2,000 and 90 percent of the next £33,000, on a per customer per bank basis. Maximum protection had thus been increased to £35,000 from £31,700, and "co-insurance" was no longer applied.

10. The allocation of respective responsibilities under the "Memorandum of Understanding" was modified in March 2006, changing the Bank's remit to one of "contributing to the maintenance of stability of the financial system as a whole." And, under the Banking Act of 2009, the Bank acquired a statutory financial stability mandate.

11. The Bank has since acknowledged that improvements in the Tripartite Arrangements are required along with the other components of the crisis management arrangements (i.e., bank insolvency arrangements and deposit insurance arrangements) (Bank of England, 2007, p. 2). And the need for a review was acknowledged by the Chancellor in his statement to the House of Commons on financial market instability on 11 October 2007.

12. The Bank's demand for the ability to mount covert support operations, in the wake of the Northern Rock fiasco, was met in the Banking Act 2009. In total, £62 billion was provided to HBOS and RBS (£37 billion) between October 2008 and January 2009, when the money was repaid.

13. On 22 October 2008 another takeover within the building society movement was announced. It concerned the Yorkshire Building Society's takeover merger of the Barnsley Building Society—concluded by end-2008—to end the uncertainty surrounding the impact of the latter's possible loss of £10 million held in Icelandic banks. As in the earlier takeover, members of the Barnsley society did not get a vote on the issue nor did they receive windfall gains. Then, on 3 November 2008, the planned merger of the Skipton and Scarborough Building Societies was announced. As in the earlier cases (including the proposed merger between the

Catholic and Chelsea Building Societies announced on 7 June 2008), the merger was completed by end-2008. Finally, in January 2009, the Britannia, the U.K.'s second largest building society, announced that it was to merge with the Co-operative Financial Services Group in April 2009 to form a "supermutual."

14. The Bank's new permanent emergency liquidity regime was unveiled a week later.

15. To include bank debt guaranteed under the new Government guarantee scheme—see Section 2.3.

16. By 8 October 2008, the following institutions had already agreed, in principle, to participate in the government-supported recapitalisation scheme: Abbey; Barclays; HBOS; HSBC Bank plc; Lloyds TSB; RBS; Standard Chartered; and the Nationwide Building Society.

17. Those already committed to the scheme and who had promised to raise their aggregate Tier 1 capital by £25 billion by end-2008 have access to a further £25 billion, if they want it.

18. A fee is charged based on the bank's median cost of protecting its bonds against default in the credit derivatives market over the 12 months to 7 October 2008—later changed to end-July 2008 to reduce the cost for banks—plus 50 basis points plus an extra fee if the debt is not denominated in sterling.

19. By the 12 November 2008, Barclays Bank (€3 billion), HBOS (nearly £3 billion), RBS (£3 billion), Lloyds TSB (£1.4 billion plus €2 billion), and the Nationwide Building Society (£1.5 billion) had all taken advantage of the government guarantee scheme.

20. A new company, U.K. Financial Investments Limited, was set up for this purpose on 3 November 2008.

21. The government, however, remains of the opinion that, despite record planned issuance of gilts—£146.4 billion in the financial year ending 4 April 2009, three times greater than in the previous year and the biggest annual amount ever, £147.9 billion in 2009–2010, and averaging £134.2 billion over the next five years—and the dramatic rise in planned global public sector bond issuance (put at around $3 trillion for 2009, three times the amount raised in 2008), it will not face particularly acute problems, on either the price or quantity front. As reasons for this relatively sanguine view they cite continued demand arising from investors' low appetite for risk; the apparent stimulus given to overseas sales by the fall in the value of sterling (36 percent of outstanding gilt issuance was in foreign hands at end-September 2008); a relatively low level for the U.K.'s current debt to GDP ratio compared with other industrialised nations; and the increased demand from domestic banks that will result from changes to the FSA's liquidity adequacy assessment regime (see FSA, 2009a). (U.K. bank holdings at end-2008 stood at £18 billion, the highest level since the third quarter of 1998.) The middle two of these factors, however, could change rapidly if market circumstances change (i.e., if fears of a deeper sterling crisis or of large-scale losses on bank bailouts, which even before the bailout package of January 2009 amounted to some 20 percent of GDP [see IMF, 2009a], emerge); and, if and when risk appetite returns, investors may not necessarily favour U.K. public sector securities over U.K. corporate or overseas debt.

As for the deficit on the balance of payments, it is hoped that the sustained fall in the value of sterling, apart from reducing the risk of deflation appearing (the costs of which are examined in Bank of England, 2009a) will eventually boost the trade account, notwithstanding the decline in global demand, and act as an offset to falling sales of North Sea oil as reserves become depleted.

22. The Pre-Budget Report, unveiled on 24 November 2008, revealed the government's intentions (see note 30 for the government's latest plans). A £20 billion fiscal stimulus, amounting to around 1 percent of GDP, would be delivered for just over a year to try and dampen the severity of the downturn (by around 0.5 percent of GDP). The main expansionary forces derive from an immediate cut in VAT—from 17½ percent to 15 percent—programmed to last until end-2009, and the bringing forward of capital expenditure from future years. To convince the markets of the government's commitment to returning to fiscal "responsibility" as soon as circumstances allow (consistent with IMF policy prescriptions, see IMF, 2009b)—2015–2016 is the suggested date—the government simultaneously announced a series of deferred tax rises and planned expenditure cuts. On its own reckoning, however, the implications of its policies for the public finances are profound. Public borrowing is forecast to hit a record level of £118 billion (equivalent to 8 percent of GDP) in 2009–2010 falling to a "prudent" level only by 2015–2016. And government net debt is forecast to reach 57 percent of GDP by 2012–2013, well above the current preferred limit of 40 percent of GDP, exceeding £1 trillion for the first time in 2012. And these projections are based on what are likely to prove wildly overoptimistic assumptions concerning growth forecasts (see IFS, 2009, and IMF, 2009c)—the economy is expected to contract by between 0.75 percent and 1.25 percent in 2009, with growth resuming in the second half of 2009 to deliver growth of between 1.5 percent and 2 percent in 2010 and 3.25 percent in 2011–2012 and thereafter—and the scale of additional "efficiency savings" that can be squeezed from the public sector. As noted in note 21, the scale of additional gilt funding that these projections imply may yet prove unsustainable; and (foreign) investors may balk at maintaining their investments at current levels even if yields are substantially raised to compensate them. (The first sign of possible difficulties to come appeared on 25 March 2009 when, for the first time in seven years and only for the fourth time since auctions began in 1986, the government failed to find buyers for all of the £1.75 billion of gilts offered for sale.)

23. While such a measure represents a further attempt to address the long-standing problem of "pro-cyclicality" within Basel II (see, for example, Hall, 2004), it is not without its critics. First, it leaves the FSA open to the charge that it has been bounced into making the move, thereby compromising its perceived political independence. And second, as the experience with the savings and loans industry in the United States in the 1980s revealed, relaxing capital requirements in a crisis is a policy fraught with danger, as is the recent decision to relax the mark-to-market requirements for some of the banks' trading book assets.

24. The full details of the Scheme were revealed on 26 February 2009. Under the Scheme, eligible participants (i.e., U.K.-authorised deposit-takers with more than £25 billion of eligible assets, e.g., corporate and leveraged loans, commercial and residential property loans, and structured credit assets such as RMBS and CDOs) can secure Treasury protection on 90 percent of the credit losses that exceed a negotiated "first loss" amount. The fee, designed to ensure appropriate protection for taxpayers and to allow the latter to share in any upside returns, can be paid through the issuance of appropriate capital instruments (e.g., nonvoting common stock) or in cash. The protected portfolio of assets must be ring-fenced and managed separately. And participants must provide legally binding commitments to increase lending to "creditworthy" homeowners and businesses and agree to abide by the FSA's new Code of Practice on remuneration policies (FSA, 2009d). The Scheme will last for at least five years and its duration will reflect the tenor of the protected assets.

As the "guinea pig" for the Scheme, the Treasury also announced on the same day the nature of RBS's participation in the Scheme, following the bank's announcement of a £24.1 billion loss for 2008, the biggest U.K. corporate loss in history! The "costs" of participation involve the bank in committing to lend £25 billion in 2009—£9 billion in the form of mortgage lending and £16 billion in the form of business lending—and a further £25 billion in 2010. It has also agreed to comply with the FSA's Code of Practice on remuneration policies. The "fee," amounting to around 4 percent of the assets protected, comprises the payment of £6.5 billion to the Treasury in the form of nonvoting equity (designed to minimise the State's voting stake in the bank) and an agreement to forego current and future tax credits on losses. In return, the bank will secure protection on £325 billion (out of a total of £2.2 trillion) of assets, with the bank bearing a "first loss" of £19.5 billion and 10 percent of the residual risk. As part of the government's commitment to financial stability, the Treasury is also to make a further capital injection, again in the form of convertible, nonvoting but dividend-paying "B" shares, of £13 billion, with RBS having the option to subscribe for an additional £6 billion if required. (If the full £25.5 billion of capital was injected, the State's economic interest in the bank would rise from 84 percent to around 95 percent, although its voting stake would be capped at 75 percent.)

As far as the impact of the Scheme on RBS's capital position is concerned (see FSA, 2009e, for full details on how the Scheme impacts on banks' capital positions), the issuance of £19.5 billion of nonvoting "B" shares to the government would boost its Core Tier 1 ratio, while the £6.5 billion of the first loss portion that is retained by the bank will have to be deducted from capital (50 percent from Core Tier 1 capital) although the risk-weighted assets of the protected portfolio would be significantly reduced—from £578 billion to £434 billion. The net impact would be to boost the bank's lending capacity and its Core Tier 1 ratio from 7 percent to 12.4 percent.

In the event, a number of revisions to the "in-principle" agreement reached in February 2009 were made in the final agreement reached in November 2009

(HM Treasury, 2009c), for implementation in December 2009. These embrace an increase in the "first loss" to be born by the bank, from £42 billion (including the 10 percent residual risk) to £60 billion—in return, the government dropped its requirement that the bank forego around £10 billion tax losses and allowances; a reduction in the size of the pool of insured assets, from £325 billion to £282 billion; a capital injection of £25.5 billion, equal to the amount agreed to in February (comprising £13 billion in upfront capital, £6 billion of capital to be drawn at the option of RBS and £6.5 billion in a fee taken as capital) but now excluding the fee element; and a change in the fee structure from one requiring payment in the form of the award of £6.5 billion of nonvoting equity to the Treasury and the foregoing of around £10 billion of current and future tax credits on losses to the payment of an annual fee of £0.7 billion to the government for the first three years followed by £0.5 billion per year for the remaining life of the scheme, plus payment of an exit fee (less any fees already paid) that will be the larger of £2.5 billion or 10 percent of the actual regulatory capital relief received by the bank while it was in the APS.

As the result of the changes, the government's economic interest in RBS will rise to 84.4 percent, consistent with February's "in principle" agreement, but the government's ordinary shareholding will be capped at 75 percent, staying at 70.3 percent for now. But, to protect against a worst-case scenario, the government will also provide a contingent capital commitment of up to £8 billion (which would take its economic interest up to 87 percent). This will be drawn down in two tranches, and only in exceptional circumstances where RBS's Core Tier 1 capital ratio fell below 5 percent. In return, RBS will pay a fee of 4 percent per year for the contingent capital.

As for Lloyds Banking Group, improved market conditions allowed the bank to escape from entry to the APS by raising £22.5 billion through a rights issue (£13.5 billion) and swapping £9.0 billion of existing debt for contingent capital. The bank, however, agreed to pay the government a fee of £2.5 billion for the implicit protection provided by the taxpayer since March 2009; and the government will subscribe £5.7 billion, net of an underwriting fee, to the rights issue to maintain its stake at 43.4 percent.

25. Indeed, the bank was so successful in meeting its targets that, controversially, staff were rewarded with bonuses of around 10 percent. In order to repay the Bank of England so quickly, however—the debt outstanding to the Bank is now down to around £11.5 billion—the bank's actions had not only fuelled the contraction in mortgage lending in the U.K. but had also indirectly caused a reduction in the amount of new funding available to first-time buyers as much of the market's lending activity comprised ex-Northern Rock borrowers remortgaging with other lenders.

26. In a statement announced on 5 March 2009, the Bank duly confirmed that just such a policy would start the following week when £2 billion of gilts would be sold in a "reverse" auction. This would be the first of up to £75 billion of purchases of gilts of between 5 and 25 year maturities planned for the next three months. And up to another £75 billion of purchases of gilts and corporate

securities (the purchase of which began on 25 March 2009)—bringing the totals to £100 billion and £50 billion, respectively—would be made if necessary. To the extent that the sellers are nonbanks (e.g., pension funds and insurance companies), the money supply will be directly increased, whereas bank sales would, at least initially, simply raise banks' capacity to lend through an increase in the banks' cash reserves held at the central bank. The aim is to get nominal spending in the economy rising at around 5 percent per annum and to help reduce corporate borrowing rates.

In the event, some £200 billion was eventually spent by the Bank, mainly on purchases of gilts, with little discernible impact on gilt or other yields or on M4, the authorities' favoured money stock indicator.

27. It should be appreciated, however, that some of the recent slowdown in domestic credit provision is due to a natural curtailment of credit demand as the recession bites.

28. The IMF argues, on the basis of simulation results using a multicountry structural model, that (temporary) expansionary fiscal policy—ideally globally coordinated—combined with accommodative monetary policy and financial stabilisation measures is required to reduce the length and severity of the global recession (IMF, 2009b). With respect to fiscal policy, the "best" elements of policy are typically shown to be increased government expenditure and/or targeted transfers, as these have the largest multiplier effects. Although calling on all governments to consider putting in place fiscal stimuli equal to at least 2 percent of GDP, the IMF recognises that certain constraints (e.g., relatively high levels of budget deficits, public debt, contingent liabilities, and real interest rates, as well as competing needs for financial sector support) may inhibit some nations from doing more, and that cross-country comparisons are complicated by such factors as the size of automatic stabilisers, the size of the output gap, and the size of multipliers (IMF, 2009c). Moreover, it warns of the need to preserve long-run fiscal discipline if increases in long-term interest rates are not to offset the expansionary effects of the fiscal stimuli undertaken, and of the importance of not adding protectionist elements to fiscal packages, particularly at a time of rapidly declining international trade.

29. In March 2009, the IMF forecast that the U.K. GDP would fall by 3.8 percent in 2009, a much larger contraction than that foreseen for any other advanced nation, and by 0.2 percent in 2010, with the U.K. being the only large economy still to be in decline that year. Moreover, it believed the U.K.'s deficit would reach 11 percent of its GDP by 2010, well in excess of that for the U.S. and EU member states (IMF, 2009d, table 2, p. 38). While most now believe growth will return to the U.K. economy in 2010, by the end of the third quarter of 2009 the U.K. economy was still in recession, unlike most of its G10 counterparts.

30. On 22 April 2009, the Chancellor unveiled a budget that provides fiscal easing, equivalent to about 0.5 percent of GDP, in 2009–2010 followed by a tightening of 0.8 percent of GDP per year until 2013–2014. The immediate stimulus reflects the support provided for industry, the housing market (including a new scheme to guarantee mortgage-backed securities) and the unemployed.

The planned fiscal tightening for the medium to long term is reflected in the forecast for public spending that, as a proportion of GDP, is expected to fall from 48 percent in 2009–2010 to 39 percent by 2017–2018. Annual growth in real public sector current spending is being cut from its current level of 1.2 percent to 0.7 percent by 2011; and capital expenditure, in cash terms, is being halved from £44 billion this year to £22 billion in 2013–2014, with public sector net investment falling to 1¼ percent of GDP by 2013–2014. While such plans imply significant cuts in future public expenditure, even deeper cuts (and/or greater tax rises) have been postponed by, once again, adopting wildly optimistic growth targets for the economy. For, although finally falling into line with independent forecasters with respect to the forecast for 2009—the U.K. economy is now expected to contract by between 3¼ percent and 3¾ percent (although this has since been thrown into doubt following the release of figures showing that the U.K. economy contracted by 1.9 percent in the first three months of 2009), compared with a figure of 3.4 percent as an average of independent forecasters and the IMF's April 2009 forecast of a 4.1 percent contraction—forecasts for 2010 and beyond are way out of line with independent forecasters. In 2010, for example, the government expects growth to resume at a rate of between 1 percent and 1½ percent, only slightly less than forecast in the Pre-Budget Review last November. In contrast, the average of independent forecasts stands at a meagre 0.3 percent; while the IMF believes the U.K. economy will actually *contract* by 0.4 percent. More worrying is the size of the bounce expected in 2011—growth of between 3¼ percent and 3¾ percent is anticipated compared with an average independent forecast of 1.9 percent. And beyond 2011, trend growth of 2.75 percent per annum is assumed. More realistic growth assumptions (as well as more conservative estimates for public sector efficiency savings and the costs of financial stabilisation policies) would see the already worryingly high public sector borrowing and debt figures spiral even higher. On the government's own estimates, Public Sector Net Borrowing is now expected to be £175 billion in 2009–2010, equivalent to 12.4 per cent of GDP, £173 billion in 2010–2011 (11.9 percent) falling to £97 billion (5.5 percent) in 2013–2014. The budget is not expected to return to balance until 2017–2018, two years later than forecast only last November. Meanwhile, public sector net debt is forecast to increase, as a share of GDP, from 59 percent to 79 percent in 2013–2014 (after allowing for potential losses on financial stabilisation initiatives already undertaken—estimated at £50 billion, or 3½ percent of GDP, compared with an IMF estimate of £135 billion, equivalent to over 9 percent of GDP [IMF, 2009e, pp. 44–45]).

The foreign exchange market's immediate reaction to this news was not encouraging for sterling—it fell by 1.1 percent against the dollar on the day, and by 1.3 percent against the euro. And the figures concerning the public finances, necessitating gross gilt issuance of £220 billion in 2009–2010 compared with £146.5 billion for 2008–2009, triggered a two-day sell-off of gilts, taking yields back above their levels prior to the announcement of the Bank of England's "quantitative easing" policy. An expansion in the latter programme plus additional bank purchases in compliance with new liquidity adequacy rules will soak up some of the additional gilt sales, however, thereby serving to limit the undesirable increase in long-term yields.

31. The IMF, however, expects U.K. banks to suffer another $200 billion of loan losses over the next two years requiring the raising of an additional $125 billion of capital if the ratio of tangible common equity to tangible assets is to return to its precrisis level of around 4 percent (IMF, 2009e, Executive Summary).

32. The authorities' outstanding proposals (see Hall, 2009c) for reforming U.K. financial regulation, as enshrined in the Financial Services Bill of November 2009, are currently before Parliament.

References

Bank of England (1998), "The Bank of England Act," *Bank of England Quarterly Bulletin*, May, pp. 93–99.

———— (2007), *Financial Stability Report*, London, October.

———— (2008), *Financial Stability Report*, no.23, London, April.

———— (2009a), "Deflation," *Bank of England Quarterly Bulletin* 49, no.1, March, pp. 37–44.

———— (2009b), *News Release: Asset Purchase Facility*, London, 6 February.

FSA (2007a), "Review of the Liquidity Requirements for Banks and Building Societies," *Discussion Paper* 07/7, 19 December.

———— (2007b), "Recent Turbulence in Global Financial Markets and Northern Rock's Liquidity Crisis," *Memorandum from the FSA to the Treasury Committee*, 5 October.

———— (2007c), "The Treasury Committee Financial Stability and Transparency Memorandum," from the Financial Services Authority (FSA) and the Financial Services Compensation Scheme (FSCS), London, December.

———— (2008a), "Strengthening Liquidity Standards," *Consultation Paper* 08/22, December.

———— (2008b), "FSA Moves to Enhance Supervision in Wake of Northern Rock," *Press Release*, 31 March (available at http://www.fsa.gov.uk).

———— (2009a), "Strengthening Liquidity Standards," *Policy Statement* 09/16, 5 October.

———— (2009b), *A Regulatory Response to the Global Banking Crisis* (the "Turner Review"), 18 March.

———— (2009c), *FSA Statement on Regulatory Approach to Bank Capital*, London, 19 January.

———— (2009d), *Code of Practice on Remuneration Policies*, 26 February.

———— (2009e), *Detailed FSA Statement on the Capital Implications of the Government Asset Protection Scheme*, 16 March.

Hall, M. J. B. (1997), "All Change at the Bank," *Butterworths Journal of International Banking and Financial Law* 12, no. 7, pp. 295–302.

———— (1998), *Financial Reform in Japan: Causes and Consequences*, Cheltenham, U.K.: Edward Elgar.

——— (2001), "How Good Are EU Deposit Insurance Schemes in a Bubble Environment?," *Research in Financial Services: Private and Public Policy* 13, pp. 145–193.

——— (2002), "Incentive Compatibility and the Optimal Design of Deposit Protection Schemes: An Assessment of UK Arrangements," *Journal of Financial Regulation and Compliance* 10, no. 2, pp. 115–134.

——— (2004), "Basel II: Panacea or a Missed Opportunity," *Banca Nazionale Del Lavoro Quarterly Review* LVII, no. 230, pp. 215–264.

——— (2008), "The Sub-Prime Crisis, The Credit Squeeze and Northern Rock: The Lessons to be Learned," *Journal of Financial Regulation and Compliance* 16, no. 1, pp. 19–34.

——— (2009a), "The Sub-Prime Crisis, the Credit Crunch and Bank 'Failure'. An Assessment of the UK Authorities' Response," *Journal of Financial Regulation and Compliance* 17, no. 4 (November), pp. 427–452.

——— (2009b), "The Sub-Prime Crisis, the Credit Squeeze, Northern Rock and Beyond: The Lessons to be Learnt," *Department of Economics Working Paper,* No. WP 2009-3, Loughborough University, February.

——— (2009c), "The Reform of UK Financial Regulation," *Journal of Banking Regulation* 11, no. 1 (December), pp. 31–75.

HM Treasury (2008a), "Financial Support to the Banking Industry," *Press Release,* 8 October.

——— (2008b), "Mortgage Finance: Final Report and Recommendations" (Crosby Report), London, November.

——— (2009a), "Statement on Financial Intervention to Support Lending in the Economy," Press Release, 19 January.

——— (2009b), "Statement on the Government's Asset Protection Scheme," Press Release, 19 January.

——— (2009c), "Implementation of Financial Stability Measures for Lloyds Banking Group and Royal Bank of Scotland," Press Release, 3 November.

——— (2009d), "Treasury Statement on Restructuring its Investment in RBS to Deliver Further Bank Lending to Industry and Homeowners," Press Release, 19 January.

HM Treasury, FSA, and Bank of England (2007), *Banking Reform—Protecting Depositors: A Discussion Paper,* 11 October, (available at http://www.hm-treasury.gov.uk).

——— (2008a), *Financial Stability and Depositor Protection: Strengthening the Framework,* Cm.7308, 30 January.

——— (2008b), *Financial Stability and Depositor Protection: Further Consultation,* Cm.7436, 1 July.

——— (2008c), *Financial Stability and Depositor Protection: Special Resolution Regime,* Cm.7459, 22 July.

House of Commons (2008a), *The Run on the Rock,* House of Commons' Treasury Committee, Fifth Report of Session 2007–08, Volume 1, HC 56-1, London, 26 January.

——— (2008b), *Banking Bill,* Bill 147, London, 7 October.

IMF (2009a), *World Economic Outlook Update: Global Economic Slump Challenges Policies,* 28 January.

———— (2009b), *The Case for Global Fiscal Stimulus*, IMF Staff Position Note SPN/09/03, 6 March.

———— (2009c), *The Size of the Fiscal Expansion: An Analysis for the Largest Countries*, February.

———— (2009d), "Global Economic Policies and Prospects," *Group of Twenty Meeting of the Ministers and Central Bank Governors* (13–14 March, London, UK), 19 March.

———— (2009e), *Global Financial Stability Report : Responding to the Financial Crisis and Measuring Systemic Risks*, Washington D.C., 21 April.

Institute for Fiscal Studies (IFS) (2009), *2009 Green Budget*, London, 28 January.

5

Financial Crisis and Regulation: The Case of Spain

*Santiago Carbó Valverde**

Abstract

There have been a number of heterogeneous and, in some cases, opposing views of how the reform of the present international financial architecture should be tackled. This chapter discusses and reassesses the principal challenges and proposals for the reform of international financial regulation, commenting upon some specific lessons for the Spanish case from recent empirical evidence. From an international perspective, consensus is broadest that the most appropriate way to avoid systemic risk escaping from the perimeter of regulation and generating shadow banking is coordination at the national/international level and prompt corrective action, which in the EU has led to a combination of both microprudential and macroprudential policies (contained in the Larosière Report). From a national perspective, the chapter provides empirical evidence suggesting the existence of a relationship between excessive credit expansion in the years prior to the crisis and the current problems of asset impairment. It can be observed that the greater demands of prudential supervision and the dynamic provisions of the Bank of Spain have so far been able to attenuate only part of the effects of asset impairment. Nevertheless, some further adjustment is still required, in the framework of the orderly restructuring of the banking sector, and this is highly likely to generate an intensive process of financial consolidation.

Introduction

The financial crisis that began in August 2007 is, due to its global nature and quantitative impact, the most important of its kind since the Great Depression of the 1930s. Over two years having passed since its onset, the crisis has evolved as a dynamic phenomenon, responding to multiple causes and processes that feed each other and are apparent with different degrees of intensity in many economies worldwide. However, none of its determining factors—asymmetrical information in the financial markets, overleveraging, excessively risky (or even fraudulent) practices that escape regulatory control, speculative bubbles in the real estate market or the exhaustion of the demand cycle, among others—are new phenomena; they have all already been observed as causes of past crises. The sole distinguishing feature of the current crisis is, precisely, the simultaneity with which some of these phenomena have emerged.

Nevertheless, it is fitting to wonder what we have learnt from historical experience, and even to what extent the present crisis will also supply lessons and transformations in regulation, supervision, and banking practices themselves that will permit further episodes of financial instability to be averted. This is the ground on which the proposed reform of the world's financial architecture is based. Throughout 2008 and, above all, 2009, a multitude of proposals and actions were launched, aimed at identifying new mechanisms for regulation and supervision that would permit the prevention and control of systemic risk as the principal source of financial instability. This chapter attempts to identify the central pillars upon which the new design of international financial regulation is seated and the difficulties facing its achievement. From both the international and national perspective, a study is made of the importance of undertaking, in the short term, adequate management of the considerable losses resulting from asset impairment. In particular, empirical evidence is supplied for Spain to show the current and potential incidence of loan default and how this has been affected by the expansion of credit in recent years and the risk provisions that banking entities have made in this regard. From these relationships and from the measures recently implemented for the restructuring of the sector, some lessons are extracted concerning the incidence and repercussion of the crisis in the Spanish banking sector.

The chapter is structured into four sections, following this introduction. Section 1 describes the financial crisis as a network mechanism—due to its global nature, its speed of transmission, and the interconnection of its own causes—while identifying the principal premises for a sufficiently far-reaching financial reform to be tackled. Section 2 offers an analysis of the international response, examining the potential alternatives for attempting to achieve coordination in international financial regulation and supervision. Empirical evidence of the causes and consequences of asset impairment in the Spanish banking sector and the actions aimed at cushioning their effects are analyzed in Section 3. Finally, Section 4 presents the main conclusions.

1. Regulation and Financial Crisis: A New Conjuncture of Recurrent Problems

1.1   A crisis of networks

Given the impact and global nature of the financial crisis, and the multitude of causes that have provoked it, it may appear that this situation is the result of new, previously unidentified, systemic risk factors. However, if the causes of the crisis are analyzed and placed in historical perspective, the phenomenon no longer appears so novel. Speculative (and even fraudulent) practices in the international financial markets, real estate bubbles, the exhaustion of the demand cycles, the consequences of the shortage of saving or excessive debt, among other factors, have already been identified as fundamental causes of past financial crises. What does, however, seem to be a distinctive feature of this crisis is the coincidence in time of many of these factors. As Reinhart and Rogoff (2009) state, the financial crises experienced since the Great Depression have been characterized by their close links to a specific cause and by their persistence and their difficulty of resolution. Although their causes are identified, crises are events, while reforms are processes and require continual efforts coordinated over time. At this point emerges the role of regulatory intervention that, following historical experience, comprises three phases, in general terms: (i) evaluation of the damage and control of the situation; (ii) corrective mechanisms using fiscal and monetary policies; and (iii) new regulation to attempt to change the systems of incentives and prevent episodes of financial instability of a similar nature.

The financial crisis unleashed in August 2007 can be termed a "crisis of networks" for three reasons. First, it is global in its incidence. Second, it is characterized by its speed of transmission. Third, because its causes (speculative bubbles, cyclical behavior, overleveraging, innovations that escape regulation, etc.), are also interrelated. On the one hand, it is possible to talk of large nuclei of concentration, in which the 25 biggest financial corporations worldwide account for half of worldwide banking business (Sheng, 2009). On the other, the activity of these large conglomerates and the need for financing and liquidity (in an environment of heavy indebtedness) generated a dependency with regard to the foreign saving of national entities.

Uncertainty has in large part been transmitted from the core of the network to the local networks, fundamentally through derivatives and securitization. These phenomena have extended the conception of the large financial entities as "too interconnected" to fail (Brunnermeier, 2009). A good example of these characteristics was the collapse of Lehman Brothers and its serious consequences in the fall of 2008.

1.2   Inherent instability and the need for a practical objective of financial stability: Guidelines

When the level of interconnection of markets and institutions is high and risk practices become generalized, financial instability may have unforeseeable consequences. Furthermore, markets have globalized while a large part of regulatory and supervisory competencies have remained at the national level. This asymmetry of competencies may prove to be even further damaging if, as Minsky (1993) stated, instability is intrinsic to financial systems as markets gain weight in relation to institutions. In particular, Minsky's so-called inherent instability hypothesis largely summarizes the mechanisms that have provoked a financial crisis such as today's, in three differentiated phases:

- In the initial phase, credit rises at a rate coherent with the collateral guarantees provided by companies and individuals, and thus the hedging of the risk can be considered adequate.
- In the second phase, credit begins to overheat and problems of liquidity and the speculative practices of investors become generalized; at the same time, a large number of borrowers cannot meet their debts. These circumstances spread unease in the financial markets and generate liquidity tensions. This generalization of uncertainty has commonly been termed the "Minsky moment."
- In the third phase, speculative practices become widespread and give rise to fraudulent schemes of all types, such as the well-known pyramid investments or "Ponzi" schemes.

In the current financial crisis, this dynamic of indebtedness and speculation is manifest in the proliferation of financial engineering mechanisms that, far from contributing value, have propagated the risk outside of regulatory control. The crisis has thus resulted, in part, from the coexistence of a principal banking system and a peripheral one, which escapes regulation and has been generically termed the "shadow banking system." This duality has meant that many institutions within the perimeter of regulation, who act principally at national level, have undertaken investments whose risk was not completely known (Diamond and Rajan, 2009). Here, it appears that the immediate response should be more regulation and intervention. However, and even when regulation is strictly necessary, it must be underlined that intervention also has disadvantages. Among other examples, since the crisis became palpable in Europe in September 2008, national interventions have largely been unilateral, creating potential distortions such as territorial asymmetries in market discipline or, even, unfair competition (Claessens, 2009). In this connection, it is clear that intervention and regulatory reform must be as global and coordinated as possible. How can financial stability be preserved at the international level? Various recent contributions have indicated some useful guidelines for undertaking regulatory reform:

(a) The perimeter for agreements upon regulation and supervision must be broad for it to be able to be efficient as a mechanism for the control of systemic risk and to be compatible among jurisdictions and institutions. This means that supervisory authorities need to identify financial stability objectives and correct asymmetries in supervision, to avoid practices of regulatory arbitrage and, above all, the creation of shadow banking systems. This requires coordination between monetary policy and financial supervision, so that, as Borio and Zhu (2008) indicate, systemic risk does not become the "missing link" of monetary policy.

(b) Effective regulation of systemic risk is that which achieves a balance between maintaining incentives to innovation and the efficiency and security of the system. This involves, especially in the case of Europe, the establishment of "joint resolution systems" that permit common rules of play for entities that operate or may potentially operate in the same market (Čihák and Nier, 2009).

(c) Another principle is that market discipline and supervision should be mutually complementary. This means that an increase in the role of the markets does not involve systemic contagion and imposes as a necessity the rescue of entities considered to be "too big to fail." On this point, it has been demonstrated that the assets securitized offered financing and investment mechanisms that weakened market discipline and escaped supervision; at the same time, having provided liquidity, they caused a certain relaxation of credit risk screening practices (Goodhart and Schoenmaker, 2006; Keys et al., 2010; Obstfeld et al., 2010).

(d) In the case of entities currently considered to be "too systemic to fail," proposals must be made that involve prompt corrective action in the face of practices of excessive risk (Mayes et al., 2008; Rose and Spiegel,

2009). Various studies have demonstrated that the proliferation of shadow systems could have been detected and corrected in time. For example, Acharya et al. (2009) show how some of the principal structured investment vehicles that provoked the outbreak of the crisis in August 2007 had already been commonly employed between five and seven years previously. On this point, equally necessary are more exhaustive accounting rules that permit the monitoring and updating of true asset values and guarantees following international financial flows (Lane and Milesi-Ferretti, 2007).

Identifying these objectives or guidelines is, nevertheless, simpler than implementing them and making them truly effective. The following section examines the principal proposals currently on offer to tackle the reform of international financial regulation.

2. The International Response: The Search for Coordination

2.1 The international banking situation: the management of losses due to asset impairment

The financial crisis has displayed various common traits internationally, of lesser or greater incidence in each economy:

- A sharp rise in private debt and an increasing dependence on foreign saving (evident in economies such as the United States and Spain).
- The channeling and extension, through structured investment vehicles, of low-quality securitized assets, given the general name of "toxic assets."
- A substantial increase in default, accompanied by a fall in the price of real estate assets with the consequent impairment of a large part of banking assets and of the securities referenced to them.
- A crisis of liquidity and of confidence, followed by a crisis of solvency and by rescue and/or restructuring plans.

From among these, default and asset impairment are of special importance in the current context, because the principal risks of failure of large international institutions are concentrated in them and because in many countries rescue or restructuring have been implemented largely in an attempt to meet such losses. In the first phase of the crisis, attention was concentrated on aid and bailout plans for financial entities with a significant proportion of "toxic assets." However, it has become progressively revealed that both mortgage loans and mortgage-backed securities have also registered considerable losses.

An international analysis, based on the Global Financial Stability Report (2009) of the International Monetary Fund (IMF) reveals the magnitude of these problems. The greatest losses have been concentrated in the United States where the IMF estimates that default in credit portfolios may have meant a loss of $700 billion, while the correction to the value of the debt instruments referenced to those assets is already approaching $400 billion. Especially noteworthy is the case of residential mortgages, where default has produced losses of 230 billion Euros and falls in the value of mortgage-backed securities of 189 billion Euros.

In Europe, the quantitative importance of the United Kingdom is striking. According to the IMF, loan default may have entailed losses of $500 billion in bank balances and of $100 billion in covered bonds linked to these loans. Worthy of particular consideration is the exposure of the United Kingdom to loans to the foreign sector, a category in which approximately half of the estimated fall in value is concentrated. In the rest of the Eurozone, loan defaults have meant losses of $500 billion (also concentrated in loans to foreign countries), while the value of the assets securitized has fallen by $300 billion (principally affecting residential mortgage securitizations). According to the above-mentioned IMF report, the increase in equity capital has been unable to prevent a considerable decline in coverage ratios, due to the magnitude of asset impairment, and thus the write-down of these securities continues to constitute the principal task for the majority of banking sectors in 2010.

These losses hinder, moreover, the recovery of confidence in the credit markets. The surveys regarding bank loans undertaken by the European Central Bank reflect the persistence of certain pessimism in the sector. Throughout 2009, net expectations were negative concerning access to market finance, liquidity, equity, or the economic situation.

With asset solvency and quality as the principal short-term challenge, the reform of international financial architecture is the subject of several areas of discussion. In the G-20 meeting held in Pittsburgh in September 2009, various proposals were put forward for a significant increase in the equity capital requirements for financial entities, establishing levels/objectives that, for 2009, were able to include regulatory capital demands that could double current levels (Mussa, 2009). In this context, as these proposals are taking shape, banking entities throughout the world are paying special attention to strategic factors such as

- Default control.
- Solvency: more exacting regulation, cushioning of asset impairment.
- Capacity for recovery of recurring business, the typical business of granting loans and capturing deposits, or "back to basics."
- Focus on the recovery of asset quality.

2.2   Coordination problems and responses:
The perimeter of regulation

While solvency and asset write-down are urgent short-term tasks, the design of new international financial regulation requires determining how to combat the duality of a regulated banking system and a shadow-banking system. Systemic risk can only be corrected if there is one sole perimeter. Market discipline and supervision must complement each other through international coordination, although difficulties arise due to the existence of multiple jurisdictions, regulators, and supervisors who evidently suffer great problems of coordination.

There exist various international proposals to achieve greater global coordination of financial regulation and supervision. As Claessens (2009) states, these proposals fall into three groups:

(i) **A single international financial supervisor:** This is the most theoretically convenient proposal but the most difficult to put into practice.

(ii) **An International Bank Charter or IBC:** The large central banks would cede sovereignty to this charter to supervise "systemic" international entities. Its scope of activity would only include international activity. For some supervisors and countries it could constitute an "excessive" loss of sovereignty, which appears to limit the possibilities of this proposal succeeding.

(iii) **A decentralized but convergent system:** This proposal attempts to improve as far as possible the current system, standardizing regulation and supervisory practices to reduce the problem of coordination, although national sovereignty in these areas is maintained. The crisis has shown that this alternative is difficult to achieve, since entities that operate internationally have no problem acting supranationally in favorable times, but in bad times it is at the national level that their problems are resolved and they are eventually rescued ("banks are international in life, but national in death").

Given the difficulties of the options proposed, the need for coordination centers on the reaching of agreements that permit the resolution of the most fundamental problems for crisis prevention, among which more restrictive solvency standards are evident, as stated earlier. However, other debates proliferate, giving rise to numerous proposals for the avoidance of the procyclicity inherent in the risk of lending activity or for improvements in corporate governance, including directors' remuneration.

Table 5.1 The revision of European financial regulation

Improvements in the Lamfalussy approach	Larosière Report
Statutes of the supervisory committees	Objectives
System of voting by qualified majority in decision-making.	Analyze the causes of the crisis and weaknesses of the current system. Its recommendations regarding regulatory, supervisory, and global matters affect the future of the structure of European financial supervision.
Presentation of accounts.	Microprudential supervision.
Presentation to the European Commission, Council, and Parliament the annual working programs.	Creation of a European System of Financial Supervision (ESFS), which transforms committees into authorities with powers.
Common formats for EU legislation.	Macroprudential supervision.
Supervisory transparency of the ESCB. Development of tables for the transposition of directives by the European Commission.	Creation of a European Systemic Risk. Council (ESRC), which reinforces the role of macroprudential supervision.
Amendments to the solvency directives.	Principal conclusions.
Permit the supervisory authorities of each country to consider the European dimension in banking activity.	Need to reinforce macroprudential supervision and its links to microprudential supervision, as the recent financial crisis has shown.
Support to supervisory committees.	
Use of the voluntary delegation of tasks and competencies to ensure cooperation and the exchange of information among supervisors, among others.	

In the case of the EU, there have been some notable recent advances toward new financial regulation, particularly the improvements in the Lamfalussy approach—in which procedures for the design of the regulation and its transfer to the member states are concentrated—and, above all, the developments of the High Level Group, created as a result of the crisis to elaborate a proposal for financial reform, which have taken shape in the so-called Larosière Report. The principal advances on both fronts are shown in table 5.1. From the Lamfalussy point of view, the mechanisms to expedite and standardize European legislation regarding solvency are noteworthy; they introduce the possibility that the member states may voluntarily cede regulatory power to the distinct committees of the EU or, at least, make an agile and exhaustive transfer of all relevant information to these committees.

The Larosière Report, in turn, is of great importance to the future of European financial regulation, in that it represents a change in the conception of supervision, with its distinction between two complementary levels of activity and the creation of various committees, some of which are already functioning:

(i) Microprudential supervision: by creating a European System of Financial Supervision (ESFS), whose principal mission is to ensure that the distinct supervisory committees in which member states participate can take decisions binding upon all.

(ii) Macroprudential supervision: by creating a European Systemic Risk Board (ESRB), which, outside the proposals resulting from the microprudential approach, can act as a delegated organ with its own capacity to adopt initiatives that can prevent systemic problems.

2.3   Coordination and problems of valuation: The mark-to-market approach

Together with the control of systemic risk, the prevention of asset impairment and its correct assumption require an efficient information (accounting) mechanism. Another of the principal areas of international discussion is the possibility of generalizing the valuation system prevailing in the Anglo-Saxon countries, the so-called mark-to-market standards. This approach requires, when in any transaction a change is produced in the value of the asset transacted, this change to be applied to all assets of the same nature held on the balance sheet. Even though this type of valuation could be of use in recognizing the asset impairment of a banking entity, it is not exempt from problems and criticisms. Baily and Elliot (2009) suggest that, on the one hand, for many analysts such accounting "at market prices" bears great responsibility for the crisis, since it involves significant changes in valuation too rapidly. However, there are two problems that may increase with mark-to-market valuation. The first is that many assets are unique and are not the subject of regular transactions in the markets (i.e., a market price by which to value them is not really available). The second is that market prices are highly volatile and can overreact upward when a bubble is formed or overreact downward when the bubble bursts.

3.   The Response in Spain: Financial Restructuring and Consolidation

3.1   Credit and asset impairment: Empirical evidence for Spain

What is the situation in Spain? What lessons can be drawn from recent empirical evidence? In the Spanish banking sector, as in the majority of

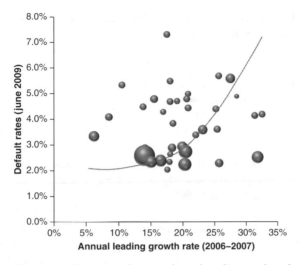

Figure 5.1   Nonlinear adjustments between lagged credit growth and current default

its surrounding countries, asset impairment constitutes the principal challenge, both for financial entities and for the authorities responsible for financial stability. In the case of Spain a significant increase in default has been observed, together with a fall in its coverage ratios, meaning many financial entities will for some time channel a large part of their profits to writing down assets and strengthening their equity capital. Asset impairment and default are explained in Spain by the financial crisis and the problems of international liquidity, the excessive assumption of risks in the real estate market (fundamentally by developers) and by the decline in economic activity and the increase in unemployment.

Spain is no exception with respect to the patterns of excessive debt and asset impairment. A simple empirical approximation illustrates the impact that the excess of credit may have exercised upon default. In particular, figure 5.1 shows the result of adjusting (through a nonlinear least square approximation) the relationship between the average annual growth rates of credit in 2006 and 2007 and the default rates registered by Spanish banks in June 2009. To perform this exercise, a sample was taken of the 60 most representative banks in Spain that, jointly, account for over 96 percent of the total assets of the banking sector. In figure 5.1, each bubble represents an entity, and its size is given by the average "core capital/total assets" ratio for the years 2006–2007, since this variable is employed as a control of the level of equity capital in the regression fit. Core capital is defined as capital plus reserves. Three interesting conclusions can be drawn from this exercise:

- A positive relationship appears to exist between the growth of credit in the years preceding the crisis and current default.
- This relationship appears to be more strongly defined above a certain threshold of credit growth. In particular, default seems to be higher in the set of institutions whose lending grew by approximately 15–20 percent in 2006 and 2007.
- Entities that displayed the highest solvency levels in 2006 and 2007 (represented by the size of the bubble) also appear to have faced lower default levels in 2009.

It is also fitting to ask to what extent the Spanish banking sector is currently affected by asset impairment, what measures it had available to deal with this type of situation and what the regulatory response to the current situation has been. As a starting point, it is useful to remember that the financial crisis arrived there later than in other countries for two reasons:

(i) Spanish financial entities did not invest significantly in the structured investment vehicles that provoked the eruption of the crisis in 2007.

(ii) The Bank of Spain had acted preventively, both in forewarning entities that investment in any structured vehicle would be penalized (due to its risk) in terms of capital requirements and, above all, in articulating so-called statistical, dynamic, or anticyclical provisions. These measures, which had been applied since the beginning of the decade, involve an additional allocation of provisions for risks in expansive phases of the economic cycle, in order to cushion impairment and default losses in recessive phases.

To what extent can asset impairment continue to affect Spanish financial entities? The situation of the Spanish banking sector merits special attention in the European context. It is estimated that Spain accounted for 27 percent of (residential) real estate assets securitized in the Eurozone in 2009. The losses in value of these securities originating in the Spanish market could be as high as 34 billion Euros, according to the IMF. These securitized assets display greater price variations than their underlying assets (the loans themselves). Furthermore, it must be remembered that some of these securitized assets are affected by the difficulty of pricing illiquid securities, where the standstill in the securitization markets has

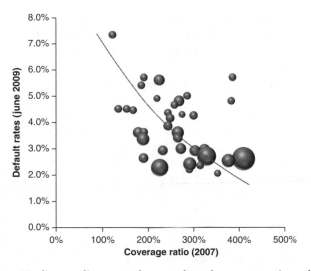

Figure 5.2   Nonlinear adjustments between lagged coverage ratio and current default

Note: The size of the bubble corresponds to the ratio "core capital / total assets".

had especially negative repercussions upon this valuation (International Monetary Fund, 2009, pp. 61–62)

In all events, Spanish banks had, in the years prior to the crisis, very high levels of risk coverage, partly due to the prudential valuation measures of the Bank of Spain and, among these, to statistical provisions. According to the data of the supervising entity itself, average default coverage in the years immediately preceding the crisis was approximately 250–300 percent, providing a cushion to soften the effects of the recession upon bank profits. Figure 5.2 shows the results of a further nonlinear least square adjustment, relating the default coverage ratio (loan provisions / default loans) in 2007 to default rates in 2009, and corroborates the existence of a sharply defined negative relationship, i.e., entities that had the highest coverage rates currently have lower default rates.

3.2   Effects and corrective measures: Bank restructuring

As in the international perspective, it cannot be stated that the determinants of the crisis in Spain are new, and neither are their consequences. Reinhart and Rogoff (2008; 2009) consider that, in an economy such as Spain's, the sharpest and longest lasting effects of the crisis are concentrated in the real estate and labor markets. In particular, they estimate that, in accordance with historical experience, the accumulated fall in housing prices could exceed 30 percent and the real estate market may take five years to recover. Similarly, unemployment could rise by 12 percentage points and the unemployment levels prior to the crisis may not return for six years. Given perspectives such as these, what measures have been proposed for the banking sector to confront the loss in value of real estate assets and the rise in loan default and return to a situation of a certain normality in lending? The response has been restructuring. The Bank of Spain's Plan for Ordered Bank Restructuring was approved in June 2009. It established a fund (FROB) that could rise to 99 billion Euros, a figure approximating the estimations of the losses in value potentially faced by Spanish financial entities. With this restructuring plan, four broad scenarios, which are not mutually exclusive, emerged:

- In the first, generalized, scenario, any entity of demonstrable solvency will be able to follow its own path and develop its own strategies for financing, growth, and integration.
- In the second, it is foreseeable that a given number of entities will not fit within the previous scenario and raise doubts as to their viability. These institutions, whether on their own initiative or that of the Bank of Spain, will have to present (within one month) a viability plan that must be approved by the supervising entity itself, which reserves the right to introduce modifications to it. On the basis of the viability plan, suggestions for the future nature of the entity are proposed, at least for the next three years, including a financing plan, in which financing from the Deposit Guarantee Fund is considered. Whatever the case, the principal path for such recapitalization plans is that of mergers and acquisitions.
- The third possibility contemplates situations of strong doubts regarding the viability of financial entities, in which the Bank of Spain intervenes directly in accordance with the legal provisos of the Law on Discipline and Intervention. Restructuring would involve merger or absorption or the total or partial transfer of the business of the entity, with the support of funds from the FROB.
- The fourth principle is more novel, and considers that those entities that do not display problems of viability but wish to merge will be able to request financial aid from the FROB in order to do so in favorable conditions of solvency, similarly to processes in other European countries. This, of course, will be tracked by the Bank of Spain.

In 2009, however, no banking entity turned to the FROB. Among other reasons, this was because the European Commission did not give the go-ahead to the Spanish restructuring plan until the end of January 2010.

Spain had arrived involuntarily late, in the sense that its banking sector resisted more strongly than that of many comparable countries the effects of the financial crisis. Throughout 2008 and a considerable part of 2009, numerous European governments rescued financial entities in their respective countries, often by direct injections of capital. The urgency of such operations and the systemic character of the entities in question were thought at that time to justify such interventions, apparently without considerations of competition being taken into account. However, in Spain this process began later, and has been designed on the basis of strict criteria and in an "ordered" way (as the very name of the FROB indicates in Spanish), and these two characteristics appear not to have benefited the country. The problem is that the European Commission appears to require a single, overall framework within which to focus possible aid, while the FROB is designed for "case by case" treatment. Furthermore, when approving the FROB, strict conditions for its implementation were established. The first and perhaps most important of these is that the time limit for aid to be awarded from this fund is June 30, 2010, giving it an emergency character. A second important aspect is that the interest rate at which entities must reimburse this fund has been established, with two options. They may pay 7.75 percent fixed interest or a rate equivalent to the return on five-year Spanish Treasury bills plus 5 percentage points. Furthermore, it must be borne in mind that although entities can reimburse this fund over a period of five years (extendable to seven), the interest rate paid increases by 0.15 percent over the above-mentioned rates for each year expiring from the date of subscription. Another of the conditions is that the minimum rating for access to FROB funds must be A (with a stable or positive perspective), a rating somewhat high for entities that have potential viability problems.

In any event, since it can apparently be deduced that increasing size is a distinctive element of the bank restructuring process in Spain, small- and medium-sized entities can have a particular part to play in the processes of financial integration, with or without intervention from the FROB, as can be observed from projects announced in 2009 and 2010 and that, together with others, must be concretized in the near future. Furthermore, there exists a factor additional to impairment, namely the excess capacity existing in the Spanish banking sector, which reinforces the need for this restructuring, in both the office networks and central services of entities.

3.3   Overall Evaluation

The various analyses included in this section permit an initial evaluation of the sequence of the crisis in Spain and the principal tasks pending, even

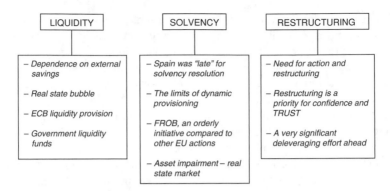

Figure 5.3   Sequence of the financial crisis in Spain

though this is a process that remains open and with consequences and impacts that are early to analyze. As figure 5.3 shows, the first problem to become evident in Spain was that of liquidity, once the collapse of the interbank and bond markets had provoked significant monetary tensions. The Spanish banking sector had not been directly affected by structured investment vehicles, into which national banks had made practically no incursions. Nevertheless, as in the United States, there exists in Spain a considerable dependence upon foreign saving, which became clear with the tensions in the money markets and which explains the increasing recourse made during 2008 and 2009 to the extraordinary liquidity facilities offered by the Central European Bank. Furthermore, the real estate bubble was important and falling property prices and defaults related to that market, as described earlier, have been responsible for a large part of asset impairment in the banking market.

However, Spanish banks initially showed stronger resistance than their European counterparts to the problems of solvency and at the close of 2009 and during 2010 began to tackle their restructuring process. Even taking into account the problems, already mentioned, that affect the FROB, facing up to restructuring is an essential task for the achievement of financial stability in the Spanish banking sector. All this must be performed within the current context of high levels of indebtedness of households, companies, and financial institutions, and the challenge of deleveraging will be considerable in coming years.

4.   Conclusions

The present article offers a review of the situation and principal problems faced by the banking sector worldwide, paying special attention to the

Spanish case and the lessons offered by empirical evidence, extracted from recent experience. In the current crisis, the management of real estate and bank asset impairment is the principal challenge faced by the majority of financial systems in rejoining the path of financial stability.

The analysis performed in this article and the empirical evidence obtained for the Spanish case permit the following conclusions concerning the reform and restructuring necessary to preserve financial stability:

- Significant problems of coordination exist at the international level; these must be resolved in critical areas such as capital requirements or the management of losses due to asset impairment.
- The perimeter of regulation must be clearly defined, eliminating *ex ante*, by prompt corrective action, any practice that significantly raises systemic risk.
- It is essential to prevent those banking entities considered as "systemic" from continuing to be so and from generating propagation mechanisms that accentuate the risks of contagion in the case of failure.
- In Europe, the Larosière Report has established a dual control system—macroprudential supervision and microprudential supervision—aimed at, precisely, balance between the control of systemic entities and the early detection of significant deviations in risk practices in member states.
- In the case of Spain, an analysis of the relationship between credit granted in recent years and current default suggests that entities whose lending increased over a certain threshold in 2006 and 2007 face higher default levels in 2009. Whatever the case, the substantial provisions made—largely due to the prudential and anticyclical measures established by the Bank of Spain—and the initial levels of coverage have been able to cushion the impact of default upon the profit and loss accounts of the Spanish banking sector.
- Asset impairment remains the principal short-term challenge in Spain. Here, the Plan for Ordered Bank Restructuring has concentrated on confronting the problem of current and potential losses due to asset impairment. In turn, it implicitly acknowledges the importance of this factor in the assumption of regulatory and competitive challenges in coming years and explicitly expresses its preference for financial integrations as a (preferably private) resolution mechanism in the case of eventual problems of viability. This restructuring is intended to facilitate the return to a degree of equilibrium in credit flows, although it will have to be undertaken with a certain balance and moderation, given that Spain is among those countries that will

have to undergo the greatest deleveraging of households, companies, and of financial institutions themselves in coming years.

*The author is Professor of Economics at the University of Granada and Head of Financial System Research of the Spanish Savings Banks Research Foundation.

References

Acharya, V. V., Brenner, M., Engle, R. F., Lynch, A. W., and M. Richardson (2009): "Derivatives: The ultimate financial innovation," in Viral V. Acharya and Matthew Richardson (eds.): *Restoring financial stability: How to repair a failed system.* New York: John Wiley.

Baily, M. N., and D. Elliot (2009): *The causes of the crisis and the impact of raising capital requirements,* mimeo.

Borio, C., and H. Zhu (2008): "Capital regulation, risk-taking and monetary policy: a missing link in the transmission mechanism?," BIS working paper 268–08.

Brunnermeier, M. K. (2009): "Deciphering the liquidity and credit crunch 2007–08." *Journal of Economic Perspectives* 23(1): 77–100.

Ĉihák, M., and E. Nier (2009): "The need for special resolution regimes for financial institutions: The case of the European Union." IMF Working Paper/09/200, IMF, Washington.

Claessens, Stjin (2009): *International exposure to US-centered credit market turmoil,* mimeo.

Diamond, D. W., and R. Rajan (2009), "The credit crisis: Conjectures about causes and remedies," mimeo.

Goodhart, C., and D. Schoenmaker (2006). "Burden Sharing in a Banking Crisis in Europe," London: LSE Financial Markets Group Special Paper Series (March).

International Monetary Fund (2009): *Global financial stability report.* IMF, Washington.

Keys, B. J., T. K. Mukherjee, A. Seru, and V. Vig (2010): "Did securitization lead to lax screening? Evidence from subprime loans." *Quarterly Journal of Economics* 125, forthcoming.

Lane, P. R., and G. M. Milesi-Ferretti (2007): "The external wealth of nations mark II: Revised and extended estimates of foreign assets and liabilities, 1970–2004." *Journal of International Economics* 73: 223–50.

Mayes, D., M. J. Nieto, and L. Wall (2008): "Multiple safety net regulators and agency problems in the EU: Is prompt corrective action partly the solution?" *Journal of Financial Stability* 4: 223–57.

Minsky, H. P. (1993): "The financial instability hypothesis," in P. Arestis and M. Sawyer (ed), *Handbook of Radical Political Economy.* Aldershot, UK: Edward Elgar.

Mussa, M. (2009): *The role of the financial sector in the Great Depression*, mimeo.

Obstfeld, M., J. C. Shambaugh, and A. M. Taylor (2010): "Financial stability, the trilemma, and international reserves." *American Economic Journal: Macroeconomics*, forthcoming,

Reinhart, C. M., and K. S. Rogoff (2009): "The aftermath of financial crises." *American Economic Review* 99: 466–72.

———— (2008): "Is the 2007 U.S. subprime crisis so different? An international historical comparison." *American Economic Review* 98: 339–44

Rose, A., and M. Spiegel (2009): *Cross-country causes and consequences of the 2008 crisis: International linkages and American exposure*, mimeo.

Sheng, A. (2009): *Global financial reform: diagnosis and prognosis (a network approach)*, mimeo.

6

Basel II Has Been a Costly Distraction on the Road to Minimizing the Societal Cost of Bank Failures and Financial Crises

*George G. Kaufman**

Introduction

As is amply demonstrated in the ongoing financial turmoil, banking (depository and similar types of institutions) crises have proven costly throughout the world. As a result, the major objective of public policy with respect to banking now is to protect against the adverse externalities from large or multiple bank failures without at the same time reducing efficiency in the banking and financial systems. Inefficient or unlucky banks should be permitted to exit, but at little if any societal loss. As cross-border barriers to the flow of financial capital have been reduced in recent years, public policy to minimize the adverse externalities of, in particular, large bank failures has added an important international component. This was reflected in the wide-spread international adoption of the minimum regulatory risk-based capital ratio requirements developed by the Basel Committee of Banking Supervision, known first as "Basel I" and then in revised form as "Basel II."

Unfortunately, both Basel protocols have had overly narrow focuses that limit their effectiveness in achieving their stated goals. Moreover, at least in the United States, the development of the complex advanced internal models approach of Basel II, which the U.S. regulators had expected to apply to the very largest, internationally active banks in 2008, has diverted substantial attention and scarce resources from the development of more efficient and comprehensive schemes for achieving the same objectives. Projects that were effectively deferred include, most importantly, the development and public dissemination of credible schemes for resolving large insolvent banks and bank-like entities that may often be viewed as "too-big-to-fail" and often operate across national boundaries; developing means to encourage prudential regulators to enforce regulations in place, such as prompt corrective action sanctions required by the Federal Deposit Insurance Corporation Improvement Act (FDICIA) of 1991, on a more timely and vigorous basis; and, outside the United States, strengthening provisions for regulators to intervene in financially troubled banks promptly and place them in receivership as soon if not before their capital turns negative. The high cost of not having resolved these issues has become evident in the financial crisis of 2007–0X.

1.   Minimizing the Cost of Bank Failures

Banks are widely considered "special" for numerous actual or perceived reasons. The adverse externalities from their failure with interruptions in the provision of their critical services are perceived to be greater than those from failures of other firms of similar size and require different public policy strategies. If failure is not prevented, it is feared that the adverse implications may be transmitted beyond the insolvent bank or banks to other financial institutions, financial markets, and ultimately the macroeconomy. This would occur primarily through two routes: (1) credit losses, and (2) liquidity losses suffered by customers of the insolvent bank(s).

Credit losses to depositor and other unsecured creditors of insolvent institutions occur when the recovery value of a bank's assets fall short of the par value of its deposits and other creditor claims at the time that the regulators officially recognize the bank's insolvency, revoke its charter, and place it in receivership or conservatorship. Liquidity losses to both depositors and borrowers at insolvent institutions occur when these parties are denied continued uninterrupted access to their claims at the time a bank is officially failed, for depositors and other creditors generally until the proceeds from the sale of the bank or its component assets are realized.[1] Thus, the bank's depositors may be denied immediate or near-immediate access to the par value of their insured deposits and the estimated recovery value of their uninsured deposits and the bank's performing borrowers, including credit card holders, may be denied access to their remaining existing credit lines. The claims are effectively frozen for a meaningful period of time. Short-term creditor claims are transformed into longer-term claims. Liquidity losses are not only a major inconvenience to the failed bank's customers, but are likely to significantly reduce the efficiency of the payments system and the value of aggregate wealth. Although, at least in the United States, liquidity losses receive less attention than credit losses, their adverse consequences are often as great or greater than credit losses. It follows that adverse externalities from bank failures may be minimized, if not eliminated, by minimizing, if not eliminating, both credit and liquidity losses. This should be a primary objective of public policy. How may this be best achieved?

Credit and liquidity losses may be eliminated, at least in theory, without reducing efficiency by imposing:

1. Prompt corrective actions (PCA) by regulators on financially troubled banks to attempt to turn them around before insolvency and regulatory takeover;
2. A mandatory prompt legal closure rule at positive capital to minimize, if not eliminate, credit losses at failure.
3. Least cost resolution of the insolvent bank to the deposit insurance fund by allocating realized or projected credit losses pro rata to all de jure uninsured claimants including the FDIC according to their legal priority to avoid protecting claimants who have equal or lower priority standing to the FDIC against loss, thereby minimizing moral hazard behavior and enhancing market discipline;
4. Brief, if any, physical closure of all but possibly small banks through a speedy sale or, more likely for large banks, through transferring the par value of insured deposits, the estimated recovery value of uninsured deposits and other claims, and loans in good standing to a newly chartered national temporary bridge bank to maintain customer access to major services on an uninterrupted near-seamless basis; and
5. Prompt reprivatization of any bridge banks that may have been chartered at sustainable capital ratios.

If these five requirements cannot be achieved for large banks for whatever reason, full protection or bailouts of all deposit and possibly other creditor claims is likely at high cost to the FDIC and possibly to taxpayers, as witnessed in the 2007–0X crisis

If successful in resolving banks before their capital turns negative, the above structure would make deposit insurance effectively redundant.[2] Losses would be limited to shareholders. By eliminating credit losses to depositors, legal closure at positive capital trumps deposit insurance that, in addition to its other well-known problems, only shifts the loss to a third party. But achievement of these objectives has a cost and requires at minimum:

1. Timely and accurate data, particularly for bank capital;
2. Useful and meaningful measures of bank capital and bank capital ratios, including risk-weights for assets;
3. Market discipline to supplement regulatory discipline;
4. Public disclosure by regulators of how insolvent banks, particularly large banks, will be resolved; and
5. Credible provisions for enforcing the timely and effective application of regulatory sanctions.

2. The Opportunity Cost of Basel

Basel standards focus on at most two of these objectives and requirements. Basel I, introduced in 1988, focused on obtaining a perceived more-meaningful measure of a bank's capital ratio by scaling capital by the bank's assets adjusted primarily for the perceived relative credit risk of different subsets of assets rather than by only total assets, as is commonly done in most other industries. Basel I designated minimum regulatory capital requirements, although it did not specify any penalties or sanctions for not meeting the minimums. These were left up to the individual participating countries. Basel II attempts to broaden the focus and builds on Basel I in two ways.[3] One, it develops a more complex and sophisticated measure of risk-based bank capital ratios, particularly for large, internationally active banks (Pillar 1). Two, it lists a set of what amounts to best practices for both bank supervision and bank disclosure (Pillars 2 and 3). Pillar 2 is intended to strengthen Pillar 1 capital requirements through supplementary supervisory monitoring and evaluation of a bank's overall capital needs, including risks not specifically specified in Pillar 1, such as interest rate risk. Pillar 3 is intended to enhance market discipline by providing investors and customers with additional information through increased public disclosure.

Although well intentioned and long in detail, Basel II still fails to provide the tools necessary to achieve the goals of minimizing the probability and costs of bank failures and significantly enhancing financial stability for a number of reasons. Among other weaknesses, it does not:

1. Include provisions for mandatory prompt corrective actions for pre-insolvency intervention to turn troubled banks around before legal closure;[4]

2. Include a mandatory legal closure rule at a given capital ratio, positive or negative;

3. Include strict enforcement and mandatory implementation of the supervisory sanctions recommended in Pillar 2;

4. Require more ex ante and ex post at-risk depositors to exploit the additional data disclosed through Pillar 3 and thereby enhance market discipline;

5. Provide evidence that the complex risk-based capital ratio measures introduced in Pillar I for the largest banks are more informative and transparent to either the regulators or the market than simpler measures, such as leverage ratios, and which are effectively used by the market in most other industries to gauge both the financial health and the likelihood of insolvency, or even the Basel I ratio, which is used currently by bank regulators for most banks; and

6. Provide rules for resolving bank insolvencies efficiently with both pro-rata loss-sharing for uninsured claimants according to their ex ante legal priorities and minimum service interruption.

In addition and much overlooked, Basel II has absorbed massive resources at high cost in terms of both highly skilled manpower, including economists, bank supervisors, academics, and consultants, and funding in the United States, the European Union, and many other countries for developing, testing, and defending as well as critiquing the recommended measures of risk-based capital. The resources involved were provided primarily by the bank regulatory agencies and central banks in these countries and the largest and most affected commercial banks, but spilled over to consultants and academics, both pro and con Basel II.

More recently, as the Basel capital measures have become more complex in an attempt to capture more completely the complexities of the "real" world; resources have been progressively directed more at mathematical refinements that have relatively little overall economic impact, indeed that often border on minutia. These revisions are as often as not motivated by perceived adverse competitive implications among banks. The results of both the quantitative impact study (QIS) 4 in the United States and QIS 5 in Europe in 2005 clearly show the questionable accuracy of the minimum capital measures generated by the models for the largest banks that could use the advanced internal models approach. In the United States, the computed minimum capital requirements for credit risk would be reduced on average by some 16 to 22 percent from Basel I values for the largest 26 banks and, possibly more importantly, vary greatly, often by 50 percent or more, both across banks that are otherwise perceived to be similar in aggregate risk profiles and for the same activities across banks.[5]

Competitive equality among banks appears to have been violated. Relative to Tier 1 minimum required leverage ratios, only two of the 26 large banks would have had sufficient capital to be classified as "adequately capitalized" under the current PCA structure and definitions, and fully 10 would be classified as "critically undercapitalized" with equity capital ratios of less than 2 percent.

The model results to date clearly show that the models for the advanced approach are not yet ready for "prime time." They do not appear to have captured the market's risk evaluations either accurately or convincingly. If these ratios had been put in effect, leverage ratios would have been lower and most large banks would have been likely to have been in even worse financial health in 2008 than they were and the severity of the financial crisis even worse. Recent testimony by Sheila Bair, Chairman of the FDIC, supports this conclusion. She noted that

> [d]uring the discussion of the Basel II Advanced Approaches, the FDIC voiced deep concern about the reductions in capital that would have resulted from its implementation. . . . It is highly likely that the advanced approaches of Basel II would have been implemented much more quickly and with fewer safeguards, and banks would have entered the crisis with much lower levels of capital. In particular, the longstanding desire of many large institutions for the elimination of the leverage ratio would have been much more likely to have been realized in a regulatory structure in which a single regulator plays the predominant role.[6]

Moreover, from 2005 to 2008, the SEC applied only the Basel II advanced model risk-based capital requirement to the largest five investment banks. Although all satisfied these requirement, the simple leverage ratios of the four that the Government Accountability Office (GAO) computed were substantially higher than those of the largest commercial banks.[7] The missing investment bank was Bear Stearns, which was known to have had an unusually high leverage ratio before its failure in 2008.

It is highly unlikely that the long-term benefits of applying additional large-scale resources to refining these models will ever approach the high costs of not redirecting these resources to more urgent aspects of reducing the societal costs of bank failures. The same criticism may be made for much of the resources devoted to Basel over the past decade. Moreover, the internal models used by the largest banks to compute their probabilities of defaults and losses, given default as input into the supervisors' model to derive required minimum risk-based capital ratios in Basel II, are proprietary. Thus, they are at best likely to be opaque to outsiders and reduce the effectiveness of market discipline relative to the more transparent simple total asset leverage ratio or even Basel I ratios, despite the emphasis on disclosure in Pillar 3.

3. Higher Priority Projects

As the recent crisis has demonstrated, bank failures have been as likely to occur and as costly today as when the Basel process began. In the United States, any pleasant surprises in commercial bank survival is due to the enactment of the FDICIA in 1991 with its higher capital requirement, not to Basel per se. To serve public policy best, the resources in the United States and elsewhere currently devoted to further Basel adjustments, be it Basel II, III, or other future versions, should be quickly redirected to, for example:

1. Developing efficient bank insolvency resolution procedures for large banks that are viewed as "too big to fail or to unwind" so that they are not. This would involve minimizing credit and liquidity losses to contain the damage. The regime developed should be publicly disclosed, so that both bankers and the public understand the new "rules of the game" and base their ex ante behavior accordingly. If publicly disclosed ex ante, regulators would also find it more difficult to change the rules ex post, in particular to provide forbearance under political pressure. Secret plans, no matter how good or well intentioned, are likely to be equivalent to no plans when the time for action occurs and political pressures build. The failure to have such a plan in force was a primary reason for the protection of most uninsured counterparties in effectively all commercial bank failures after 2007.

2. Preparing and publishing periodic financial stability reports and participating in the IMF-World Bank Financial Sector Assessment Program (FSAP), as nearly all other industrial countries do. As the crisis has amply shown, the United States was not above it all.

3. As was belatedly started, exploring the possibility of extending aspects of the bank insolvency resolution regime in the Federal Deposit Insurance Act (FDIA) to large bank holding companies and other large financial institutions. The bank regime differs significantly from the bankruptcy regime for other corporations in a number of important areas.[8] For banks, initiation of insolvency or bankruptcy and placing the bank in receivership or conservatorship is by the bank regulators rather than by large creditors or the firm voluntarily. Losses are allocated to minimize cost to the FDIC according to absolute priority rather than by negotiation among the claimholders and the courts, except when the systemic risk exemption is invoked to permit bank regulators to protect totally or partially some uninsured claimants, if necessary, to prevent financial

instability. This exemption should, however, be difficult to receive. The FDIC also had the authority to advance payments to uninsured depositors based on the estimated recovery value of the bank's assets. The FDIC, rather than a court appointed administrator, administrates the receivership or conservatorship, including the sale of assets and settlement of liabilities. These provisions help to permit the regulators to fail banks more quickly even before insolvency, to resolve insolvencies at low cost, and to allocate losses so as to better maintain critical bank services of failed banks on a near seamless basis and minimize adverse externality.

4. Outside the United States, developing a credible and enforceable legal closure rule and efficient process for resolving regulatory insolvencies, possibly using as a base the FDICIA-introduced PCA and legal closure rule provisions in the United States. This implies both establishing the necessary prerequisites in terms of a legal and institutional framework and collecting the required input data for imposing prespecified discretionary and mandatory sanctions, including legal closure, on a timely basis. Few countries outside the United States have the effective legal and regulatory provisions in place that attempt to require supervisors to discipline banks when their capital ratios, however measured, decline to or below a series of minimum trigger values before legal closure, and eventually to invoke legal closure if these measures fail to turn a bank around.

5. In EU countries, developing a process by which insolvent banks that engage in cross-border branching within the EU can be resolved efficiently and fairly without home-host country conflicts that arise from the present system of home country responsibility for deposit insurance and legal closure of branches in host countries, which bear part of the cost of the home country actions. Solutions may involve cross-border loss sharing arrangements and are likely to involve consideration of transnational deposit insurance systems and legal closure rules. Indeed, until a time that these problems are thoroughly addressed, cross-border branching within the EU may generate greater costs over the cycle than benefits, particularly with respect to using subsidiary banks.

3. Conclusion

The above argument strongly suggests that the Basel process has been overly costly. It has lacked a sufficiently wide focus and has been a costly distraction. The process has misallocated large-scale scarce resources from fully addressing the more important and urgent problem of minimizing the adverse externalities of either single or multiple bank failures to developing more complex but not necessarily more accurate measures of risk-based capital ratios in an attempt to better capture the complexities of the real world but with little guidance as to how these measures should be used to reduce the likelihood and cost of bank failures, even if they were more meaningful and transparent than simpler measures. In the United States, this has resulted in a more fragile banking system that was less prepared to absorb large adverse shocks when they occurred after 2007 and regulatory agencies that were less prepared to deal with the fallout at a high cost to the economy. Outside the United States, this has contributed to the delay in developing a more comprehensive prompt corrective action structure for regulatory actions both to reduce the probability of bank insolvencies through requiring progressively harsher and more mandatory sanctions as a bank approaches insolvency and to legally close those institutions whose capital ratios, however defined, decline to a prespecified low but positive value, particularly when operating across one or more national borders. As a result, most countries were in no better shape to address this problem in 2008 than they were in the early 1990s, when the exercise of refining Basel I began. This is a high cost. It is time to curtail the scale of the ongoing Basel II–and-beyond exercises by redirecting resources to more productive avenues.

* The author is the John F. Smith Professor of Economics and Finance at Loyola University Chicago, and consultant to the Federal Reserve Bank of Chicago. This chapter was initially prepared for presentation at a "Symposium on the U.S. Implementation of Basel II," jointly sponsored by the FDIC and *Journal of Financial Services Research* in Washington, D.C., on September 13, 2006, and circulated as a working paper dated July 10, 2007. I am thankful to Edward Kane, participants at the symposium, and readers of the earlier working paper for helpful comments. The views presented are solely those of the author and do not necessarily represent those of the Federal Reserve Board or the Federal Reserve Bank of Chicago.

Notes

1. Kaufman and Seelig (2002).
2. A more detailed description of this program appears in Kaufman (2006).
3. Basel Committee on Banking Supervision (2005). See also Kaufman (2004).
4. Kaufman (2005).
5. Powell (2005).
6. Bair (2009), p. 3.
7. GAO (2009).
8. Bliss and Kaufman (2007).

References

Bair, Sheila C, 2009. "Statement Before the Committee on Bank, Housing and Urban Affairs," U.S. Senate, Washington, D.C.: FDIC, August 4.

Bliss, Robert R., and George G. Kaufman, 2007. "U.S. Corporate and Bank Insolvency Regimes: A Comparison and Evaluation." *Virginia Law and Business Review* (Spring): 143–77.

Basel Committee on Banking Supervision, 2005. *Basel II: International Convergence of Capital Measurement and Capital Standards: A Revised Framework*, Basel, November.

Kaufman, George G., 2004. "Basel II: The Roar That Moused," in Benton E. Gup, ed., *The New Basel Capital Accord*. New York: Thomson, pp. 38–52.

———, 2005. "Basel II vs. Prompt Corrective Action: Which is Best for Public Policy?" *Financial Markets, Institutions, and Instruments* (December): pp. 349–58.

———, 2006. "Using Efficient Bank Insolvency Resolution to Solve the Deposit Insurance Problem." *Journal of Banking Regulation* (October): 40–50.

———, 2010. "The Financial Turmoil of 2007–09: Sinners and Their Sins." *Policy Brief 2010-PB-01*, Networks Financial Institution at Indiana State University, March.

Kaufman, George G., and Steven Seelig, 2002. "Post-Resolution Treatment of Depositors at Failed Banks." *Economic Perspectives* (Federal Reserve Bank of Chicago), 2nd Quarter, pp. 27–41.

Powell, Donald E., 2005. "Testimony: Development of the New Basel Capital Accords Before the Senate Committee on Banking, Housing and Urban Affairs." Washington, D.C.: FDIC, November 10.

U.S. Government Accountability Office (GAO), 2009. *Financial Markets Regulation: Financial Crisis Highlights Need to Improve Oversight of Leverage at Financial Institutions and across System* (09–739), July.

7

Fannie Mae and Freddie Mac: Creatures of Regulatory Privilege

*David J. Reiss**

Introduction

As part of its response to the ongoing credit crisis, the federal government placed Fannie Mae and Freddie Mac, the government-chartered, privately owned mortgage finance companies, in conservatorship. These two massive companies are profit-driven, but as government-sponsored enterprises (GSEs) they also have a government-mandated mission to provide liquidity and stability to the United States mortgage market and to achieve certain affordable housing goals. How the two companies should exit their conservatorship is of key importance to the future of federal housing finance policy. Indeed, this question is of pressing importance as the Obama Administration has signaled that it would rely heavily on Fannie and Freddie as part of the short-term response to the foreclosure epidemic that has swept across America in the last couple of years. Once the acute crisis is dealt with, however, the Administration will need to put American housing finance policy on the right track for the long-term health of the system. This will require a framework for analyzing the needs of that system, a framework that this chapter provides.

Fannie and Freddie are extraordinarily large companies: together, they own or guarantee more than 40 percent of all the residential mortgages in the United States. This amounts to over $5.4 trillion in mortgages. By statute, Fannie and Freddie's operations are limited to the "conforming" portion of the mortgage market, which is made up of mortgages that do not exceed an annually adjusted threshold ($417,000 in 2009 and significantly higher in high-cost areas). The two companies effectively have no competition in the conforming sector of the mortgage market because of advantages granted to them by the federal government in their charters. The most significant of these advantages has been the federal government's implied guarantee of Fannie and Freddie's debt obligations. The implied guarantee allowed Fannie and Freddie to borrow funds more cheaply than their fully private competitors and thereby offer the most attractive pricing in the conforming market. As the two companies grew and grew, numerous commentators and government officials called for their reform. Fannie and Freddie's powerful lobbying forces, however, had kept these reformers mostly at bay until they entered conservatorship.

As a result, Fannie and Freddie continued to grow at a rapid rate through the early 2000s, until they were each hit by accounting scandals. In response to those scandals, Congress and the two companies' regulators began to take various steps to limit their growth. But once they stabilized in 2007, the current credit crisis commenced and their market share began to increase once again as other lenders could not raise capital to lend to borrowers. At first, many commentators believed that Fannie and Freddie would ride the crisis relatively unscathed, but it turned out that they had much more exposure to the problems in the toxic subprime and Alt-A portions of the mortgage market than they had let on in their public disclosures.

Because of their poor underwriting, the two companies started posting quarterly losses in 2007 that ran into the billions of dollars, with larger losses on the horizon. As a result, they were having trouble complying with the capital requirements set by their regulator. Their problems began to spiral out of control along with those of the rest of the financial sector until then-Secretary of the Treasury, Henry M. Paulson. Jr., asked that Congress give the Treasury the authority to take over the two companies if they were not able to meet their financial obligations. Congress, with remarkable alacrity, passed the Housing and Economic Recovery Act of 2008 (the Act) in the summer of 2008. Soon thereafter, Paulson decided that the two companies were flirting with insolvency and placed them in conservatorship, pursuant to the Act.

While the American taxpayer will likely be required to fund a bailout of the two companies that will be measured in the hundreds of billions of dollars, the current state of affairs presents an opportunity to reform the two companies and the manner in which the mortgage market is structured. Though the need for reform is evident, few scholars have considered the issue systematically. Scholars have, however, built up a significant base of knowledge about what works well and what does not work well with public/private hybrids like Fannie and Freddie.

Contemporary theories of regulation persuasively argue that special interests work to bend the tools of government to benefit themselves. This chapter, relying on regulatory theory, provides a framework with which to conceptualize the possibilities for reform by viewing Fannie and Freddie as creatures of regulatory privilege. A critical insight of regulatory theory is that regulatory privilege should be presumed to be inconsistent with a competitive market, unless proven otherwise. The federal government's special treatment of Fannie and Freddie is an extraordinary regulatory privilege in terms of its absolute value, its impact on its competitors and its cost to the federal government. As such, regulatory theory offers a fruitful resource for academics and policymakers considering reform of Fannie and Freddie's privileged status because it clarifies how Fannie and Freddie have relied upon their hybrid public/private structure to obtain and protect economic rents at the expense of homeowners as well as Fannie and Freddie's competitors.

Once analyzed in the context of regulatory theory, Fannie and Freddie's future seems clear. They should be privatized so that they can compete on an even playing field with other financial institutions, and their public functions should be assumed by government actors. While this is a radical solution and one that would have been considered politically naïve until the current credit crisis, it is now a serious option that should garner additional attention once its rationale is set forth.

In an earlier study (Reiss, 2008), I provided a comprehensive analysis of the regulatory privilege that Fannie and Freddie enjoy. This chapter builds on that work to situate that privilege within a broader understanding of regulatory theory and to explain the rare hybrid public/private nature of the privilege that Fannie and Freddie enjoy. In doing so, this chapter argues that the existing regulation of the two companies should be brought in line with our current understanding of how government should be deploying its power in the private sector.

This chapter proceeds as follows. Part 1 will describe Fannie and Freddie's role in the secondary market for residential mortgages. After describing what happened to the two companies in the credit crisis that commenced in 2007, it will outline the key provisions of the Housing and Economic Recovery Act of 2008, which authorized the federal government to place Fannie and Freddie in conservatorship.

Part 2 then shifts to construct a theoretical framework with which to evaluate Fannie and Freddie. Part 2.A presents Fannie and Freddie's assessment of their own roles in the secondary residential mortgage market. Part 2.B reviews how other scholars have conceptualized the role of Fannie and Freddie in the housing finance market. Part 2.C then evaluates the operation of Fannie and Freddie in the context of six policy goals that derive from contemporary regulatory theory: (i) maintaining competition; (ii) efficiently allocating society's goods and services; (iii) promoting innovation; (iv) preventing inappropriate wealth transfers; (v) preserving consumer choice; and (vi) preventing an overly concentrated economy. It finds that Fannie and Freddie come up short under nearly all of those goals.

Based on the conclusion of Part 2 that Fannie and Freddie no longer have a net positive impact, Part 3 argues that the two companies should be privatized. It also argues that the benefits that Fannie and Freddie produce in the residential mortgage market should be maintained through alternative means, including financial regulation, consumer protection legislation, and increased subsidies for affordable housing.

1.   Fannie and Freddie and the Credit Crisis

This part begins by explaining what Fannie and Freddie do in the mortgage markets. It then describes how they fared in the credit crisis that commenced in 2007. This brief history opens with the early phase of the credit crisis in which the two companies were perceived as potential white knights, mounting a defense of the distressed secondary mortgage market. It then details their own troubles that led to the enactment of the Housing and Recovery Act of 2008. It concludes with the government placing them in conservatorship as the financial condition of the two companies rapidly disintegrated.

1.1   Fannie and Freddie's business

Fannie and Freddie have two primary lines of business. First, they provide credit guarantees so that groups of residential mortgages can be packaged as residential mortgage-backed securities (RMBS). Second, Fannie and Freddie purchase residential mortgages and related securities with borrowed funds. Because of the federal government's implied guarantee of their debt securities, Fannie and Freddie have been able to profit greatly from this second line of business. This is because they can make money on the spread between their low cost of funds and what they must pay for the mortgage-related investments in their portfolios.

Fannie and Freddie's charters restrict the mortgages they may buy. In general, they may only buy mortgages with loan-to-value ratios of 80 percent or less unless the mortgage carries mortgage insurance or other credit support and may not buy mortgages with principal amounts greater than an amount set each year. Loans that Fannie and Freddie can buy are known as "conforming" loans. Loans that exceed the loan amount limit in a given year are known as "jumbo" loans. Most of the remainder of the

RMBS market belongs to "private label" firms which securitize (i) jumbo mortgages and (ii) subprime mortgages that Fannie and Freddie cannot or choose not to guarantee or purchase for their own portfolio.

Because Fannie and Freddie have so dominated the conforming sector of the mortgage market, they have standardized that sector by promulgating buying guidelines that lenders must follow if they want to sell their mortgages to either of the two companies. Such standardization has led to increases in the liquidity and attractiveness of mortgages as investments to a broad array of investors.

The government guarantee of Fannie and Freddie's debt obligations is a regulatory privilege that arose from Congress' efforts to create a national secondary residential mortgage market in the 1960s and 1970s. It is the characteristic that allows them to borrow more cheaply than other financial institutions, the characteristic that allows them to completely dominate the prime conforming mortgage market, and the characteristic that poses the greatest threat to the federal government and the American taxpayer. One must therefore properly account for it in order to understand Fannie and Freddie.

Unlike true monopolists, Fannie and Freddie's market power is limited by the nature of their competitive advantage: in an otherwise efficient market, the maximum amount that they can retain as economic rent is the spread between the interest rates they must pay and those that their competitors must pay. Nonetheless, Fannie and Freddie share a key characteristic in common with government-granted monopolies: a legally created and overwhelming competitive advantage in a particular market, which translates into higher prices for consumers than would exist if Fannie and Freddie did not retain a portion of their economic rent for themselves.

Because of their government guarantee, Fannie and Freddie were thought to be well situated when the current credit crisis commenced. As other lenders began to fail and the secondary market for subprime mortgages dried up in 2007, a Citigroup report suggested that Fannie and Freddie could easily ride out the turmoil in the mortgage markets (Hagerty, 2007). Even more, some commentators were arguing that Fannie and Freddie would be able to bail out other mortgage market players by buying additional mortgages. At the same time, however, some were raising the alarm that Fannie and Freddie could face some of the same problems that other mortgage lenders had been facing. But this view was overtaken in 2007 by the more dominant one that saw Fannie and Freddie as saviors of the mortgage markets.

This was a happy development for Fannie and Freddie because it meant that the terms of the debate regarding their appropriate role in the mortgage markets went from one in which the Executive Branch was beating the drums to limit their growth to one in which politicians and mortgage executives were calling for their role to be significantly expanded. Fannie and Freddie quickly tried to capitalize on this change in their political fortunes, advocating for an increased role in the crisis. At the earliest stage of the credit crisis, the Bush Administration continued to oppose an expansion of Fannie and Freddie's roles. As the crisis progressed, the regulator of the two companies began to signal that they were considering some expansions in Fannie and Freddie's role. The Federal Reserve, which had also been calling for limitations on Fannie and Freddie before the credit crisis struck, also began to publicly consider a greater role for the two firms.

1.2   The crisis deepens

As Fannie and Freddie's political star began to appear ascendant, troubling accounts of possible losses started to appear: their underwriting models had been too optimistic and had not accounted for the possibility of severe reductions in housing prices across the nation. These fears were confirmed soon thereafter, as Fannie and Freddie began to report very large losses. These losses meant that Fannie and Freddie did not have the capital to expand their role in the mortgage markets and that their political star began its descent once again. The large losses led both companies to seek infusions of fresh capital. By this point, the federal government was now concerned both with Fannie and Freddie's viability as well as the health of the overall market. Nonetheless, the federal government was running out of policy responses to the credit crisis and Fannie and Freddie were seen as some of the few remaining possible agents that could execute federal policy.

By the beginning of 2008, the Bush Administration and Congress were seriously considering various initiatives to create more funding for mortgages, a number of which were implemented. As part of the Economic Stimulus Act of 2008, enacted in February 2008, Fannie and Freddie were temporarily allowed to buy or guarantee mortgages with principal amounts as high as $729,750 in order to restore liquidity to at least a portion of the jumbo sector. Fannie and Freddie's safety and soundness regulator, the Office of Federal Housing Enterprise Oversight (OFHEO), also lifted Fannie and Freddie's portfolio accounts caps and repeatedly lowered capital requirements in order to help respond to the housing slump and expand the supply of credit for mortgages.

These steps seemed to have had the intended effect of increasing the supply of credit available for mortgages. Some commentators, however, were still warning that Fannie and Freddie continued to be heavily exposed to losses resulting from the housing slump that they were supposed to be alleviating. The market also began to worry about Fannie and Freddie's solvency, as the yields on their debt widened by 30 basis points to trade at a historically high 40 basis points above the London interbank offer rate (LIBOR) in mid-March. By May, more and more parties were concerned about the solvency of the two companies and Congress and the Bush Administration were seriously negotiating an overhaul of Fannie and Freddie's safety and soundness regulator, OFHEO, to increase its ability to oversee and regulate the two companies.

By mid-July, the market's serious concerns about Fannie and Freddie's viability were reflected in their stock prices, which were at their lowest levels in more than 16 years. The federal government, on the heels of the Bear Stearns bailout, took decisive action to prevent another acute crisis in the financial markets. The Treasury Department announced that it was seeking broad authority from Congress to support Fannie and Freddie through acquisition of its debt and equity securities. At the same time, the Federal Reserve announced that it was authorizing emergency lending to the two companies on the same terms that it has historically lent to its regulated banks and, since the Bear Stearns bailout, to primary dealers. The Bush Administration kept up the pressure to move the bailout plan forward, even in the face of Republican hostility in Congress based on opposition to a taxpayer bailout of the two entities. The bailout plan was enacted as part of the Housing and Economic Recovery Act of 2008. While this gave confidence that debt-holders would be bailed out in the case of insolvency, shareholders could not feel the same way, particularly since Fannie and Freddie's massive portfolios were still in trouble. It also did not offer much hope to those who had hoped that Fannie and Freddie would continue to support the housing market.

1.3   Congress responds: The Housing and Economic Recovery Act of 2008

The Housing and Economic Recovery Act of 2008 (the Act) was one of the major legislative responses to the credit crisis that had begun in 2007. Among other things, the Act revamped the regulatory oversight for Fannie and Freddie and provided the Treasury with the authority to bail out Fannie and/or Freddie if they faced insolvency. Prior to the passage of the Act, Fannie and Freddie's financial safety and soundness regulator was OFHEO, which was an independent agency located within the Department of Housing and Urban Development (HUD). OFHEO had limited power over Fannie and Freddie to establish capital standards; conduct financial examinations; determine capital levels; and appoint conservators.

Two provisions of the Act are most relevant here: (1) one that strengthens Fannie and Freddie's financial safety and soundness regulation and (2) one that temporarily increases government support for the two companies.

1.3.1   Improved financial safety and soundness regulation

The Act replaces OFHEO with a new independent Federal Housing Finance Agency (the Agency). The Agency has general regulatory authority over the two companies and the Federal Home Loan Banks. The Agency's role mirrors that of OFHEO, but grants it significantly more power to regulate financial safety and soundness issues. The Agency is intended to be a top-notch financial regulator along the lines of the Federal Deposit Insurance Corporation.

The Agency is run by a director appointed by the president, with the advice and consent of the Senate. The director's mandate is to ensure that both entities operate with sufficient capital and internal controls, with a mind toward the public interest, such that Fannie and Freddie accomplish their purpose of providing liquidity to the mortgage markets. The director is assisted in his duties by the Federal Housing Finance Oversight Board, which advises the director about strategies and policies. In addition to the director, the Board includes the Secretary of the Treasury, the Secretary of Housing and Urban Development, and the Chairman of the Securities and Exchange Commission.

The Act addresses the possible actions to be taken by the Agency should Fannie and/or Freddie become undercapitalized, significantly undercapitalized, or critically undercapitalized. An undercapitalized entity falls under greater monitoring and restriction of activities. A significantly undercapitalized entity may have its board replaced and/or executive officers fired. This is also grounds to withhold executive bonuses. A critically undercapitalized entity may have the Agency named as conservator or receiver.

1.3.2   Temporary government support

The Act temporarily authorizes the Secretary of the Treasury to make unlimited equity and debt investments in Fannie and Freddie securities. This appears to be the first time that the Treasury has been authorized to invest in the equity of privately held companies. This will only be done by mutual agreement between the relevant GSE and the Secretary of the Treasury. In order to purchase obligations, an emergency determination must be made by the Secretary of the Treasury. This determination must address whether such actions are necessary to provide stability to the financial markets, prevent disruptions in the availability of mortgage finance, and protect the taxpayer.

The director must consult with, and consider the views of, the Chairman of the Board of Governors of the Federal Reserve System, with respect to the risks posed by the regulated entities to the financial system, prior to issuing any proposed or final regulations, orders and guidelines with respect to the exercise of the additional authority provided in the Act regarding prudential management and operations standards for; safe and sound operations of; and capital requirements and portfolio standards applicable to Fannie and Freddie.

In addition to the two provisions discussed above, the Act has two more that are of some importance to this discussion. These two provisions relate to how the two firms seek to expand their market share and how they engage in political horse-trading to achieve their ends, which in turn relate to the argument in favor of privatization set forth in Part 3 below. The first provision provides funding for affordable housing through an assessment on Fannie and Freddie. The second provision increases the conforming loan limits. This increase expanded the companies' market and increases the availability of mortgage credit during the crisis.

The Act requires that Fannie and Freddie "set aside an amount equal to 4.2 basis points for each dollar of unpaid principal balance of its total new business purchases" (Housing and Economic Recovery Act of 2008, codified at 12 U.S.C. §1337). When the Act was passed, it was generally agreed that this provision would raise upward of $500 million each year for affordable housing initiatives.

The Act also raises the conforming loan limits in some areas. Such limits shall be increased in areas for which 115 percent of the median house price exceeds the conforming loan limits, to the lesser of 150 percent of such loan limit or the amount that is equal to 115 percent of the median house price in such area.

1.4   Fannie and Freddie enter conservatorship

Within days of the passage of the Act, Fannie and Freddie faced demands to raise more capital, pressures that they would not be able to meet. Within a few weeks, the markets were expecting the federal government to bail out the two companies. And within a couple of months, Paulson announced that he was placing the two companies in conservatorship because they were not able to raise the capital they needed to continue operating. Throughout the credit crisis, their reported losses have continued to increase.

One important consequence of conservatorship is its impact on the implied guarantee. Some commentators argue that the implied guarantee is now an explicit one. The government and the market have not yet embraced this view. How the two companies exit their conservatorships will help shape the nature of the government guarantee as well.

As the credit crisis unfolds, there is much speculation as to what form Fannie and Freddie should take upon exiting conservatorship once the credit crisis has passed. Part II proposes a theoretical framework to help determine the answer to that question.

2.   Evaluating Fannie and Freddie

There is very little controversy over the overwhelming benefits that Fannie and Freddie brought to the national mortgage market during the 1970s. Indeed, they, along with Ginnie Mae, effectively created it. But at least since the early 1990s, there has been much disagreement with Fannie and Freddie's claims that they continue to provide overwhelming benefits to America's homeowners. There has also been an exploration of the costs that the two companies impose on the American government and on the mortgage markets. This part begins by reviewing how Fannie and Freddie claim to benefit the residential housing finance market and how "independent scholars"[1] evaluate their success at reaching these goals. It then draws on theories of regulation and monopoly to propose a more comprehensive mode of evaluation that untangles their hybrid public/private structure to demonstrate how that structure gives them extraordinary benefits that undercut competition in the mortgage markets as well as their statutorily mandated public missions.

2.1   Fannie and Freddie's self-assessment

Fannie and Freddie set forth four standards by which they believe they should be judged: (a) they lower overall interest rates for homeowners; (b) they offer systemic stability and liquidity to the market; (c) they increase the supply of affordable housing; and (d) they have increased consumer protection in the residential market. I will review evidence for each of these claims in turn. I find that independent research challenges some of these claimed benefits. Moreover, these four standards are ad hoc and fail to account for many other impacts that the two companies have on the housing market.

(a) *Lower Overall Interest Rates for Homeowners.* Fannie and Freddie claim that they lower interest rates for homeowners. There is nearly universal agreement that this is true. While Fannie and Freddie describe these lower rates as significant, independent scholars describe them as modest.

Various studies have measured the benefit to conforming borrowers as being between 24 and 43 basis points. Assuming an increased 34 point spread (halfway between the two figures) on a $200,000 mortgage, a borrower would pay an additional $57 dollars a month in interest. This figure, while significant for the average American homeowner, is not an extraordinary benefit, particularly for those who can itemize their home mortgage interest deduction to further reduce the after-tax bite of such interest payments.

Moreover, Froomkin (1995, p. 618) identifies a hidden cost that the Fannie and Freddie financing model imposes: in many ways the federal government is borrowing at a higher cost than it needs to if it wants to subsidize residential mortgages. Instead of borrowing through a GSE, the federal government could act directly at a lower cost to assist favored constituencies like homeowners. For instance, the federal government could directly provide or guarantee certain kinds of mortgages at a cheaper cost than Fannie and Freddie, much like it directly provides student loans at a cheaper cost than private educational lenders. This hidden cost has come into sharper relief during the current credit crisis, where Fannie and Freddie's borrowing costs remained for quite some time stubbornly high, even after they entered conservatorship. Thus, the Fannie and Freddie model may not be the most cost-effective means by which the government can achieve the goal of lower interest rates for homeowners.

(b) *Systemic Stability and Liquidity.* Congress gave Fannie and Freddie the task of providing liquidity and stability to the secondary mortgage markets. In 2003, OFHEO issued a report titled *Systemic Risk: Fannie Mae, Freddie Mac and The Role of OFHEO* that evaluated their role in the broad financial markets. The report argued that the systemic implications of Fannie or Freddie's financial difficulties would depend on the circumstances: "Any systemic disruption would likely be minimal as OFHEO took prompt corrective action and other market participants filled the short-term market void. Alternatively, in the unlikely circumstance that an enterprise experienced severe financial difficulties, they could cause disruptions to the housing market and financial system" (OFHEO, 2003).

While the secondary mortgage markets generally function well and without liquidity crises, the credit crunch of 2007–2009 has provided a rare opportunity to evaluate the impact of Fannie and Freddie on liquidity. At early stages in the crisis, Fannie and Freddie promoted themselves as white knights and lobbied for access to a broader swath of the mortgage market in order to stabilize them. But as the credit crisis developed, it became clear that Fannie and Freddie were subject to the same forces that had led to the insolvency and massive write-downs of private mortgage lenders, until the government stepped in quite forcefully to bolster the government-supported mortgage market.

In early 2008, the federal government authorized Fannie and Freddie to purchase loans with significantly higher principal amounts in high-cost areas like New York and California, again in order to provide additional liquidity. But at around the same time, Fannie and Freddie revealed that they faced billions of dollars in losses caused by their poor underwriting. Fannie Mae issued additional shares to raise billions of dollars of capital to ensure that they complied with the OFHEO capitalization requirements and Freddie Mac planned to do the same. But, as noted above, Fannie and Freddie ultimately required a bailout in order to prevent a crisis that would have spread far beyond the American residential mortgage market to infect the entire global credit market, if left unchecked. The net effect is that Fannie and Freddie did provide some temporary liquidity and stability but their long-term impact was very harmful to the broad financial system and will likely cost the American taxpayer many tens of billions of dollars to resolve the harm they ultimately caused.

(c) *Affordable Housing Goals.* The Federal Housing Enterprises Financial Safety and Soundness Act of 1992 established three affordable housing goals for Fannie and Freddie, those for (1) low- and moderate-income housing; (2) special affordable housing; and (3) central cities, rural areas, and other underserved areas housing. Pursuant to this statute, HUD is responsible for monitoring, adjusting, and enforcing these housing goals. These goals represent what should be the percentage of housing units financed by Fannie and Freddie each year.

Fannie and Freddie typically meet these goals, although they sometimes may use financing shenanigans (such as buying a portfolio of loans solely to meet affordable housing goals) to do so. Independent research, however, has challenged whether these goals actually increase the net amount of affordable housing. A number of studies have indicated that Fannie and Freddie actually cannibalize the Federal Housing Administration (FHA) loan market by lending to borrowers who would have otherwise received FHA mortgages. The U.S. General Accounting Office has also questioned whether Fannie and Freddie, notwithstanding their particular affordable housing mandate, do any more than any other lenders to promote affordable housing.

(d) *Consumer Protection.* Fannie and Freddie argue that they have helped to standardize the conforming mortgage to the benefit of consumers. Many, including this author, have praised this standardization as a positive, something that on the whole reduces bad options for consumers. This generally positive development is not without some costs to consumers, however, as it reduces the financing choices available to them. For instance, Fannie and Freddie have effectively banished prepayment penalties from the prime conforming mortgage market, which sounds like a good thing for consumers. But some consumers might have preferred to take a loan with a prepayment penalty if it meant that the loan would have had a lower interest rate.

Moreover, recent news about Freddie's role in the subprime and Alt-A markets undercut Fannie and Freddie's consumer protection argument to some extent. Apparently, the two firms had a much greater exposure to the disastrous Alt-A subsector than they had previously let on. In Congressional testimony in late 2008, Fannie's former chief credit officer reported that the two companies "now guarantee or hold 10.5 million nonprime loans worth $1.6 trillion—one in three of all subprime loans, and nearly two in three of all so-called Alt-A loans, often called 'liar loans'" (Browning, 2008). As these two sectors were rife with predatory lending practices, Fannie and Freddie may be seen as complicit with these practices even though they did not engage in them directly.

2.2   Existing theories of the government-sponsored enterprises

Alice Rivlin, as then-director of the Office of Management and Budget, has stated that "GSEs were created because wholly private financial institutions were believed to be incapable of providing an adequate supply of loanable funds at all times and to all regions of the nation for specified types of borrowers" (OMB, 1995). This is certainly the primary reason that Congress employs GSEs, even if, as Thomas Stanton notes, "market imperfections are much more difficult to find today" than they were when Fannie and Freddie were created (Stanton, 2002, p. 10).

Froomkin (1995, pp. 557–59) has suggested four additional reasons behind Congress' decision to create federal government corporations like Fannie and Freddie: (a) they are believed to be more efficient at achieving market-related goals; (b) they are believed to be more insulated from politics than a division of a large federal agency; (c) they are believed to be effective at delivering targeted subsidies; and (d) they are a useful subterfuge for Congress because their borrowing is typically not counted as part of the federal deficit. As seen in this chapter, there is good reason to doubt that the first three reasons are as compelling as Congress would have liked. There is also good reason to believe that Congress was spot on regarding the fourth. Rivlin and Froomkin outline the major reasons that Congress creates GSEs, but they do not offer a comprehensive theory of the GSE. Existing efforts to do that are reviewed below.

Finance and economics scholars have proposed a variety of cost/benefit frameworks with which to evaluate Fannie and Freddie, although this is no mean task. These frameworks have often relied upon various *ad hoc* metrics, such as whether Fannie and Freddie actually lower interest rates for homeowners or how much of the Fannie/Freddie subsidy is passed on to homebuyers. There is general agreement that the two companies do lower interest rates to some extent and that they do so by passing on a portion of the subsidy that derives from the government's guarantee of their obligations on to homeowners.

Fannie and Freddie, of course, argue that they still provide an array of benefits, while others vigorously dispute this claim. Fannie and Freddie know that this debate is fundamentally one about their right to exist as GSEs. Their critics, on the other hand, have become increasingly strident in their criticism of the Fannie and Freddie business model as these companies have grown way beyond the expectations of anyone who had studied them in the 1970s and 1980s.

While this body of literature has provided many insights into Fannie and Freddie, it does not provide an overarching theoretical framework that would help determine their value. Such a framework should describe the ecology of Fannie and Freddie as well as the incentives and structural limitations that drive the development of the two companies. It should also provide guidance as to how they should be treated going forward.

2.3   Fannie and Freddie evaluated through the lens of regulatory theory

Given Fannie and Freddie's monstrous size and market power, there are no comparable public-private hybrid entities. As products of regulation, however, they fit well within existing theories of regulation. This section evaluates their value as agents of public policy through the lens of regulatory theory.

Two oft-stated objectives of government economic policy are to maintain and encourage competition between firms in order to increase "the material welfare of society" (Brodley, 1987) as well as to maximize consumer welfare "through lower prices, better quality and greater choice" (U.S. Department of Justice Antitrust Division website, n.d.). Cass Sunstein has rightfully noted that many regulatory regimes therefore reflect "a belief that regulatory enactments might simultaneously promote economic productivity and help the disadvantaged" (Sunstein, 1990, p. 3). But Sunstein has also noted, along with many others, that one of the main criticisms of regulation is that it is "only purportedly in the public interest" and that it "turns out on inspection to be interest-group transfers designed to protect well-organized private groups . . . at the expense of the rest of the citizenry" (p. 32)

Indeed, modern theories of regulation stem from the insight that firms attempt to use regulation as a device "to establish or to enhance monopoly power" (Crew and Rowley, 1989, pp. 6–7). Assessing the role of regulation in a particular market is necessary to understand whether that market is functioning competitively and equitably. Fannie and Freddie, although born of regulation themselves, claim to act competitively. Theories of regulation thus provide a useful framework with which to understand the market in which Fannie and Freddie operate, one that allows us to evaluate whether the companies increase "the material welfare of society" and maximize consumer welfare. This part will analyze Fannie and Freddie as creatures of regulatory privilege within the context of regulatory theory.

The core of Fannie and Freddie's regulatory privilege is the government's guarantee of their obligations, which was initially granted to create a national secondary residential mortgage market. This implied guarantee drives any competition from the conforming mortgage market because the two companies can borrow money so much more cheaply than their competitors. This lower cost of funds means that that they can outcompete fully private financial institutions in the conforming market, thereby keeping the conforming sector to themselves.

The government guarantee is a variant on the longstanding government practice of spurring private investment in various arenas by granting some privilege or monopoly power to a party that will infuse the activity with needed capital or bring focused attention to it. For example, government-granted monopolies can take the form of a charter granting a monopoly on trade, such as the one granted by Queen Elizabeth I to the English East India Company in 1600 in order to increase English trade with Asian nations. They can take the form of a system such as that governing American patents, granting patent-holders the sole right to exploit a patent for a certain period in order to encourage innovation. Or they can take the form of a regulated natural monopoly, like a utility company, that is regulated not only to protect consumers from monopoly pricing but also to ensure that the company can make a fair return on its investment.

Unlike true monopolists, Fannie and Freddie are limited by the nature of their competitive advantage: in an otherwise efficient market, the maximum amount that they can retain as economic rent is the spread between the interest rates they must pay and those that their competitors must pay. Notwithstanding this cap on profits, Fannie and Freddie share an important characteristic with government-granted monopolies: a legally created and overwhelming competitive funding advantage in a particular market that derives from their special charters. This advantage translates into higher prices for consumers than would exist if Fannie and Freddie did not retain a portion of their economic rent for shareholders and management.

Regulatory theory identifies six goals that are relevant to a study of Fannie and Freddie, including (i) maintaining competition; (ii) efficiently allocating society's goods and services; (iii) promoting innovation; (iv) preventing inappropriate wealth transfers; (v) preserving consumer choice; and (vi) preventing an overly concentrated economy. The first three goals related to economic efficiency concerns. The second three goals address additional public policy objectives. As shall be seen below, Fannie and Freddie do little to effectuate these goals. Indeed, in some cases they act contrary to them.

(i) *Maintaining Competition.* Maintaining competition is one of the most important goals of economic regulation. But applying this goal to Fannie and Freddie's activities is a bit difficult as there was no real national mortgage market when they were created. Indeed, they were formed in order create a new product: a fungible mortgage security. So, to begin with, there was barely any competition with which Fannie and Freddie could interfere. And now, because of their funding advantage, they have no competitors in the prime conforming market. This state of affairs presents two questions regarding competition in the modern residential mortgage market: should there be more competition in the conforming mortgage market; and should Fannie and Freddie be allowed to expand the markets in which they compete while maintaining their funding advantage?

With regard to the first question, it is noncontroversial to answer that competition is considered healthy in almost all markets, except for those that are better suited to natural monopolies like the utilities market. While Fannie and Freddie maintain that they compete with each other, independent commentators describe their behavior more as that of duopolists than competitors. With regard to the second question, it again is non-controversial to state that introducing subsidized firms like Fannie and Freddie into a generally efficient nonsubsidized mortgage market like the jumbo market would distort pricing in that market.

And Fannie and Freddie are entering that jumbo market: the rapidly increasing size of the conforming loan limit, a product of furious lobbying by the two firms, allows Fannie and Freddie to claim more of the overall mortgage market for themselves as opposed to their jumbo-originating competitors. As Fannie and Freddie both operate without competition in the conforming market and expand their markets through political action, they seem to operate contrary to the goal of maintaining competition.

Moreover, if one believes that Fannie and Freddie were primarily created to develop the national mortgage market, then it follows that their government-granted privilege should be revoked after they have completed that task. That is, Fannie and Freddie's regulatory privilege should be treated more like the privilege granted to patents, which only allows for a temporary monopoly for the express purpose of encouraging innovation, rather than a natural monopoly like that of a utility company that is typically regulated in perpetuity because it has no potential competition.

(ii) *Efficiently Allocating Society's Goods and Services.* In a productively efficient system, each unit of a product is produced at the lowest possible cost. If a producer in a competitive market fails to produce its product at the lowest possible cost, it would likely fail. This result would not typically apply to a monopolist because it does not face competition in its market. Monopolists thus typically lack "sufficient incentive to hold production costs at low levels" (Breyer, 1982, p. 16).

The competitive advantage provided by Fannie and Freddie's regulatory privilege is limited, as discussed above, by the fact that they would face competition if the price (interest rate and fees) in the conforming market was equal to or higher than the price in the private label market. But so long as they keep the price lower than the price in the private label market, they are able to extract some economic rent. Thus, they are not efficiently allocating society's goods and services.

Regulatory privilege imposes certain additional social costs. Its beneficiaries incur costs to retain and expand it, often through campaign contributions, lobbying, and bribery. Such firms are also more likely to dissipate their rents through expenditures like advertising in order to protect their privileged status. Fannie and Freddie are thus best understood as rent-seekers who expend resources to obtain favorable regulation in order to obtain rents.

(iii) *Promoting Innovation.* Recipients of regulatory privilege may have less impetus to innovate because of their competitive advantage. Fannie and Freddie claim, however, that they continue to innovate as the secondary market matures. Indeed, they have executed a number of innovations that allow them to profit from aspects of the mortgage market that had traditionally fallen outside of the scope of their activities. These include, for instance, the development of automated underwriting systems and underwriting guidance systems for third parties. It is no coincidence that these innovations allow the two companies to enter new markets, thereby pushing against the limitations on their expansion into new markets contained in their charters. The Mortgage Banking Association argues that in the area of underwriting technology, Fannie and Freddie have actually squelched the innovations of others, much as Microsoft has squelched its competitors by tying new products to its operating software.

Private label competitors have innovated at a far greater rate than Fannie and Freddie, introducing a dizzying array of products for consumers to choose from and securities for investors to choose from although much of that innovation now seems foolish, greedy, and wrongheaded. At a minimum, there is no evidence that Fannie and Freddie innovate more than they would if they faced a marketplace filled with many competitors. That being said, as the subprime crisis unfolds, the once vaunted innovation of private-label lenders has taken on a decidedly morbid pall. Engel and McCoy (2007) argue quite convincingly how the business model of these private-label lenders led directly to much of the abusive lending of the last ten years. One might have argued that this goal of regulatory theory should weigh in favor of Fannie and Freddie if they themselves did not invest so heavily in subprime and Alt-A mortgages originated by the very same private label lenders that engaged in such dangerous innovations.

(iv) *Preventing Inappropriate Wealth Transfers.* Monopolists are willing to forgo sales for increased profits. Similarly, Fannie and Freddie forgo offering the lowest possible price for mortgages; they do this by retaining a portion of their subsidy, instead of passing it on to borrowers as they would in a perfectly competitive market. This is reflected in the outsized profits that Fannie and Freddie have historically enjoyed as compared to other financial institutions. It may also be reflected in the generous pay packages that management awards itself before turning over the remainder of the economic rent to shareholders. Furthermore, monopoly pricing dissuades some buyers who would have purchased a good at a competitive price from doing so at the monopoly price, which is allocatively inefficient. Fannie and Freddie's retention of a portion of their subsidy likewise keeps some potential borrowers from borrowing.

(v) *Preserving Consumer Choice.* Government regulates businesses that operate in markets that are not fully competitive, in part, to achieve fairness for consumers. Because of their competitive advantage in the conforming loan market, consumers effectively only have the choice of Fannie or Freddie. As noted above, Fannie and Freddie argue convincingly that they have helped to standardize the prime, conforming mortgage to the benefit of consumers.

There is no question that private label firms would enter the conforming market if they were able to borrow funds at rates comparable to those at which Freddie and Fannie can borrow. The pros and cons of those private-label firms have been well documented in the jumbo and subprime markets: they expand consumer choice but often at the expense of the consumer protection inherent in a standardized market place. More competitors would, of course, mean more consumer choice of lenders. It would also likely mean more choice of mortgage products. But in the context of mortgage lending, more consumer choice is a two-edged sword, as the implosion of the subprime market attests.

Fannie and Freddie also argue that they implement the government's policy of increasing homeownership; indeed, Fannie's slogan is "Our Business is the American Dream." They claim that they have thereby helped the nation achieve a great increase in the rate of homeownership. This claim is undercut in a variety of ways. First, the credit crunch has made some question whether homeownership is a good in and of itself for all households. Second, some scholars argue that America over-invests in housing and that Fannie and Freddie are part of that problem. Third, it is unclear whether they actually help to fund affordable housing for low- and moderate-income homeowners, who should presumably be the main beneficiaries of such a government initiative. Fourth, the amount that the typical homeowner saves because of Fannie and Freddie is relatively modest.

(vi) *Preventing an Overly-Concentrated Economy.* Regulation may be employed to reduce over-concentrations of market power. Fannie and Freddie argue, however, that their vast size provides stability to the mortgage market; independent scholars disagree. Recent events further disfavor the Fannie/ Freddie perspective. Taken individually, Fannie and Freddie each present an over-concentration of risk that is perhaps unsurpassed by any other private firm operating anywhere in the world. Because the two companies have the identical, undiversified business model, that risk is only magnified. Thus, any substantial operational risk or mistaken hedging strategy at either of those firms, poses a systemic risk to the international economy, a risk that has already become a reality.

*   *   *

Fannie and Freddie do not do well when these six regulatory goals are taken together. As to the three economic efficiency goals, the conforming market is not as competitive or efficient as it would be if there were more competitors. There is also no evidence that the market is more innovative than it would be if there were more competitors. Thus, merely on economic efficiency grounds, Fannie and Freddie's regulatory privilege does not serve the public interest. Nor do Fannie and Freddie do particularly well with the other public policy goals. The two companies engage in rent-seeking, limit consumer choice, and keep other firms from competing with them.

The two areas where Fannie and Freddie seem to offer some clear and significant benefits are in (i) providing short-term liquidity and stability to the mortgage market during an acute crisis and (ii) promoting consumer protection, at least in the prime, conforming sector. This second point is underscored by the events leading up to the credit crisis that have demonstrated that too much consumer choice in the mortgage arena can lead to horrible results. If the benefits offered by Fannie and Freddie could be undertaken through alternate means, one might conclude that Fannie and Freddie are not particularly beneficial agents of public policy.

In sum, regulatory theory helps to untangle Fannie and Freddie's intended market function from their intended public mission and to explain how the two purposes do not work well individually or taken together. Because Fannie and Freddie are creatures of federal regulatory privilege, and not independent firms that are operating in a relatively unregulated market, the federal government has broad latitude in setting new goals for these two firms and modifying the regulatory privileges awarded to them.

3. Fannie and Freddie's GSE Status Should Be Terminated

Identifying the weaknesses of Fannie and Freddie as agents of public policy is very different from identifying what should be done with them. The two companies have two of the most powerful lobbying machines in Washington. Moreover, the nature of Fannie and Freddie's privileges makes it unlikely that they will be revisited by Congress with any regularity. Because Fannie and Freddie are poor agents of public policy and are political powerhouses with unmatched influence, the two companies should be fully privatized.

3.1 Fannie and Freddie are political powerhouses

Koppell (2003, pp. 97–121) has thoroughly documented how Fannie and Freddie have been able to exercise unparalleled influence in Washington. Mirroring the hybrid analysis in this chapter, he concludes that it is the combining of elements of public instrumentalities and private companies that gives them the "best of both worlds"—in terms of the political influence the two companies can marshal. Thus, any policy proposals relating to the two companies must be evaluated in the context of the political environment in which they operate.

Given that Fannie and Freddie have outsized influence in Washington, one must be cautious in recommending half-measures in reaction to their limitations as agents of public policy. Unfortunately, most of the reforms floated in the last few years would seem to fall within this category. They include

- limiting the size of their mortgage portfolios;
- limiting their debt issuance;

- stripping the two companies of some of their unique privileges to signal to the market that the implied guarantee has been weakened;
- freezing the conforming loan value to limit the size of mortgages they can buy, thereby limiting their overall size;
- requiring them to obtain ratings from rating agencies for their debt issuances that discount the implied guarantee;
- imposing user fees; and
- strengthening their subordinated debt programs.

If any of these half-measures were adopted, however, Fannie and Freddie's lobbying juggernaut would be sure to undercut them as soon as Congress' focus moved on to another pressing issue.

3.2   The government guarantee is a reckless budgeting device

Froomkin (1995, p. 618), among others, has identified the encouragement of federal budget shenanigans as a hard to quantify "cost" of the Fannie and Freddie hybrid business model. This is because the federal government's contingent liability for its guarantee of Fannie and Freddie's obligations is off-budget, allowing Congress to avoid having that liability trigger debt ceiling limits. If off-budget accounting is a bad sign when found in corporations such as Enron, it is at least as bad for the federal government. For, while the federal government was ultimately able to investigate Enron, who will watch the watchers? Indeed, if the federal government had to quantify and account for this contingent liability in its budget, it would most certainly reduce Congress' ability to increase net spending.

Fannie and Freddie thus pose four serious budgetary problems. First, the cost of the government's guarantee is hidden because it is historically treated as off-budget. Second, the cost of the guarantee is particularly difficult to quantify. Third, the cost of the guarantee is not capped by the federal government, given that the federal government has not imposed any meaningful limits on Fannie and Freddie's growth. Finally, Fannie and Freddie's charters and the costs they might pose to the federal government are infrequently revisited by Congress. Indeed, Congress only takes a serious look at them every ten years or so.

Block (2003–2004, pp. 900–904), in her work on the federal tax budget, proposes a set of principles that should guide the budget legislative process. These principles are built on those relied upon by the General Accounting Office and are (1) budget formation as a democratic exercise; (2) enforceability; (3) accountability; (4) transparency; and (5) openness and durability. These five principles help to clarify the manner in which the contingent liability of the government's guarantee should be treated in the federal budget process.

The government's guarantee of Fannie and Freddie's obligations, when viewed as an item in the legislative budgetary process, fails to abide by any of these principles. Because the government guarantee of Fannie and Freddie's obligations was effectively created decades ago, it is generally not part of the annual debate surrounding the budget. Because the size of the guarantee is uncapped and contingent, it fails the enforceability and accountability principles: it operates outside of the budget, its cost is hard to estimate, and the trigger for the federal government's obligation to make good on it is in itself an unexpected event. Similarly, the guarantee, because of its contingent nature, is quite confusing to those outside of the budget process. Finally, it fails to meet the openness and durability principles because it is not typically part of the annual budget deliberations.

In sum, the budgetary implications of the government's guarantee provide an additional public policy argument against Fannie and Freddie's hybrid structure, one that even on its own weighs heavily against them as agents of public policy.

3.3   Fannie and Freddie should be privatized

There are four broad positions regarding the appropriate role of Fannie and Freddie in the housing finance market. First, Fannie and Freddie are generally doing the job that they were designed to do, although their powers and that of their regulators should be tweaked. Second, Fannie and Freddie are generally doing their job, but they are retaining too much of the value of the government guarantee for the benefit of shareholders and management at the expense of their affordable housing goals. Third, Fannie and Freddie should be nationalized because the federal government has taken on most of the risk associated with them already. And finally, Fannie and Freddie pose a systemic risk to the financial system, unfairly benefit from their regulatory privilege, and do not create net benefits for the American people.

This chapter has taken the fourth position. In particular, it argues that the government guarantee should be terminated and the two companies should be privatized. Until they entered conservatorship, this position has been considered a political nonstarter, particularly because Fannie and Freddie have many allies in the Republican and Democratic parties. Due to recent events, it is now one of the options on the table for a post-conservatorship Fannie and Freddie.

One taking the first view—that Fannie and Freddie are generally doing the job that they were designed to do—might argue that "[t]he penetration of competitive markets by laws and regulations is a highly durable and robust intrusion in the U.S. economy . . . [which] is arguable as tightly regulated as the more socialistic economics of Western Europe" (Crew and Rowley, 1988). Thus, there is no need to extricate the federal government from its relationship with Fannie and Freddie because the government has similar relationships with many other private companies. Proponents of this view typically recommend the limited reforms outlined in Section 3.1 above.

Affordable housing providers and advocates often take the second position: Fannie and Freddie are pretty much doing their job of making housing more affordable to Americans, but they are retaining too much of the value of the government guarantee for the benefit of the shareholders and management, at the expense of their affordable housing goals. Given the shared agenda of Fannie and Freddie, on the one hand, and affordable housing providers and advocates, on the other, this position should not come as a surprise to a student of regulation. Thus, these parties favor proposals that redirect some of the excess profits of Fannie and Freddie from their shareholders and management to affordable housing programs.

And, indeed, in a plan subsequently suspended by federal conservatorship, Congress had implemented an affordable housing fund in which the two firms would deposit upward of $500 million of their income each year. These monies were to be invested in affordable housing projects throughout the country. Affordable housing advocates saw this as a painless way to dramatically increase the supply of affordable housing. The ongoing bailout of the two companies demonstrates that the initiative was not painless, just pain deferred.

Fannie and Freddie supported this proposal in exchange for expanding their market. This expansion was implemented by increasing the conforming loan limit in high-cost parts of the country, which allowed the two companies to expand into the bottom part of the jumbo market. It is of note, of course, that Fannie and Freddie's support for such an extraordinarily costly initiative as the affordable housing fund came at a low point of their public prestige and was widely seen as a political compromise that brought together a broad set of special interests whose goals are aligned with those of Fannie and Freddie. These interests included affordable housing advocates, local governments, and the construction industry.

The dynamics of this position are complex. Housing advocates are concerned with the sustained lack of attention that federal and state governments have paid to affordable housing policy and see any dedicated housing dollars as a long overdue priority. Implicit in this view is that the risk of a Fannie and/or Freddie bailout to the typical American taxpayer is worth the benefit of the affordable housing dollars that the affordable housing fund could direct to low- and moderate-income families. The real debate, from this perspective, is how much of the golden egg of the economic rents resulting from the implied subsidy (as revealed by Fannie and Freddie's profits that consistently and greatly exceed their industry average) can be redirected to these affordable housing objectives without killing the Fannie and Freddie geese.

The third position, nationalization, had only begun to be taken seriously as the Fannie and Freddie bailouts become more and more likely. Indeed, then-Secretary Paulson has raised the idea, one which would seem to be anathema to a fiscal conservative like himself. Paulson proposed merging the two companies with the Federal Housing Administration, a government agency, which already insures certain mortgages. He did note, however, that such a plan would place much of the underwriting in the hands of the government, which is unlikely to do that task well (not that the private sector has done so either in recent years!).

As noted above, this chapter advocates for the fourth view: Fannie and Freddie pose a systemic risk to the financial system, unfairly benefit from their regulatory privilege, and no longer create meaningful net benefits for the American people. In speaking of regulatory reform, Sunstein (1990, p. 109) notes that a good first step "would be to adopt a presumption in favor of flexible, market-oriented, incentive-based, and decentralized regulatory strategies. Such strategies should be focused on ends . . . rather than on the means of achieving those ends." Fannie and Freddie are holdovers from an earlier philosophy of government action, one that has seen its day. Indeed, if one were to create from scratch a new system of federally supported residential mortgage finance, it is quite clear that the model would not be Fannie and Freddie, which are relatively inflexible and centralized solutions to the complex and fluid problems posed by the housing finance market. And while there is an argument to be made that Fannie and Freddie are market-oriented and incentive-based, it is a stronger argument to say that they are beneficiaries of regulatory privilege with incentives that have benefited their shareholders and management disproportionately.

Privatization is needed to remedy this state of affairs. Notwithstanding Fannie and Freddie's potency in Washington, this is not merely some fanciful policy proposal. Theories of regulation and rent-seeking identify erosions of government-granted monopolies over time as part of their natural lifecycle. And, as the credit crisis continues to worsen, more and more previously unthinkable solutions are being taken quite seriously.

Four concrete plans have been proposed to fundamentally change Fannie and Freddie's structure, each involving different degrees of government involvement. First, convert them into cooperatives owned by lenders. Second, break the companies up into a number of smaller companies (or charter a number of similar competitors). Third, leave them intact, but regulate them like public utilities. Fourth, convert them into generic financial holding companies.

The first proposal, converting Fannie and Freddie into cooperatives, has precedent. There are two other privately owned GSEs that are cooperative lenders: the Federal Home Loan Bank System (FHLB System) and the Farm Credit System. Some commentators have called for the FHLB System to take over Fannie and Freddie. This proposal has some initial attraction as it might attenuate the short-term profit-maximizing culture that characterizes publicly traded corporations like Fannie and Freddie. But history does not give comfort that such a GSE structure is superior to that of Fannie and Freddie's. Indeed, Congress had to bail out the Farm Credit System in 1987. And there are rumblings that the FHLB System may face problems similar to those of Fannie and Freddie.

The second proposal, chartering additional housing finance competitors, has some initial attraction. Indeed, one might consider the federal deposit insurance system to be a model of this: numerous recipients of regulatory privilege (access to federally guarantee insurance) who must compete among themselves. If the Fannie/Freddie duopoly could be diluted with enough similar competitors, the amount of economic rent that Fannie and Freddie retain from their government guarantee subsidy should reduce significantly. In addition, one might think that a more competitive market would spread risk among more firms.

Upon further reflection, however, this proposal also reveals significant flaws. The benefit of GSE competition is less compelling now that we have experienced a bubble where so many financial institutions demonstrated herd-like behavior in their business models. And, as with the first proposal, the American taxpayer is still left with the contingent liability of the government guarantee.

The third proposal, regulating them like utilities, appears to be favored by Paulson and taken seriously by the likes of the former Federal Housing Finance Agency director, James Lockhart. One worries, however, how the common regulatory problem of capture would be avoided in this situation in which the two companies to be regulated are so clearly skilled in the art of politics.

The fourth proposal, converting them into generic financial services holding companies along the lines of institutions like Citigroup, J. P. Morgan, and Bank of America, has the attraction of simplicity. It also terminates the contingent liability of the government guarantee and allows the conforming mortgage market to function like other sectors of the overall mortgage market. There is also a precedent for this approach: Sallie Mae was successfully converted from a GSE to a private company. This approach would also send the message that the American mortgage markets have grown up and are now to be integrated with the rest of the financial sector.

This proposal has its own limitations that must be addressed if it were to be implemented. First, because Fannie and Freddie can offer at least a short-term stabilizing role in the residential mortgage markets, the federal government would need to implement other policies to take on that role. Possible policy responses to market disruptions could include providing targeted federal mortgage guarantees; authorizing the Treasury to make mortgage-backed securities purchases; and allowing mortgage lenders to access the Federal Reserve's discount window. Policies like these can ensure that the residential mortgage market functions during a panic.

Second, homeowners will pay slightly higher interest for conforming mortgages if the two companies were privatized. If Congress determines that this increase were too much, particularly given the current condition of the economy, it could reduce the burden by modifying the deduction for mortgage interest or by providing a tax credit relating to mortgage interest. While such a strategy will decrease federal revenues it will be offset by the liability that Fannie and Freddie impose on the federal government, a liability that is already on its way to costing taxpayers hundreds of billions of dollars as part of the current bailout.

Third, if the federal government wanted to increase funding for affordable housing as contemplated in the Act, it would need to do so through direct expenditures. Again, this direct cost would be offset by terminating the contingent liability of the government guarantee.

Finally, Fannie and Freddie have imposed pro-consumer terms on the prime conforming mortgage market. These must be maintained and built upon through new consumer protection regulation in order to avoid the nasty and brutish environment of the subprime mortgage market. And, indeed, it is hard to imagine that privatization would be politically feasible if such protections were not built into the privatization proposal.

Notwithstanding these limitations, the full-privatization proposal has the most going for it. It avoids the problem of the government guarantee that remains with the other three proposals. It leaves to the private sector what the private sector is supposed to do best: evaluate risk. And it leaves to the government what it is supposed to do best: protect against systemic risk, protect consumers, and provide affordable housing to those who could not otherwise afford it.

4. Conclusion

The main problem with GSEs is well-documented: they take on a life of their own and can survive well after they have achieved the purposes for which they are created. Alice Rivlin, in her then-capacity as the director of the Office of Management and Budget, stated that "GSEs should only be created with a clearly articulated 'exit strategy' and an express sunset date in their charter" (OMB, 1995). Unfortunately, this is almost never the case.

The typical result of poor GSE design is that the GSE ends up driving much of the legislative and regulatory agenda regarding its own fate. Stanton and Moe (2002, p. 105) argue that this can lead to "increasing dominance over the governmental process" by GSEs; the inability "of the government to supervise GSE safety and soundness and the government's resulting financial exposure;" as well as government inability "to induce GSEs to serve public purposes that conflict with the interests of shareholders."

Fannie and Freddie reflect what is worst in GSE design. After fulfilling their purpose of creating a national mortgage market, they have taken on monstrously large lives of their own. In the midst of their bailout, Congress should take the opportunity to convert them to fully private status. Congress should also enact appropriate financial regulation, consumer protection legislation, and affordable housing programs. And Congress should remember the lessons of Fannie and Freddie when it considers using the GSE as a tool of government in the future. It should reflect on the appropriate design for such a hybrid tool, a design informed by a theoretical understanding of the GSE based on regulatory theory and sound federal budget policies.

* The author is Professor of Law at Brooklyn Law School. This chapter is based in large part on "Fannie Mae and Freddie Mac and the Future of Federal Housing Finance Policy: A Study of Regulatory Privilege," *Alabama Law Review* 61, (forthcoming 2010).

Note

1. Fannie and Freddie have funded directly or indirectly most of the research that pertains to them. That research typically supports Fannie and Freddie's own agendas. In addition, many of the scholars writing about Fannie and Freddie have worked or do work for one of the two companies. Again, much of their research is supportive of the two companies. I use the terms "independent scholars" and "independent research" to distinguish scholarly work produced by those without a connection to the two firms as well as research by Fannie- or Freddie-affiliated researchers that does not appear to have a pro-Fannie and pro-Freddie bias.

References

Block, C. (2003–2004). Congress and accounting scandals: Is the pot calling the kettle black? *Nebraska Law Review 82*: 365–459.

Breyer, S. G. (1982). *Regulation and its reform*. Cambridge, MA: Harvard University Press.

Brodley, J. F. (1987). The economic goals of antitrust: Efficiency, consumer welfare and technological progress. *New York University Law Review 62*: 1020–53.

Browning, L. (2008, December 10). Ex-officer faults mortgage giants for "orgy" of nonprime loans. *The New York Times*, p. B3.

Crew, M. A., and C. K. Rowley, (1988). Dispelling the disinterest in deregulation. In C. K. Rowley, R. D. Tollison, G. Tullock, G. (eds.) *The political economy of rent-seeking*. Boston, MA: Kluwer Academic Publishers.

————— (1989). Feasibility of deregulation: a public choice analysis. In M. A. Crew, (ed.), *Deregulation and diversification of utilities*. Boston, MA: Kluwer Academic Publishers.

Engel, K .C., and P. A. McCoy (2007). Turning a blind eye: Wall street finance of predatory lending. *Fordham Law Review 75*: 2039–2104.

Froomkin, M. (1995). Reinventing the government corporation. *University of Illinois Law Review 1995*: 543–634.

Hagerty, J. R. (2007, July 28). Fannie, Freddie are said to suffer in subprime. *The Wall Street Journal*, p. A3.

Housing and Economic Recovery Act of 2008, Pub. L. No. 110-289 (2008). 122 Stat. 2654.

Koppell, J. G. (2003). *The politics of quasi-government*. Cambridge, UK: Cambridge University Press.

OFHEO (2003). *Systemic risk: Fannie Mae, Freddie Mac and the role of OFHEO*. Washington, DC: Office of Federal Housing Enterprise Oversight.

OMB (1995). *Memorandum on government corporations* (M-96-05). Retrieved from www.whitehouse.gov/omb/assets/omb/memoranda/m96-05.pdf.

Reiss, D. (2008). The federal government's implied guarantee of Fannie Mae and Freddie Mac's obligations: Uncle Sam will pick up the tab. *Georgia Law Review 42*: 1019–1083.

Stanton, T. H. (2002). *Government-sponsored enterprises: Mercantilist companies in the modern 2d*. Washington, DC: AEI Press.

Stanton, T. H., and R. Moe (2002). Government corporations and government-sponsored enterprises. In L. M. Salaman, (ed.), *The tools of government: A guide to the new governance* (80–116). New York: Oxford University Press.

Sunstein, C. (1990). *After the rights revolution: Reconceiving the regulatory state*. Cambridge, MA: Harvard University Press.

U.S. Department of Justice (n.d.). *About the division: Antitrust division*. Retrieved January 21, 2010 from http://www.justice.gov/atr/about/mission.htm.

Part II

Other Issues in Financial Regulation

8

Uncertainty and Transparency of Monetary Policy

*Giorgio Di Giorgio and Guido Traficante**

Abstract

What is the proper degree of central bank transparency? This chapter investigates the issue in a framework characterized by (a) common uncertainty on potential output and (b) imperfect knowledge of the central bank target by the private sector. We show that full transparency is socially beneficial under a variety of parametrizations. Our results confirm, in a different setup, those of Faust and Svensson (2001, 2002), and Svensson (2006).

Introduction

Monetary policy transparency has considerably increased across countries in the last decade. This development is probably linked with the fact that many central banks have recently adopted (more or less explicitly) an inflation targeting regime, where it is essential for the central bank to be able to anchor the private sector's expectations. In a forward-looking environment, it would seem natural to be pro-transparency, as extensively argued in Woodford (2003).

However, Morris and Shin (2002) have seriously challenged this belief and opened a lively debate in the economic literature.[1] They argue that there can be a cost in providing more accurate public information, as agents may overreact to such information. In this framework, agents formulate expectations based on the underlying fundamentals, but a coordination motive arises from strategic complementarity in their actions. As a result, agents may be too sensitive to forecast errors in public information. Svensson (2006) underlines that Morris and Shin's result in favor of opaqueness can be misleading, because it was obtained for a very particular functional form of social welfare and for unreasonable parameter values. Morris and Shin modeled public information as a signal of exogenous disturbances; however, economic agents mainly receive endogenous signals, that is, signals about the state of the economy that depend on economic policy objectives, actions, and on public and private assessments of the overall economic conditions. Examples of such signals are the short-term policy rate set by central banks or their economic forecasts. The introduction of transparency issues along these lines leads Walsh (2007) to show that more *economic* transparency is not always welfare beneficial. The optimal degree of transparency depends on the relative quality of the signals available to the central bank and the private sector and on the relative central bank's ability to forecast aggregate demand and supply shocks: if the central bank obtains more accurate signals on cost shocks, optimal transparency increases, whereas if it obtains more accurate signals on demand shocks, optimal transparency decreases. In modeling the information structure within the private sector, Walsh allows for firm-specific shocks and follows Cornand and Heinemann (2006), who introduce a rationale for partial transparency, in the sense of partial release of information. They find that extensive release of public information may induce excessive sensitivity of agents' expectations to noises in public information (as in Morris and Shin). However, if public information can be released only to a proportion of agents, there is only a limited effect on the higher-order expectations, thereby avoiding coordination failures and restoring positive values of (partial) transparency.

In this chapter we investigate whether central bank's political transparency is desirable in the presence of incomplete information about the state of the economy. We will assume that the central bank and the private sector share the same incomplete information on potential output. Moreover, the private sector does not observe the policy targets and cannot exactly infer the policy reaction function, linking the choice of the policy instrument to the final objectives. Orphanides (2001, 2003a) widely documented the relevance of a common noise in the measure of potential output for central bank's policy. Cukierman and Lippi (2005) showed that, even if the policymakers efficiently estimate potential output, this does not avoid persistent retrospective policy errors. An interesting question is, therefore, if a more transparent central bank can limit the welfare cost of having incomplete information about potential output.

From a methodological point of view, this chapter contributes to the literature that analyzes problems of incomplete information in DSGE models. In most papers an information structure featuring a common information set for the private sector larger than the central bank's one has been assumed (Svensson and Woodford 2004; Boivin and Giannoni 2008).[2] We start by observing that policy objectives and intentions are not always revealed explicitly and truthfully to the public. Hence, we assume asymmetric information about policy targets in favor of the central bank and we analyze whether disclosing such policy targets could be beneficial in a framework of incomplete common information on potential output.

The chapter is organized as follows: we describe the model in Section 1, and we solve it in its state-space form in Section 2. In Section 3 we show the numerical properties of the model and check the robustness of our findings. Section 4 summarizes and concludes.

1. The Model

We will focus on the informational side of a microfounded DSGE model featuring nominal rigidities and monopolistic competition. The supply-side of the economy is modeled according to a New Keynesian Phillips curve[3]

$$\pi_t = \beta E_t \pi_{t+1} + \frac{(1-\omega\beta)(1-\omega)}{\omega} \kappa (y_t - \bar{y}_t) + \frac{(1-\omega\beta)(1-\omega)}{\omega} s_t \qquad (1)$$

where β is the discount factor, $1 - \omega$ is the constant fraction of firms adjusting their prices (Calvo's parameter), κ is the sum of the coefficient on relative risk aversion and the inverse of the wage elasticity of labor supply, and s_t is a cost-push shock. The cost-push shock is assumed to be an AR(1) process:

$$s_t = \rho_s s_{t-1} + \varepsilon_t \qquad (2)$$

Since only cost-push shocks posit policy trade-offs, we follow Faust and Svensson (2002) and Walsh (2006, 2007) and work with a simplified version of the demand side. We assume that the central bank has imperfect control over the level of output (treated as a policy instrument, see below) and, in turn, over the output gap. More precisely, the following stochastic structure is adopted:

a) an autoregressive error term η_t makes the intended output gap $y_t^I - \bar{y}_t$ deviate from the actual output gap $y_t - \bar{y}_t$;

$$y_t - \bar{y}_t = y_t^I - \bar{y}_t + \eta_t \qquad \eta_t = \rho_\eta \eta_{t-1} + \mu_t \qquad (3)$$

b) potential output is autoregressive: $\bar{y}_t = \rho_y \bar{y}_{t-1} + g_t$;
c) The central bank and the private sector share a distorted observation of the true potential output because of a measurement error:

$$y_t^\circ = \bar{y}_t + v_t \tag{4}$$

where v_t is normal white noise with variance σ_v^2.

Considering y_t as the policy instrument of the central bank is only a simplifying assumption. In the standard case of an IS equation derived from first principles, with consumption dynamics depending on real interest rates, we could treat either inflation or output as a control variable and subsequently derive the interest rate that is coherent with the prescribed relationship between output and inflation.[4]

The central bank is assumed to minimize the following loss function:

$$L_t = \frac{1}{2}\left[\left(\pi_t - \pi_t^*\right)^2 + \alpha\left(y_t - \bar{y}_t\right)^2\right] \tag{5}$$

where π_t^* is a stochastic inflation target, with the following AR(1) representation:

$$\pi_t^* = \rho_\pi \pi_{t-1}^* + \varsigma_t \tag{6}$$

The assumption of a stochastic inflation target reflects the idea that the true central bank's target hardly remains constant over time. This seems to hold, for example, in the case of the Federal Reserve, which does not have any explicit inflation target. In a recent paper, Ireland (2007) estimates a New Keynesian model able to capture the behavior of the Federal Reserve's unobserved inflation target. His results show that that the target rose from 1.25 percent in 1959 to 8 percent in the late 1970s before falling back below 2.5 percent in 2004. In this exercise, the time-varying inflation target has a lagged component and it is a function of both supply shocks[5] and a purely exogenous shock to the inflation target. The estimation provides evidence in favor of a relevant contribution of supply shocks, even if it is not possible to reject the null hypothesis according to which the movements in the inflation target are purely random.[6]

The information structure is as follows: the central bank and the private sector are assumed to share the same incomplete information set on potential output. Such incompleteness stems from the noise present in observing potential output and the consequent difficulty in distinguishing cost-push shocks from potential output shocks. An asymmetric feature regards the central bank's inflation target, which is not perfectly known by the private sector. Transparency is therefore related to how the private sector perceives intended output, the central bank's policy instrument, which is related to the true inflation target. More specifically, the private sector is assumed to receive a signal ψ_t of y_t^I satitsfying the following condition:

$$y_t^I = \psi_t + \chi_t \tag{7}$$

ψ_t is independent of χ_t, which is assumed to be a mean-zero normal shock. The private sector observes the central bank's signal ψ_t: the more transparent the central bank is about the signal, the better will be the private sector's perception about the central bank's intended output and its true inflation target.

In the following section we characterize the problem in state-space form, and we derive the solution of the model in terms of (a) the central bank's optimal policy and estimation of the state of the economy and (b) the private sector's estimation of the state of the economy and the inflation target. The latter, in turn, will depend upon the degree of central bank transparency.

2. State-Space Form and Model Solution

The model described in the previous sections can be summarized in a canonical state-space representation with three blocks. The first block characterizes the economy according to a VAR representation; the second contains the loss criterion; and the third block the measurement equation.

2.1 State-space form

The economy can be described by

$$\begin{bmatrix} X_{t+1} \\ E_t \pi_{t+1} \end{bmatrix} = A \begin{bmatrix} X_t \\ \pi_t \end{bmatrix} + B y_t^I + C_u u_{t+1} \tag{8}$$

where X_t is a vector containing the predetermined variables y_t, s_t, η_t and π_t^*; y_t^I is the intended policy that corresponds to output unless for a shock η_t; and, finally, u_{t+1} is a composite vector of structural shocks with covariance matrix given by Σ_u. All the matrices are of appropriate dimensions.

The period loss function is a quadratic form of the goal variables Y_t in which W is a positive-semidefinite weight matrix:

$$Y_t = C \begin{bmatrix} X_t \\ \pi_t \end{bmatrix} + C_y y_t^I \quad C \equiv \begin{bmatrix} 0 & 0 & 0 & -1 & 1 \\ -1 & 0 & 1 & 0 & 0 \end{bmatrix} \quad C_y \equiv \begin{bmatrix} 0 \\ 1 \end{bmatrix} \quad (9)$$

where $W = \begin{bmatrix} 1 & 0 \\ 0 & \alpha \end{bmatrix}$ so that the policymaker aims at minimizing the loss function

$$L_t \equiv Y_t' W Y_t.$$

The third block deals with the measurement equation:

$$Z_t = D \begin{bmatrix} X_t \\ \pi_t \end{bmatrix} + \Sigma_t^i \qquad (10)$$

The matrix D selects the elements of the vectors X_t and π_t that can be observed; the central bank, in fact, can observe inflation target without noise, while potential output is observed with a noise v_t. On the other hand, the private sector has a different information set than the central bank since its measurement error of potential output is still given by v_t, but it does not observe the inflation target. In (10), the i over the matrix Σ_t indicates that the measurement errors are different for the private sector and the central bank because of the different information sets available to each of them.

In two very different environments, Faust and Svensson (2001, 2002) and Svensson and Woodford (2004) have shown that when there exists asymmetric information between the private sector and the policymaker, the estimation of the state of the economy depends on the policy followed by the central bank. The solution is therefore more complex than in the case with symmetric partial information. However, we know from Svensson and Woodford (2004) that the certainty equivalence principle holds. Hence, the policy set up by the central bank does not depend on the information structure available, and in particular it does not depend on the shocks represented in the state-space form.

2.2   Non inertial policy rule and signal-extraction problems

In order to solve the signal-extraction problem for both the agents involved in the model, we first need to solve the policy problem. We concentrate on a discretionary, non inertial equilibrium as in Faust and Svensson (2001, 2002). In this case, the central bank follows a linear rule where its intended output is a function of the contemporary states of the economy:

$$y_t^I = \gamma_1 s_t + \gamma_2 \bar{y}_t + \gamma_3 \eta_t + \gamma_4 \pi_t^* \tag{11}$$

The private sector has to learn the time-varying policy target without observing y_t^I and π_t^* directly. This learning process will be contingent on the signal ψ_t on the intended output received by the private sector. Since π_t^* and y_t^I are unobserved by the private sector, we can go through (11) and (7) and solve the estimation-problem.

The variable

$$\gamma_1 s_t + \gamma_2 \bar{y}_t + \gamma_3 \eta_t - \psi_t \tag{12}$$

would allow us to pin down the observation of the inflation target if monetary policy is fully transparent. In this case, in fact, $\chi_t \to 0$, hence the signal ψ_t coincides with the intended output and, in turn, the difference between (12) and (11) amounts to $-\gamma_4 \pi_t^*$.

Since the inflation target is not observable, however, (12) minus (11) includes also an error term, given by χ_t. Therefore, for a given policy (11) chosen by the central bank, the private sector will infer the inflation target by using the following expression:

$$\iota_t = -\gamma_4 \pi_t^* + \chi_t \tag{13}$$

Notice that the private sector's inference about the inflation target depends on the central bank decision to reveal its intended output. In other words, it is not necessary for the central bank to explicitly reveal π_t^* in order to be transparent about its inflation target

Solving this policy problem, we get a policy function, that is, a matrix F constituted by the γ coefficients in (11) and a matrix G that links inflation to the states of the economy. We can plug these two matrices into (8) and then combine the resulting state-space form with the corresponding relevant measurement equation. The latter will be different if we analyze the signal-extraction problem of the central bank or of the private sector.

The measurement equation for the central bank is given by:

$$
Z_t^{CB} = \begin{bmatrix} 1 & 0 & 0 & 0 & 0 \\ 0 & 0 & 1 & 0 & 0 \end{bmatrix} \begin{bmatrix} \bar{y}_t \\ s_t \\ \eta_t \\ \pi_t^* \\ \pi_t \end{bmatrix} + \begin{bmatrix} v_t \\ 0 \end{bmatrix} \tag{14}
$$

whereas, for the private sector it will be the following:

$$
Z_t^{PS} = \begin{bmatrix} 1 & 0 & 0 & 0 & 0 \\ 0 & 0 & 0 & -\gamma_4 & 0 \end{bmatrix} \begin{bmatrix} \bar{y}_t \\ s_t \\ \eta_t \\ \pi_t^* \\ \pi_t \end{bmatrix} + \begin{bmatrix} v_t \\ \chi_t \end{bmatrix} \tag{15}
$$

3. Parametrization and Numerical Results

Faust and Svensson (2001) show how to derive an analytical expression for the policy coefficients using the methods of undetermined coefficients. However, to study the properties of the model and evaluate the effect of varying the degree of transparency, they had to follow numerical methods. We will solve the model numerically. Our calibration relies on standard numerical values in the literature (see Woodford 2003; and Giordani and Söderlind 2004). The discount factor β is set equal to 0.99, and the degree of price stickiness ω is set equal to 0.66. We set the coefficient of constant relative risk aversion equal to 2 and the inverse of labor-supply elasticity equal to 1.5: hence, the implied value for κ is 3.5.[7] The autoregressive coefficient of potential output is assumed to be 0.7, while for both the cost-push and the demand shock we pick a value of 0.4. The autoregressive coefficient for the inflation target is 0.05, a value consistent with the evidence of Ireland's estimates about the statistical properties of the time-varying inflation target for the Federal Reserve. Furthermore, we think that even in presence of a constant inflation target, as in the case of the European Central Bank, there can be phases in which it is not possible to strictly adhere to the target because of extraordinary external shocks.

Given this set of structural parameters, we simulate the stochastic properties of the shocks and the measurement errors. We solve the model for

100,000 draws of a uniform distribution for the variance of potential output, cost-push shock, demand shock, and the inflation target. Specifically, we let $\left[\sigma_g^2, \sigma_\varepsilon^2, \sigma_\mu^2, \sigma_\varsigma^2\right] \in [0,5]$, while the measurement shocks are simulated in a different way depending on whether we are considering the central bank's or the private sector's perspective. Since the central bank is assumed to observe the inflation target, we capture its uncertainty about potential output by taking 100,000 points drawn uniformly from the parameter space $[0, 5]$.

With respect to the private sector, we take the same values drawn before for the central bank and derive the values for σ_χ^2 as a function of the central bank's degree of transparency. Namely, we define the degree of transparency $\tau \equiv \dfrac{\sigma_\psi^2}{\sigma_\psi^2 + \sigma_\chi^2}$ and compute inversely the value of $\sigma_\chi^2 = \dfrac{\sigma_\psi^2(1-\tau)}{\tau}$.
Of course, for high levels of transparency (i.e., $\tau \rightarrow 1$), σ_ψ^2 coincides with σ_η^2, while the less transparent the central bank is, the less informative ψ_t is about the intended policy y_t^I. We distinguish three regimes of transparency and for each of them we draw 100,000 points from a uniform distribution and, in turn, for the value of σ_χ^2. In particular, we consider a low level of transparency for $\tau \in [0,0.3]$, a medium level of transparency if $\tau \in [0.3,0.6]$ and finally a high level of transparency when $\tau \in [0.6,1]$. For each of these parameter spaces, we draw 100,000 points uniformly and then compute residually the value of σ_χ^2 before computing the loss functions. Then the model is solved both for the central bank and the private sector. The average values of all the losses computed for these draws are shown in table 8.1: the loss function for the central bank turns out to be independent of the degree of transparency, while that of the private sector is computed for each of the three different levels of central bank transparency.

As these loss functions can be considered a natural measure of welfare for the households,[8] we compare the outcomes arising when the central bank decides to be more or less transparent. Table 8.1 shows that, given a loss function equal to 267.11 for the central bank, the private sector

Table 8.1   Numerical simulation

Regime	Central bank's loss	Private sector's loss
$0 \leq \tau < 0.3$	267.1082	317.4385
$0.3 < \tau \leq 0.6$	267.1082	306.5697
$0.6 < \tau \leq 1$	267.1082	285.4359
$\tau = 0$	267.1082	320.8341
$\tau = 1$	267.1082	267.1125

is better off when it is able to disentangle the error component in the instrument set by the central bank. In fact, the loss function for the private sector amounts to 317.44 for the first range of transparency that we consider; it is sufficient to increase the degree of transparency to the range (.3, .6] to make the private sector better off, since in this case loss drops to 306.57, a value which is further reduced in the most transparent regime we examine: specifically, when $\tau \in [0.6,1]$, the loss amounts to 285.44. Increasing transparency, therefore, is beneficial in terms of the private sector's welfare, as it is also confirmed by solving the model for extreme values in the degree of transparency: with a regime that is not transparent at all, the loss function for the private sector reaches its maximum value, while a completely transparent regime allows the private sector to reach almost the same welfare level as the central bank, the difference being due only to the partial observation of the inflation target.[9] Similarly to what was found by Faust and Svensson (2001), higher transparency may improve the outcome of discretionary policy. However, our result has been derived in a completely different setup, where agents are forward-looking and the central bank does not have any incentive to create unexpected inflation. On the other hand, Faust and Svensson's analysis is conducted entirely in a backward-looking model, where there exists a specific role for central bank's credibility. Faust and Svensson show that increasing transparency makes the discretionary policy closer to the social optimum by assuming that the central bank responds to both the actual time-varying policy target and the private sector's perception of the target.

In our setup, we solve a standard DSGE model under discretion and show that a more transparent regime is beneficial for the private sector even in the presence of incomplete information on potential output. The latter finding suggests a reflection about a common claim according to which if the central bank has limited knowledge of the state of the economy, it would help to be more opaque in order to make the private sector react less than it would do in case of explicit announcements about policy objectives, forecasts, and policies. Here, we interpret the notion of transparency as related to how easily policy intentions can be grasped by the private sector. We show how the presence of incomplete information, in the form of unobserved potential output, cannot be considered a good reason for the policymaker to follow a less transparent regime.

3.1   Alternative scenarios and robustness

In this section, we undertake robustness analysis and check whether our results hold true when considering (a) heterogeneity in the information set within the private sector, and (b) heterogeneity in the information set between the central bank and the private sector with respect to observation of potential output.

We believe it is worthy to consider the effects of different information sets within the private sector for two reasons. First, following Cornand and Heinemann (2006) and Walsh (2007), it is possible that partial release of information, à la Morris and Shin (2002), is beneficial. In case of a wide release of information, the economic agents are induced to coordinate their expectations by taking into account the public information released by the policymaker: this can make the economy too sensitive to any noise in the public information itself. This information cost, however, can be limited if the central bank decides to provide information only to a fraction of agents because a low level of publicity reduces the incentive to overreact to the public signal, as the latter reaches only a fraction of agents. Second, partial release of information may be interpreted as a particular kind of rational inattention: even if the central bank disseminates its public signal to everyone without any discrimination within the private sector, only a fraction of agents incorporate the new information into their decisions. As a consequence, this strand of literature finds an optimal degree of transparency that does not generally coincide with full transparency. Taking that into account, we perform the following experiment: for each given degree of transparency τ, only a fraction P of agents in the private sector observes the inflation target as a function of the degree of transparency. In a separate appendix (available on request), we show in detail how to introduce heterogeneity in the private sector. Here we simply report graphically the effects of differentiating the information set within the private sector. Again, we simulate the model for the same values of shocks and measurement errors in the interval [0, 5], considering, as above, three regimes of transparency and $P \in [0,1]$. Introducing heterogeneity within the private sector's information set should not be confused with varying the degree of the central bank's transparency: in this exercise, we simulate the outcomes for both different levels of transparency and the fraction of informed agents. Then we derive the private sector's loss function as a weighted average of the fraction of the loss of informed and uninformed households. We believe that this experiment allows us to overcome a limit in the literature about policy transparency. Up to now, many contributions (including Walsh 2007), justified the presence of a fraction of uninformed agents by invoking rational inattention à la Sims, and considered the latter as a perfect substitute for low transparency. However, this equivalence is not obvious, as central bankers may be unable to inform only a fraction of agents. Figure 8.1 shows the percentage change in social loss relative to the case of full transparency.

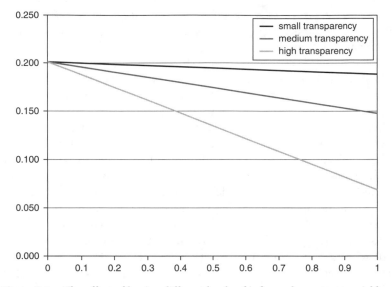

Figure 8.1   The effect of having different levels of informed agents on social loss (percent change relative to having full transparency for the entire private sector)

We find that partial release of information is never optimal, unlike some previous results in the literature. In figure 8.1 the slope of the relative change in social loss monotonically increases with the degree of transparency. Under low transparency the cost of having only a fraction of informed agents is almost constant since even the informed agents observe π_t^* very noisily. Under high transparency, on the contrary, the relative loss decreases rapidly as the information released by the central bank can improve significantly the learning process on the part of private sector. Therefore, providing information about the policy target reduces global uncertainty and, in turn, increases social welfare, in line with Faust and Svensson (2001, 2002), Svensson (2006), and Woodford (2005).[10]

We believe that there exists another reason why, in the present setup, being completely transparent enhances social welfare without any cost in terms of excessive sensitivity to the public signal. The private sector's information set has been modeled as a subset of the central bank's one; specifically, given that the central bank has incomplete information about potential output, the private sector shares this kind of incomplete information and, furthermore, does not perfectly observe the inflation target. Therefore, by releasing a precise signal about the inflation target, the private sector's loss decreases. However, information released by the central bank can be noisy, due to the imperfect knowledge about both the structure of and the shocks affecting the economy. For robustness purposes, we analyze whether these results hold under the assumption that the private sector is better informed on potential output. Such new informative asymmetry could reintroduce a problem of excessive reaction to public signals and reduce incentives for central bank transparency. We simulate the model for different degrees of uncertainty in the measurement of potential output. We take the same 100,000 values of $\sigma_v^2 \in [0,5]$ for the central bank, while for the private sector we take 100,000 values in the uniform distribution $[0, 2.5]$. We assume that the private sector's forecast about potential output is a linear combination of the signal received by the central bank and its own observation. Under an assumption of asymmetric information set about potential output by the private sector, we reexpress the observation equation (4) for the central bank and the private sector:

$$\bar{y}_t^{CB} = \bar{y}_t + v_t^{CB} \quad E\left(v_t^{CB}\right) = 0 \quad Var\left(v_t\right) = \sigma_{v,CB}^2 = \frac{1}{\vartheta} \tag{16}$$

$$\bar{y}_t^{PS} = \bar{y}_t + v_t^{PS} \quad E\left(v_t^{PS}\right) = 0 \quad Var\left(v_t^{PS}\right) = \sigma_{v,PS}^2 = \frac{1}{\varpi} \tag{17}$$

where ϑ and ϖ indicate the precision of the signals received by the central bank and private sector, respectively. Under the assumption of uncertainty about the quality of the two signals (16) and (17), the private sector's learning process uses a linear combination of these:

$$S_t = \varphi \bar{y}_t^{CB} + \left(1 - \varphi\right)\bar{y}_t^{PS} \quad \varphi \equiv \frac{\vartheta}{\vartheta + \varpi} \tag{18}$$

Table 8.2 shows the numerical properties of this modification to our baseline model, for different levels of transparency as defined above. We still obtain that the private sector's loss is decreasing in the degree of central bank transparency, even when the private sector's signal on potential output is more precise.

Finally, in figure 8.2 we show the percentage change in social loss relative to the case of full transparency as a function of the number of informed agents. The message remains coherent with that of figure 8.1 above. Social welfare improves when all the agents are informed. Hence, it is not sufficient to assume that the private sector's measurement error of potential output is lower to modify the conclusion in favor of full transparency and full release of information.

Table 8.2 Numerical simulation with the private sector having a more precise signal about potential output

Regime	Private Sector's Loss
$0 \leq \tau < 0.3$	294.8310
$0.3 < \tau \leq 0.6$	284.6931
$0.6 < \tau \leq 1$	262.9250
$\tau = 0$	298.2852
$\tau = 1$	244.2209

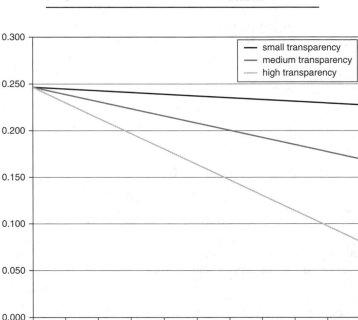

Figure 8.2 The effect of having different levels of informed agents on social loss with different perception of the potential output between the central bank and the private sector (percent change relative to having full transparency for the entire private sector)

4. Concluding Remarks

In the last two decades we have observed a sharp increase in the degree of central bank transparency. In this chapter, we justify this choice by numerically simulating a DSGE model featuring uncertainty on potential output and imperfect knowledge of the central bank's inflation target by the private sector. Our welfare criterion includes a stochastic inflation target, following the analysis of Ireland (2007). We assume that the private sector does not observe the inflation target and it observes a noisy measure of potential output, identical to what is observed by the central bank. If the central bank follows a noninertial optimal policy, the private sector's estimation of the state of the economy also depends on the degree of central bank transparency.

Under higher transparency, private sector's forecasts become more accurate and its welfare increases. This finding is robust in assuming heterogeneity of the information set within the private sector, unlike some previous examples in the literature (Cornand and Heinemann 2006; Walsh 2007). Moreover, it also holds when the private sector is assumed to have better information on potential output with respect to the central bank.

From a methodological point of view, the major contribution of this chapter is to extend the analysis of informational asymmetries in a DSGE model to the case of an unobservable policy goal.

* The authors are, respectively, Professor of Monetary Economics and Dean of the Faculty of Economics at Università LUISS Guido Carli, in Rome, and an Economist at the Development and Strategy Department of Eni and Research Fellow at Università LUISS Guido Carli, in Rome. This chapter has been presented at the 2009 WEAI–IBEFA Vancouver Conference, in July, and at the 50th Annual Meeting of the Italian Economists Society, at LUISS University, Rome, in October. We thank S. Nisticò and participants of the mentioned events for their comments and suggestions.

Notes

1. Actually, Morris and Shin's paper was commented upon and discussed also outside the academia. *The Economist,* for example, in 2004 published an article that was inspired by the result found by Morris and Shin and entitled "It's Not Always Good To Talk."
2. Svensson and Woodford (2004) claim that the only case of asymmetric information in which it is coherent to assume a common information set for all members of the private sector is the case in which the private sector has complete information about the state of the economy and the central bank does not. In fact, only in this case "the model's equations can be expressed in terms of aggregate equations that refer to only a single private sector information set, while at the same time, these model equations are treated as structural, and hence invariant under the alternative policies."
3. See Woodford (2003) for an extensive discussion of the complete microfoundation of DSGE models.
4. To that extent, a clear explanation is given in Clarida, Galí, and Gertler (1999) and Svensson and Woodford (2003).
5. The supply shocks are connected to the New Keynesian model used as the reference model constituting the theoretical background of the estimation.

In particular, the supply shocks are linked to the elasticity of demand for the intermediate goods and the aggregate technology shocks, respectively.

6. The policy implication is, hence, that a time-varying inflation target had relevant implications in terms of actual observed inflation: the American inflation in the 1970s would have been lower if the Federal Reserve had maintained a constant inflation target.

7. The slope coefficient of the new Keynesian Phillips curve can be expressed according to the following representation:

$$\frac{(1-\omega)(1-\beta\omega)}{\omega}(\sigma+\phi)$$

where σ stands for the coefficient of relative risk aversion and ϕ is the inverse of labor supply elasticity.

8. In particular, Woodford (2003) derives a loss function like (5) as a second-order approximation of the representative household's utility.

9. Namely, even without measurement error, the private sector observes a fraction γ_4 of π_t^*.

10. In our setup, differently from Morris and Shin (2002) and other contributions, public information is not a focal point for private actions, because private agents are not forced to coordinate on the public signal, neglecting private information even if the latter is more accurate than the former. Nevertheless, Woodford (2005) and Svensson (2006) show the fragility of the Morris and Shin results to some relevant points like changing the welfare measure, or by calibrating their model with more realistic parameters.

References

Amato, Jeffery D., and Hyun Son Shin (2003). "Public and private information in monetary policy models." *BIS Working Papers,* 138.

Baeriswyl, Romain, and Camille Cornand (2007). "Monetary policy and its informative value." *Mimeo.*

Boivin, Jean, and Marc P. Giannoni (2008). "Optimal monetary policy in a data-rich environment." *Mimeo.*

Clarida, Richard, Jordi Galí, and Mark Gertler (1999). "The science of monetary policy: A new Keynesian perspective." *Journal of Economic Literature* 37: 1661–1707.

Cornand, Camille, and Frank Heinemann (2006). "Optimal degree of public information dissemination." *Mimeo.*

Cukierman, Alex (2007). "The limits of transparency." *Mimeo.*

Cukierman, Alex, and Francesco Lippi (2005). "Endogenous monetary policy with unobserved potential output." *Journal of Economic Dynamics and Control* 29(11): 1951–83.

Dale, Spencer, Athanasios Orphanides, and Pär Österholm (2008). "Imperfect central bank communication: Information versus distraction." *Mimeo.*

Economist (2004). "It's not always good to talk," 22 July, 71.

Ehrmann, Michael, and Marcel Fratzscher (2007a). "Social value of public information—Testing the limits of transparency." *ECB Working paper series,* 821.

——— (2007b). "Communication and decision-making by central bank committees: Different strategies, same effectiveness?" *Journal of Money, Credit and Banking* 39: 509–41.

——— (2007c). "Transparency, disclosure and the Federal Reserve." *International Journal of Central Banking* 3(1): 179–225.

——— (2007d). "The timing of central bank communication." *European Journal of Political Economy* 23: 124–45.

Ehrmann, Michael, and Frank Smets (2003). "Uncertain potential output: Implications for monetary policy." *Journal of Economic Dynamics and Control* 27: 611–38.

Faust, Jon, and Lars Svensson (2001). "Transparency and credibility: Monetary policy with unobservable goals." *International Economic Review* 42: 369–97.

———(2002). "The equilibrium degree of transparency and control in monetary policy." *Journal of Money, Credit and Banking* 34: 520–39.

Geraats, Petra M. (2002). "Review: Central bank transparency." *Economic Journal* 112: 532–65.

Giordani, Paolo, and Paul Söderlind (2004). "Solution of macromodels with Hansen-Sargent robust policies: Some extensions." *Journal of Economic Dynamics and Control* 28: 2367–97.

Ireland, Peter N. (2007). "Changes in the Federal Reserve's inflation target: Causes and consequences." *Journal of Money, Credit and Banking* 39(8): 1851–82.

Morris, Stephen, and Hyun Son Shin (2002). "Social value of public information." *American Economic Review* 92: 1521–34.

Orphanides, Athanasios (2001). "Monetary policy rules based on real-time data." *American Economic Review* 91(4): 964–85.

——— (2003a). "Monetary policy with noisy information." *Journal of Monetary Economics* 50: 605–31.

——— (2003b). "The quest for prosperity without inflation." *Journal of Monetary Economics* 50: 633–63.

Svensson, Lars E. O. (2006). "Social value of public information: Morris and Shin (2002) is actually pro transparency, not con." *American Economic Review* 96: 448–51.

Svensson, Lars E. O., and Michael Woodford (2003). "Indicator variables for optimal policy." *Journal of Monetary Economics* 50: 691–720.

——— (2004). "Indicator variables for optimal policy under asymmetric information." *Journal of Economic Dynamics and Control* 28: 661–90.

——— (2006). "Transparency, flexibility and inflation targeting." In *Monetary Policy under Inflation Targeting*, ed. Frederic Mishkin and Klaus Schmidt-Hebbel, Santiago, Chile: Banco Central de Chile.

——— (2007). "Optimal economic transparency." *The International Journal of Central Banking* 3(1): 5–36.

Woodford, Michael (2003). *Interest and Prices: Foundation of a Theory of Monetary Policy.* Princeton, NJ: Princeton University Press.

——— (2005). "Central-bank communication and policy effectiveness." NBER Working Paper, 11898.

9

Privatization and Governance Regulation in Frontier Emerging Markets: The Case of Romania[†]

*Gilles Chemla, Adrian Pop, and Diana Pop**

Abstract

This chapter investigates the link between the regulation of control transactions and the institutional and corporate features of public companies, by analyzing the massive delisting activity in the Romanian capital market. The peculiar ownership reforms involving a large number of listed companies offer a unique opportunity to verify Bebchuk and Roe's (1999) theory of path dependence. Over time, the Romanian authorities have undertaken wide-ranging institutional reforms, most of which favor blockholders over small and dispersed shareholders. Our empirical approach, based on logit and duration models, allows us to analyze the evolution of public companies over this period and sheds light on the likely events causing frontier emerging markets' eclipse. Our main findings reveal that delisting is more likely to occur when (i) the shareholdings acquired from the privatization authority by circumventing the capital market are high; (ii) the company experiences frequent takeover bids; and (iii) the stock liquidity is low.

Introduction

The question of how to deal with conflicts that has risen among the various protagonists of public companies has been recently restated within the context of the ownership reforms undergone in the European emerging markets. The vast privatization programs addressed to millions of citizens in the early 1990s and the subsequent trading of distributed free shares on new revived markets were viewed as genuine steps forward to the implementation of financial discipline in deficient corporations. The very existence of small shareholders, often confusedly called "dispersed shareholders," had for a long time been considered a trump card in the reforming process involving former state-owned enterprises. While a large number of shareholders could justify to some extent the use of the "public corporations" label, it represents at best a sine qua non condition for restructuring privatized companies. Particularly, corporate refocusing on higher valued uses of resources asks often for the involvement of institutional shareholders or industries' leaders likely to have expertise in the area of financial engineering and substantial financial resources for acquiring control in those companies. The ownership structure "majority owner–small individual shareholders" that originated from partial or complete privatization was a compromise that further raised a growing debate about the role of regulation governing property rights and the adequate corporate governance mechanisms that could address conflicts opposing market players. In this respect, facilitating the emergence of a sound private sector requires specific regulatory measures insulating minority shareholders from expropriation by the controlling ones. In emerging markets, the authorities considered that leveling the playing field among corporate claimants could be achieved simply by transposing some of the rules applicable in well-established financial markets. Whether the "imported" legal texts have reflected the evolving domestic institutional issues and have had the expected wealth effects remains an open question whose answers are likely to be contextual.

In Central and Eastern Europe (CEE), the combination of circumstances in which the corporate structures have emerged and evolved provides singular opportunities to analyze the design of explicit rights of minority shareholders in blockholder regimes. The continuous dilution inflicted on minority shareholders in public companies led the Organization for Economic Cooperation and Development (OECD) to recommend delisting as one of the remedies that could restore the confidence in the private economic sector of some transition economies. We address this issue by focusing on the main institutional and corporate factors explaining the decision to change the companies' public status, before and after the OECD report (2001) on the Romanian capital market. In this respect, we analyze the massive delisting activity on the over-the-counter market RASDAQ (Romanian Association of Securities Dealers Automated Quotation) between 1997 and 2006. Our evidence shows that the controversy around shareholders rights finds its roots in the proliferation of deals with large blocks made by circumventing the market. It reveals that private status—considered as an extreme form of concentrated ownership—depends on the initial ownership structures, thus confirming the structure-driven path dependence conjecture of Bebchuck and Roe (1999).

Prior studies on buyouts frame some nonmutual exclusive hypotheses individualizing the main factors likely to drive the delisting decision (see Renneboog et al. 2007, for an extensive review). Most of the findings used as benchmarks concern the Leverage Buyout (LBO) waves that have taken place in developed markets. The studies that have examined the likelihood of delisting in the European emerging markets reveal the limited scope of several hypotheses and point to the investigation of specific characteristics pertaining to regulation that should bear directly on the decision to go private. Atanasov et al. (2009) provide evidence that the minority freeze-out at large discounts proliferated on the Bulgarian market represents an extreme form of financial tunneling facilitated by poor legal protection. Jackowicz and Kowalewski (2005) confirm that agency conflicts that occurred in the postprivatization period explain the delisting decision in Poland. While similar in intuition, this study distinguishes from the previous works in that it addresses the concern that corporate governance regulation could dissimulate the protection of minority shareholders in emerging markets behind "politically correct" texts. Our approach exploits hand-collected firm-level characteristics and institutional features for 2,729 public companies. Particularly, the empirical specifications of selected companies controlling for the outcomes of privatization, take-overs, and share capital changes on the decision of whether to remain public give additional insights on the exposure of minority shareholders to potential expropriation, which could enhance our understanding of emerging market's finance.

The remainder of the chapter is structured as follows. In Section 1, we briefly present the history of corporate structures formation and market regulation in Romania, with a focus on the main challenges raised by the implementation of fair price standards in freeze-out bids. Section 2 outlines the main testable hypotheses, presents the empirical methodology, and describes our sample selection procedure and the selected independent variables. In Section 3, we discuss the results of logistic and duration analyses, explaining the likelihood of a company changing its public status into a private one. The final section concludes.

1.   Institutional Setting and Legal Provisions Regulating Control Transactions

1.1   Initial patterns of corporate ownership structures

The peculiar experience of the Romanian stock market has been fuelled by the controversial mass privatization policy. Unlike other countries from CEE, where the transfer of State property into private hands involved private financial intermediaries that competed for collecting privatization vouchers (e.g., Poland, the Czech Republic, Bulgaria), in Romania the authorities preferred to institute direct contact between companies and citizens. In this respect, each adult citizen could exchange the free voucher received for the shares of a single company. In 1995, when the mass privatization program was relaunched, they could opt for one of 3,905 companies included in the official list, based on some basic information (industry code, share capital, sales, gross profit, and the maximum percentage of share capital to be privatized). During the subscription period, the vouchers could not be bilaterally exchanged, and thus, nobody could gather more vouchers. At the end of the subscription period, the Privatization Authority (AVAS) assigned a certain number of shares to individual shareholders based on the subscription degree: (1) if the offer was oversubscribed, it made a pro-rata distribution without exceeding the initial offered percentage; (2) if the offer was undersubscribed, it allotted the corresponding shares, while keeping the unsubscribed ones. Those who could not decide themselves were allowed to exchange their privatization vouchers for the shares of one of the five private property funds administratively created in 1991. The stock market emerged at this stage of the restructuring process as a "natural" result of the mass privatization program. All companies included in that program were compulsory listed either on the Bucharest Stock Exchange (1995) or on the over-the-counter market, RASDAQ (1997). The distributed shares to citizens formed the free float of companies, considered from then-on as public companies. According to the number of listed companies, the Romanian market has become the largest market in the region overnight.[1] Nonetheless, the mass privatization concerning thousands of industrial companies created 18 million small shareholders but very few companies with dispersed shareholdings. As of the end of 1998, Earle and Telegdy (2002) report a mean and median ownership of shareholders who received shares within the mass privatization program of 24.5 percent and 18.4 percent, respectively. As, on average, the individual shareholders could not make any corporate decision even with perfect coordination, they have been for a long time regarded as a class of tolerated passive investors. Paradoxically, the stock market was viewed as a platform where "voucher" shareholders could sell their holdings and thus enjoy the last free lunch proposed by the government, rather than as an institutional structure facilitating capital raising.

Despite its scope, the mass privatization was only one piece in the puzzling restructuring program of the Romanian government. Meanwhile, AVAS had been continuing to sell the State property to individual and institutional investors either by means of direct deals or market bids. According to AVAS data, 9,258 blocks were dealt between 1993 and 2003, more than 45 percent of the transactions involving majority stakes.

The broad picture of the very way the AVAS holdings were sold credibly signals that the Romanian government aimed principally at attracting large investors. While investments in controlling positions aroused interests in making the needed changes, the pervasive block-holdings obstruct the portfolio investments, thus calling into question the endurance of market structures. Fama and Jensen (1983), Maupin et al. (1984), Jansen and Kleimeier (2003), and Atanasov et al. (2009) argue that high ownership concentration makes companies decide to go private. According to this broad picture, a gradual eclipse of public companies in blockholders regimes is reasonably predictable. Our contention is that the Romanian stock market is an excellent candidate for identifying and analyzing the peculiar conditions in frontier emerging markets[2] that could have a major influence on delisting decisions.

1.2   Imported or tailored corporate rules?

The vast majority of companies listed on the Romanian capital market were under the control of a major shareholder from the very first day of their public episode. The low free floats had a negative impact on trading and created scope for market price manipulations that further deepened the market illiquidity. The OECD (2001) report provides anecdotal evidence on expropriation practices used by a major shareholder in small- and medium-sized enterprises, especially changes to share capital and related-parties transactions. Under this view, the main redress available for minority shareholders was to create the premises for ownership consolidation and delisting of illiquid companies by instituting an equitable system of tender offers. In this respect, the OECD recommended that the Romanian market authority determine a reasonable threshold triggering the squeeze-out procedure and assure the implementation of a fair price standard.

In Romania, the control transactions between private investors have been regulated drawing on the EU legislation. According to the regulation enacted from the very inception of the capital market, an investor must make a nondiscriminatory, voluntary, or mandatory tender offer whenever he/she seeks to acquire 33 percent and 50 percent of the voting rights in a listed company, respectively. As a practical consequence of this rule, more than 1,500 takeover bids leading to the acquisition or reinforcement of control have been approved by the market authority (CNVM) over a ten-year period. However, before 2001, a public company was allowed to delist only (a) after concluding a tender offer initiated in the name of the majority of shareholders to buy back the outstanding shares, and (b) if the General Assembly of Shareholders of the company, having afterwards fewer than 500 shareholders or a share capital lower than ROL 1 billion, decided to transform the company into a private one. The main objective of this regulation was to maintain a minimal functionality of the capital market on behalf of small shareholders willing to trade their stocks. Beginning with 2002, the updated takeover rules, in line with the recommendations made in the OECD (2001) report, state the "obligation" for the largest shareholder owning at least 90 percent of the capital to cash-out the minority shareholders. The law regulating the capital market promulgated in 2004 redefines this "obligation" as a "right" of controlling a shareholder owning 95 percent or having received more than 90 percent of the target shares in a previous takeover bid to delist the company.

However, the appraisal remedy granted to the minority shareholders has raised a lot of controversy. From 1996 to 2002, the buyout price was based exclusively on the net asset value. Beginning in March 2002, when the first draft of a new market law was proposed, the calculation details of the exit price had been changed at least five times until the promulgation of the law. According to its final version, the buyout price had to be compounded based on three distinct values: (1) the average market price in the 12 months preceding the going-private transaction; (2) the maximum price paid by the acquirer for the target shares over the same period; and (3) the equity per shares valuated based on the International Accounting Standards. The ambiguity created by the frequent change of the market law made some major shareholders interpret their obligation only in respect to the buyout of the controlled company but not to the minimum price to be paid to minority shareholders. In 2004, the market authority modified once again the squeeze-out price provision that states this time that the price paid in a previous tender offer in which at least 90 percent of the remaining shares were tendered is a fair price.[3] Unless the controlling shareholder does make use of his right in the next three months following the acquisition of such a stake, the fair price will be valued by an independent expert. Besides, according to the market law of 2004, the minority shareholders were given the right to sell out the remaining shares[4] to the dominant shareholder owning 95 percent of share capital either according to the terms of the bid preceding the acquisition of such a stake[5] or based on the valuation made by an external expert. However, if an external valuation of the minority holdings is necessary, the small shareholder contesting the bidding price is obliged to bear the valuation costs. When small shareholders are wealth constrained and the valuation costs are likely to be higher than stock value, such a fairness principle becomes simply unfeasible.

The acquisition literature argues that providing an acquirer with a squeeze-out right is an alternative to voluntary dilution when target shareholdings are dispersed (see Yarrow 1985). In such cases, "allocational" acquisitions are possible only if acquirers can either limit the access of atomistic shareholders to postacquisition gains (via dilution, private benefits of control, or squeeze-out rights) or build a toehold in the target. The exclusion mechanisms have a socially desirable function because they allow the market for corporate control to play its disciplinary role. However, on capital markets where blockholdings prevail, the regulator should first assess whether acquirers and target shareholders still play a zero-sum game, in which the latter systematically have positive gains.

Furthermore, the valuation criterion based on the previous bidding prices seems highly inadequate in emerging markets. According to the "theory of bid capture" (Bates et al. 2006), the minority shareholders need protection mainly because of the ability of major shareholder to structure binding bids. The freeze-out right is regarded as an important source of private benefits, whenever the controlling shareholder uses private information having a downside effect on the company value. In illiquid markets, the investors possessing private information have the ability to exploit the inefficiencies caused by the low free float (Lehn and Poulsen 1989). Bebchuk and Kahan (2000) argue that there is an adverse selection effect that results from the use of market prices as benchmark for the no freeze-out value of minority shares.

In emerging markets, the freeze-out regulation should address, besides financial considerations, the matter of "fair dealing" that implies analyzing how some control transactions, including privatization, were initiated, structured, and disclosed to the minority shareholders in the previous stages. Particularly, the mandatory bid rule, while deemed to be a public regarding, was tailored to meet privatization objectives and the interests of groups dominating the corporate realm. Thus, an investor who buys a stake that triggers the mandatory bid rule directly from the Romanian privatization authority is exempted from the obligation to make a tender offer for the remaining shares. These direct deals, called "excepted transactions" in the legal text, allow the investors to build up high toeholds in public targets, even to control them, outside the market mechanism. Under these circumstances, the market prices cannot convey any information about the valuation of potential bidders. Pop (2006) stresses the ineffectiveness of the mandatory public offers made on the Romanian market from the point of view of minority shareholders of the target company, especially when a dominant shareholder exists and the insider trading is unbounded. In public-to-private transactions, the minority shareholders run the danger of being under-compensated despite the premium paid above the market price. Consequently, in markets fraught with opportunities to exert substantive coercion on minority shareholders, the authorities should avoid imposing the price paid in the previous tender offers as the exclusive benchmark of fair value.

Because of the regular changes of legal details and fair-price standards, as well as the looser intervention of the market authority against the abuses proliferated by majority shareholders, we wonder whether benchmarking regulation against modern takeover laws is sufficient to meet the general objectives of "efficiency" and "fairness" in minority freeze-outs.

2.   Data, Sample Selection and Empirical Methodology

Maximizing the firm value often requires the revision of the business organization of firms: from public to private ownership. A going-private transaction usually refers to a buyout transaction of a public company by one or a handful of the target's shareholders, its management, or external investors. Typically, the remaining stocks are paid in cash, sometimes raised by issuing debt securities backed by the target's assets and serviced by its operating cash flow. The intent of the offering party to take a company private is materialized in a tender offer for the outstanding shares. One can prefer a two-step deal with similar economic terms: (1) a tender offer directly to the target's stockholders; (2) conditioned on the acquisition of 90 percent of the target's stock, a squeeze-out of minority stockholders who did not tender in the previous offer. While it is acknowledged that going-private transactions create some benefits, there is a broad disagreement around the sources of the gain arising from leaving the market. In the studies conducted on developed markets, the following hypotheses were tested: (1) the agency costs-related hypotheses, including the free cash flow hypothesis, incentive realignment hypothesis, and control hypothesis; (2) the undervaluation hypothesis; (3) the takeover defense hypothesis; (4) the transaction costs hypothesis; (5) the tax benefit hypothesis; and (6) the wealth transfer hypothesis (see Renneboog et al. 2007). A broad reading of international evidence shows that the assumptions made in the related literature for explaining why private status is preferred to the public one are not necessarily mutually exclusive. To get a better view on the range of conditions likely to defy those provisions, we analyze empirically whether specific trades (privatization, public offers, and capital transactions) could explain the choice for a private status of controlled companies, as well as the timing of the delisting decision.

From the universe of 3,596 companies that were delisted between 1997 and 2006, we excluded all those justifying their decision based on the following reasons: (1) merger with other companies; (2) divestiture; (3) bankruptcy; (4) radiation from the Commerce Registry; (5) administrative decision of the market authority; (6) transfer to the Bucharest Stock Exchange. We further eliminated the companies having the one-digit NACE code "A.— Agriculture, forestry, and fishing," as far as the judicial regime of the land had been ambiguous during the period analyzed. Consequently, we identified 2,081 delisted companies having either "withdrawn" or "closely held company" reasons as their stated argument on the official market reports. In order to reveal the rationale behind the decision to delist, we construct a control sample, which includes 1,240 industrial companies that were still listed on RASDAQ on December 31, 2006. As in the previous case, we excluded from the control sample all agricultural firms. Of 3,321 observations meeting the selection criteria, we lost 592 observations because financial reports or detailed market data for those companies were not publicly available.

For each of these companies we collect detailed information about privatization, public offers, share capital changes, stock market data, as well as financial data during the public status episode. In order to construct our independent variables, we explored and cross-examined several sources of information: RASDAQ, the Romanian Minister of Finance, AVAS, CNVM, and the Romanian Universe Database. The raw stock market information regarding the transaction history of the peer companies was kindly provided by Broker S. A., a Romanian investment firm.

As our main inquiry is whether the privatization policy of AVAS influenced the decision to take a company private, we construct three alternative variables: (1) *AVAS_major*, which is a dummy variable taking the value of 1 if the size of the block sold directly by AVAS exceeds 50 percent and 0 otherwise; (2) *AVAS_maxdir*, representing the maximum size of the block dealt with AVAS by circumventing the stock market; and (3) *Privatization rounds*, defined as the total number of privatization rounds in which the company was involved. To test whether the ability to restructure, or conversely to divert resources, depends on the identity of the major shareholder, we include in our empirical models two dummy variables, *ESOP* and *Individual*, that equal 1 if the maximum block of AVAS was sold to the company's employees or individuals, respectively, and 0 otherwise.

The takeover activity is captured by constructing the following variables: (1) *First Bid_Submitted,* representing the ratio of the number of shares submitted to the number of targeted shares in the first takeover bid; (2) *Nb. Bids,* representing the total number of takeover bids made for the company's shares; (3) *Bid_Av Price,* expressed as the ratio of maximum biding price to average price over the considered period.

To control for market conditions, we used the *Stock Turnover* variable, measuring the ability of firms to attract the market participants' interest, computed as the ratio of trading volume to the average number of outstanding shares. The denominator of this variable is compounded by taking into account the duration between two subsequent changes to share capital made over the considered period. Moreover, we control for the stock market conditions by including in the analysis the proxy *Market Trend,* computed as the ratio of the closing price on the last transaction day of the considered period to the average market price over the same period. For the peer companies, we construct the market specific variables with respect to December 31, 2005, in order to avoid an implicit bias in the size of transaction volume linked to their continual public status.

In the related literature it is argued that new share issues might represent a subtle strategy for adjusting the position of large shareholders to the detriment of the small ones. The OECD (2001) report provides anecdotal evidence about practices aiming to dilute minority shareholders' rights through share capital increases without prior revaluation of existing assets or through in-kind contributions by the majority shareholders. A priori increasing the share capital does not necessarily imply an ownership adjustment. Over the analyzed period all listed companies were allowed to revalue their assets because of the losses incurred from high inflation. In order to update the assets value, the shareholders could decide to modify either the number of outstanding shares or their face value. In the last case, companies may not have to issue any additional shares. As we have no information about the evolution of ownership structure, we control for financial tunneling by considering two proxies: (1) the number of times a company changed its total number of shares, *Nb. Capital Changes*; and (2) the total percentage of share capital increases between the listing date and the delisting or "censored" date, *Capital Change.*

The relationship between the financial characteristics and probability of delisting is expressed by the following variables: (1) *Size,* the logarithm of total assets; (2) *ROE,* the ratio considered whenever the equity value is negative—100 percent; (3) *Leverage,* computed as the ratio of debt to total assets; (4) *Assets Turnover,* equal to sales divided by total assets; and (5) *FATA,* representing the proportion of fixed assets to total assets. All financial variables are based on the financial statements reported by companies at the end of the year preceding the delisting/"censored" year.

In order to analyze the determinants of the delisting process for the Romanian companies listed on RASDAQ, we use three different empirical specifications. The first specification is based on a standard logit model as follows:

$$Proba \ [STATUS_t = 1] = F \ (\beta_0 + \beta_1 X_1 + \beta_2 X_2 + \ldots + \beta_n X_n)$$

where $F(.)$ represents the cumulative logistic distribution, $X_1, \ldots, X_n$ a set of explanatory variables, and

$$STATUS_t = \begin{cases} 1 \text{ if the firm was delisted at time t} \\ 0 \text{ otherwise} \end{cases}.$$

Our second specification is based on a Cox proportional hazard (PH), which allows for censoring in the sense that not all companies included in our sample were delisted during the analyzed period (see Kalbfleisch and Prentice 1980, for more details on the estimation of survival models). A crucial assumption behind the Cox proportional hazards specification is that the hazard ratio is proportionally distributed over time. To evaluate this assumption, we performed a test of nonzero slope in a generalized linear regression of the scaled Schoenfeld residuals on various functions of time (see Grambsch and Therneau 1994, for additional details). The test is equivalent to evaluate the hypothesis that the log hazard ratio function is constant over time. After estimating each Cox proportional hazard model, we generated the matrix of Schoenfeld residuals (scaled adjusted), tested the null hypothesis that the slope is equal to zero for each covariate in various models, and performed the global test recommended by Grambsch and Therneau (1994). Although the null hypothesis of zero slope in the appropriate regressions was accepted for some *individual* covariates of interest, the *global* test indicated in most cases deviations from the proportional hazards assumption. Consequently, our third specification is based on an alternative modeling choice: the *accelerated failure-time* (AFT) model. The AFT specification supposes a linear relationship between the logarithm of the survival time and the covariates. As usual, the assumption on the distributional form of the error term determines the class of the regression models. Particularly, assuming a normal, logistic, extreme-value, or three-parameter gamma distribution for the error term, the corresponding regression models are lognormal, log-logistic, Weibull, and generalized gamma, respectively. In this chapter, we opted for the generalized gamma model for two distinct reasons. First, as it is well known, the hazard function implied by the generalized gamma specification is extremely flexible, allowing for a large specter of possible shapes (in particular, the Weibull and lognormal distributions can be viewed as special cases of the generalized gamma density). Second, to discriminate between various AFT models, we computed for each model the log likelihood and the *Akaike Information Criterion* (AIC). According to our comparisons, the gamma generalized model appears to be the best-fitting model (i.e., exhibiting the largest log likelihood) and the one with the smallest AIC value.

The two classes of regression models used in our empirical analysis (*logit* and *survival—PH & AFT—*models) help to shed light on two distinct facets of our main research question. On the one hand, the logit methodology allows us to conclude on the *unconditional* predictive power of the various determinants of the decision to delist. On the other hand, the *survival analysis* allows us to obtain estimates of the impact of the covariates on the *conditional* probability to delist; that is, the probability to delist *conditional* on being listed to a certain point in time and exhibiting certain values for the covariates in the previous period. The later methodological issue is highly relevant to the literature on the decision of public companies to delist.

3.   Empirical Results

The empirical results presented in Table 9.1 reveal a positive and significant relationship in all logit specifications between the variables used as proxies for the government involvement in the course of capital concentration and the probability of going private. Firms involved in direct privatization end up with lesser investor participation, as long as the block owned by AVAS is dealt with by a single or a small group of investors. This result lends support to Bates et al.'s (2006) thesis that the likelihood of having minority shareholders "left out in the cold" increases whenever there is discrepancy between them and the controlling shareholder. By linking this result to the theory of bid capture, we validate indirectly the control hypothesis indicating that the delisting decision and wealth of minority shareholders are negatively related. While highly significant in the logistic regression, the size of the block obtained by avoiding the market, irrespective of its level, has no impact on the duration of public status. However, this is a common-sense result. On the one hand, in closely held companies, few private investors would accept to continue to have the government as partner. On the other hand, bearing in mind the strong dealing position of AVAS, it is hard to imagine that it could behave like a usual shareholder and tender voluntarily its shares in a regular takeover bid. The stylized

Table 9.1 Results from logistic and duration models

Independent Variables	Logistic models			Cox Proportional Hazard models			Generalized Gamma Duration models		
	1	2	3	4	5	6	7	8	9
AVAS_ major	0.222** (0.020)			0.981 (0.720)			0.006 (0.764)		
AVAS_ maxdir		0.006*** (0.000)			1.000 (0.622)			+ 0.000 (0.525)	
Privatization rounds			0.208*** (0.002)			1.025 (0.501)			-0.006 (0.704)
ESOP	-0.358*** (0.001)	-0.345*** (0.002)	-0.376*** (0.001)	0.789*** (0.000)	0.802*** (0.001)	0.787*** (0.000)	0.096*** (0.000)	0.087*** (0.001)	0.093*** (0.000)
Individual	0.103 (0.460)	0.100 (0.489)	0.115 (0.425)	0.987 (0.840)	1.024 (0.731)	1.008 (0.903)	0.006 (0.831)	-0.010 (0.719)	-0.004 (0.868)
First Bid_ Submitted	1.233*** (0.000)			1.578*** (0.000)			-0.181*** (0.000)		
Nb. bids		0.600*** (0.000)	0.581*** (0.000)		1.252*** (0.000)	1.254*** (0.000)		-0.093*** (0.000)	-0.094*** (0.000)
Bid_ Av price	0.058** (0.053)	0.011 (0.520)	0.013 (0.461)	>1.000** (0.035)	1.000** (0.034)	>1.000** (0.035)	-0.000* (0.057)	-0.000* (0.056)	-0.000* (0.058)
Nb. capital changes	-0.206*** (0.000)	-0.202*** (0.000)	-0.203*** (0.000)	0.774*** (0.000)	0.782*** (0.000)	0.781*** (0.000)	0.099*** (0.000)	0.096*** (0.000)	0.096*** (0.000)
Capital change[a]	0.021 (0.760)	0.018 (0.816)	0.016 (0.786)	>1.000*** (0.000)	>1.000*** (0.000)	>1.000*** (0.000)	-0.000*** (0.000)	-0.000*** (0.000)	-0.000*** (0.000)

(Continued)

Table 9.1 Continued

Independent Variables	Logistic models			Cox Proportional Hazard models			Generalized Gamma Duration models		
	1	2	3	4	5	6	7	8	9
Size	-1.101***	-1.179***	-1.171***	0.760***	0.750***	0.750***	0.106***	0.112***	0.112***
	(0.000)	(0.000)	(0.000)	(0.000)	(0.000)	(0.000)	(0.000)	(0.000)	(0.000)
ROE	0.016	0.013	0.015	1.047*	1.048*	1.046*	-0.013	-0.012	-0.012
	(0.353)	(0.435)	(0.339)	(0.069)	(0.071)	(0.081)	(0.142)	(0.159)	(0.166)
Leverage	0.058	0.074*	0.078*	0.989***	0.989***	0.989***	0.005***	0.005***	0.005***
	(0.153)	(0.081)	(0.071)	(0.005)	(0.006)	(0.006)	(0.001)	(0.002)	(0.002)
Asset turnover	0.137***	0.125**	0.117**	1.037***	1.035***	1.035***	-0.016***	-0.016***	-0.016***
	(0.006)	(0.012)	(0.018)	(0.001)	(0.002)	(0.002)	(0.000)	(0.001)	(0.001)
FATA	0.435**	0.429**	0.426**	1.679***	1.684***	1.672***	-0.204***	-0.206***	-0.204***
	(0.027)	(0.031)	(0.032)	(0.000)	(0.000)	(0.000)	(0.000)	(0.000)	(0.000)
Stock turnover	-0.095**	-0.104**	-0.125***	0.949*	0.930**	0.934**	0.021*	0.031**	0.029**
	(0.015)	(0.018)	(0.008)	(0.060)	(0.020)	(0.022)	(0.057)	(0.015)	(0.017)

facts show that AVAS has always cashed out its minority positions in distinct deals and has defined distinct transactions terms. A similar effect on government stakes is reported in Atanasov et al. (2005), in their analysis of the Bulgarian market, but they explain their results through political-costs arguments. As direct privatization leads to high ownership concentration, the shareholder base of companies cannot be unexpectedly changed. Under these circumstances, the takeover defense hypothesis is less plausible in our case.

The probability and conditional probability to delist are lower when companies are controlled by employees' associations compared with those firms where AVAS's shareholdings were dealt with industrial companies or financial institutions. The negative sign of this variable can be explained by the peculiar conditions stated in the privatization contracts concluded between AVAS and employees' associations. In the majority of cases, employees could defer the complete payment of the negotiated acquisition price for several years but were forbidden to resale the acquired block to other investors during the teasing period.

The significant positive effect of *First Bid_Submitted* shows that companies whose shareholders massively accepted the conditions of the first takeover bid are taken private sooner than their counterparts. The positive and significant coefficient of the *Nb. Bids* variable reveals that when bidders intend to obtain complete participation in the target, the company has more chances to end its public episode.

The change in the organizational form becomes less likely for companies that modify their total number of shares more often. The sign of variable *Nb. Capital Changes* is negative and highly significant in all empirical specifications. We have also controlled for the amplitude of these changes through the ratio of the number of outstanding shares before the delisting/"censored" date to the initial number of outstanding shares, but the estimated results based on this variable are not conclusive. One possible explanation could be that in the case of very intensive assets firms, the revaluation process could cause a steep increase in the total number of shares. As in such cases in which existing shareholders receive free shares proportionally with their holdings, such a decision could be followed by improved market liquidity. Another way of explaining why the estimated coefficients of this variable are not significant concerns the distribution of dividend shares. It is worth underlining that the two types of decisions leading to the increase of share capital do not trigger any change in the ownership structure. Even if the stylized facts reported by the OECD show that the dilution inflicted by major shareholders through in-kind contributions was a recurrent practice in small- and medium-sized enterprises, tracing such strategies based only on the history of capital changes is practically impossible.

In order to distinguish between "benign" and "malign" operations, we would have to control for the ownership structure before and after such an event (unavailable data). However, when we control for this influence in the hazard models, our intuition is confirmed by the results; that is, within companies experiencing a steeper increase in the total number of shares, the decision to end the public episode is made sooner than in the peer companies.

As one of the main concerns of our study is to test how the conflicts of interest over the use of companies' resources influence the decision to go private or dark, in the empirical models we control for financial conditions. Financial literature predicts that companies that expand their activity but sacrifice profitability are more likely to face conflicts of interest. By using the operating decision against small shareholders' interest, the blockholders seek to affect minority discounts paid in going-private transactions or to simply influence their willingness to delist the company. Gilson and Gordon (2003) argue that by taking the company private, the large shareholders can capture the capitalized value of future private benefits over the value of a noncontrolling share. Moreover, there is a strong link between those gains and the level of benefits likely to be expropriated by operational means. If so, the positive sign of *Assets Turnover* and the nonsignificant influence of the financial performance (proxied by *ROE*) can be interpreted as an indication of the use of such stratagems, that is, disadvantageous transfer prices between the public companies and other companies owned by the controlling shareholder. The positive and significant coefficient of the *FATA* variable lends support to the conjecture that companies in which expropriation behavior is more likely choose to leave the stock market and exit sooner than their competitors. As companies listed on the stock market were seriously undervalued, significant gains could be realized by taking over the company and by later selling its physical assets in pieces. This finding is consistent with the hypothesis that dilution inflicted on the small shareholders can be a practice associated with the decision to go private. The low market capitalization made the debt a useless source of financing and going to private transactions neutral events with respect to taxes. Consequently, the conditions needed for testing the traditional tax benefit and the wealth transfer (from bondholders) hypotheses are not validated within the peculiar context of the Romanian market. According to our findings, the probability of delisting decreases with the company's size. The inherent difficulty to completely acquire companies of large size is a common result in the literature.

One of the previous influences, namely ownership concentration, creates scope for insider trading based on proprietary information and consequently for market misevaluation. The negative and significant coefficient of the

Stock Turnover variable lends additional support to our intuition that the delisting decision concerns mainly public companies obliterated by the investors' ignorance. This finding is in line with those reported by Jackowicz and Kowalewski (2005) and Atanasov et al. (2009) for other CEE emerging markets and proves that the absence of scrutiny from small investors could be critical for the survival of public companies.

All in all, our results validate the control and undervaluation hypotheses. The delisting practices prevailing in the Romanian market bring into attention the operations involving control positions and the subsequent effects of the low free float. As privatizing public companies is an arbitrary choice that decisively affects the investment incentives of private players, our results provide empirical proof that the regulation is in reality adapted to fit the institutional environment.

4. Conclusion

In this chapter we provided additional evidence about the causes of delisting by focusing on the expropriation of minority shareholders, one of the main stated concerns as well as an empirical regularity found in previous studies on emerging markets (Atanasov et al. 2009; Jackowicz and Kowalewski 2005). Our approach emphasizes the possibility that the incentives to take advantage of outside shareholders are explained by the very way the initial shareholdings of controlling shareholders were chosen. The interest groups that emerged in the early privatization period weakened the regulatory response to corporate governance failures in the Romanian market. Even if the law regulating going-private transactions taken as a whole could be public regarding, the details of the fair price standard, the frequent changes of those details, as well as the exemptions to the rule in the case of the transactions involving State majority or minority ownership make this law less effective in preventing the expropriation of minority shareholders.

The main findings of this study are that delisting is likely to occur especially when (1) the block obtained by circumventing the market is large; (2) the companies are more often involved in capital transactions; and (3) the companies are less scrutinized by investors and therefore market prices are less informative. In the light of our empirical findings, the regulatory provisions seem to perversely defend the sticky concentrated ownership structures.

The significant phenomenon of delisting experienced by the Romanian capital market, including even blue-chip companies, after the issue of the OECD (2001) report brings into question the likely effectiveness of the introduction of squeeze-out rights. Unfortunately, the implementation of the acquis communautaires has too often reflected the political decisions made during privatization and the interests of politically influential shareholders. In the long run, beyond the fairness principle, a matter of serious reflection should be the shrink of capital markets caused by massive delisting.

* The authors are, respectively, the Head of the Finance Group at Imperial College Business School, a research director at Centre National de la Recherche Scientifique at the University of Paris-Dauphine; Associate Professor of Banking and Finance at the University of Nantes; and Associate Professor of Finance in the Economics Department of the University of Angers.

Notes

† JEL Classifications: G34, G38, K22

1. Berglöf and Pajuste (2005) and Pajuste (2002) present a comparative analysis among the markets of Central and Eastern Europe that could provide the reader with further details.
2. In order for a market to be considered as "emerging," several criteria have to be met: (1) the market is localized in an emerging country; (2) the market does not exhibit financial depth; (3) there exist broad-based discriminatory controls for non-domiciled investors; (4) it is characterized by a lack of transparency, depth, market regulation, and operational efficiency. Wilshire Consulting provides an annual report classifying the emerging markets in two distinct categories: (1) "investable" emerging markets; and (2) "frontier" emerging markets. The aim of this classification is to identify those markets that are able to support institutional investments and not to evaluate the current attractiveness for investment managers. For the time being, the only European emerging markets classified as "investable" are Hungary, Poland, and the Czech Republic.
3. According to the acquisition literature, establishing a price for the going-private transaction equal to that paid in the previous stage of a two-stage bid conditioned by the acquisition of 90 percent of the voting rights is argued by the free-rider behaviour of atomistic shareholders. If the final price were higher than this limit, all the minority shareholders would wait for the final stage of the offer. Besides, as each stockholder has a choice of whether to tender the shares to a prospective investor, such a price could not be considered coercive.
4. According to Holderness and Sheenan (1988), such a fair-price provision restricts ex ante the scope of bidders' opportunism and insulates the small investors from excessive expropriation.
5. An extensive discussion about the mirroring characteristics of the rights of controlling shareholders and minority shareholders, respectively, is provided in Burkart and Panunzi (2004).

References

Atanasov, Vladimir, Conrad S. Ciccotello, and Stanley B. Gyoshev, 2005. How does law affect finance? An empirical examination of tunneling in an emerging market. The William Davidson Institute Working Paper 742.

————, 2009. How does law affect finance? An examination of equity tunneling in Bulgaria. *Journal of Financial Economics,* forthcoming.

Bates, Thomas W, Michael L. Lemmon, and James S. Linck, 2006. Shareholder welfare and bid negotiation in freeze-out deals: Are minority shareholders left out in the cold? *Journal of Financial Economics* 81: 681–708.

Bebchuk, Lucian Arye, and Mark J. Roe, 1999. A theory of path dependence in corporate ownership and governance. *Stanford Law Review* 52: 127–70.

Bebchuk, Lucian Arye, and Marcel Kahan, 2000. Adverse selection and gains to controllers in corporate freezeouts. In *Concentrated Corporate Ownership* ed. Randall Morck, 247–59. University of Chicago Press.

Berglöf, Erik et Anete Pajuste, 2005. What do firms disclose and why? Enforcing corporate governance transparency in Central and Eastern Europe. *Oxford Review of Economic Policy* 21(2): 178–97.

Burkart, Mike, and Fausto Panunzi, 2004. Mandatory bids, squeeze-out, sell-out and the dynamics of the tender offer process. In *Reforming Company and Takeover Law in Europe,* ed. Guido Ferrarini, Klaus J. Hopt, Jaap Winter, and Eddy Wymeersch. Oxford University Press, Oxford.

Earle, John S., and Álmos Telegdy, 2002. Privatization methods and productivity effects in Romanian industrial enterprises. *Journal of Comparative Economics* 30: 657–82.

Fama, Eugene, and Michael Jensen, 1983. Separation of ownership and control. *Journal of Law and Economics* 26: 301–25.

Gilson, Ronald J., and Jeffrey Gordon, 2003. Controlling controlling shareholders. *University of Pennsylvania Law Review* 152: 785–843.

Grambsch, Patricia M., and Terry M. Therneau, 1994. Proportional hazards tests and diagnostics based on weighted residuals. *Biometrika* 81: 515–26.

Holderness, Clifford G., and Dennis P. Sheehan, 1988. Constraints on large-block shareholders, NBER working paper no. 6765.

Jackowicz, Krzysztof, and Oskar Kowalewski, 2005. Why companies go private in emerging markets? Evidence from Poland. Working paper, Leon Kozminski Academy of Entrepreneurship & Managment.

Jansen, Karsten, and Stefanie Kleimeier, 2003. Motives for going private in Germany. Limburg Institute of Financial Economics, LIFE Working Paper 03–016.

Kalbfleisch, John D., and R. L. Prentice, 1980. *The Statistical Analysis of Failure Time Data.* New York: John Wiley.

Lehn, Ken, and Annette Poulsen, 1989. Free cash flow and stockholder gain in going private transactions. Journal of Finance 44, 771–88.

Maupin, Rebekah J., Clinton M. Bidwell, and Alan K. Ortegren, 1984. An empirical investigation of the characteristics of publicly held corporations that change to private ownership via management buyouts. *Journal of Business Finance & Accounting* 11: 435–50.

OECD (2001). Report on Corporate Governance in Romania.

Pajuste, Anete, 2002. Corporate governance and stock market performance in Central and Eastern Europe: A study of nine countries, 1994–2001. SSEES Working Paper no.22.

Pop, Diana, 2006. M&A market in transition economies. Evidence from Romania. *Emerging Markets Review* 7(3): 244–60.

Renneboog Luc, Tomas Simons, and Mike Wright, 2007. Why do public firms go private in the UK? The impact of private equity investors, incentive realignment and undervaluation. *Journal of Corporate Finance* 13: 591–628.

Yarrow, George K., 1985. Shareholder protection, compulsory acquisition and the efficiency of the takeover process. *Journal of Industrial Economics* 24, 3–16.

10

Universal Access, Cost Recovery, and Payment Services

Sujit Chakravorti, Jeffery W. Gunther, and
*Robert R. Moore**

Abstract

We suggest a subtle, yet far-reaching, tension in the objectives specified by the Monetary Control Act of 1980 (MCA) for the Federal Reserve's role in providing retail payment services, such as check processing. Specifically, we argue that the requirement of an overall cost-revenue match, coupled with the goal of ensuring equitable access on a universal basis, partially shifted the burden of cost recovery from high-cost to low-cost service points during the MCA's early years, thereby allowing private-sector competitors to enter the low-cost segment of the market and undercut the relatively uniform prices charged by the Fed. To illustrate this conflict, we develop a voter model for what begins as a monopoly setting in which a regulatory regime that establishes a uniform price irrespective of cost differences, and restricts total profits to zero, initially dominates through majority rule both deregulation and regulation that sets price equal to cost on a bank-by-bank basis. Uniform pricing is dropped in this model once cream skimming has subsumed half the market. These results help illumine the Federal Reserve's experience in retail payments under the MCA, particularly the movement over time to a less uniform fee structure for check processing.

Introduction

The Monetary Control Act of 1980 (MCA) required the Federal Reserve (the Fed) to provide all banks with equal access to payment services, not just member banks, and to price those services with explicit fees. The legislative history of the MCA suggests this mandate had the twin purpose of promoting competition in the provision of payment services and generating revenue for the Treasury.

We analyze the interplay between two of the MCA's most salient features in the area of retail payment services. The first is the requirement that the fees charged for Fed services should in total cover both the costs of providing those services and an adjustment factor designed to reflect the taxes that would have been paid and the return on capital that would have been generated had the services been provided in the private sector. The second is the requirement that, in setting its prices, the Fed should strive to ensure that an adequate level of payment services is provided nationwide. This latter provision suggests the Fed may need to set prices for payment services in some regions below the cost to provide those services, if necessary, to ensure equitable access for banks in all areas of the country.

We contend these two requirements are inconsistent, essentially promoting, if not entailing, a partial shift in the burden of cost recovery from high-cost to low-cost service points, thereby allowing private-sector competitors to enter the low-cost segments of the market and undercut the relatively uniform prices charged by the Fed. To clarify the ultimate implications of this legislative environment, we develop a voter model for what begins as a monopoly setting in which a regulatory regime that establishes a uniform price irrespective of cost differences, and restricts total profits to zero, initially dominates through majority rule both deregulation and regulation that sets price equal to cost on a bank-by-bank basis. The uniform price rule is dropped in this model once cream skimming has subsumed half the market, and the alternative regulatory regime that ensures the equality for individual banks of service fees and costs is never selected by the voting mechanism.

These results suggest the MCA set the stage for a declining role of the Fed as a provider of retail payment services, including check processing, and the losses in Fed check volume that began in the early 1990s may have reflected the provision of universal access, in addition to private-sector competition, as heightened by structural change.[1] Our model then points to the increasing complexity of the Fed's fee structure as a relaxation of, but not departure from, the universal service objective, necessitated by the tension between universal service and cost recovery.

We proceed as follows. The first section provides an account and interpretation of the MCA's relevant provisions. In the second section, we develop a voter model of payment services regulation. The third section offers empirical support for our arguments in the area of check processing. The fourth section concludes.

1. Pricing Provisions of the MCA

1.1   Cost recovery

The MCA required the Fed to establish a fee structure for payment services that recovered not only its overall direct and indirect operating costs, but also any additional costs faced by private-sector providers of retail payment services.[2] These additional costs are imputed through a private-sector adjustment factor designed to reflect the taxes that would have been paid and the return on capital that would have been generated had the services been provided in the private sector.[3] In this manner, MCA was intended to promote private-sector competition in check collection and other payment services provided by the Fed.[4]

1.2   Universal service

Along with the requirement that the Fed cover costs with revenue, the MCA also included in Section 107 a universal service objective directing the Fed to adopt pricing principles that "give due regard to competitive factors and the provision of an adequate level of such services nationwide." This latter provision suggests the Fed may need to set prices for payment services in some regions below the cost of providing them.

While this universal service objective is subject to a greater amount of interpretation than the relatively straightforward requirement that revenues cover costs, its spirit is nevertheless fairly clear. And, that spirit is reflected in the Fed's description of its business practices, as published in *Federal Reserve Regulatory Service 7− 137*: "Federal Reserve services will be offered on a fair and equitable basis to all depository institutions on similar terms and conditions." Similarly, as stated in *Federal Reserve Regulatory Service 7− 143*: "Federal Reserve payment services are available to all depository institutions, including smaller institutions in remote locations that other providers might choose not to serve."

In this manner, the MCA's universal service objective entails the provision of payment services for all depository institutions, including smaller institutions in remote locations, where volumes are typically low and costs are high. In addition, the MCA's emphasis on fairness, equity, and inclusiveness may be interpreted as encouraging a tendency toward charging relatively uniform prices for these services, even if significant differences in costs exist between different users, as indicated in *Federal Reserve Regulatory Service 7−137*, as cited above.

1.3   Potential price undercutting

However, with the mandate in place for the Fed to match overall cost and revenue in providing payment services, its ability to partially shift costs away from high-cost users depends on its ability to set fees for low-cost users in excess of the levels associated with the recovery of costs for that user category. As a result, through its universal service objective, the MCA may have done more than simply promote private-sector competition in the provision of payment services. Rather, it potentially exposed the Fed to price undercutting by competition focused on low-cost users.

These considerations are relevant to the Fed's role in check processing and other areas of payment services as well. A useful example is documented in the policy discussions surrounding the implementation of the MCA in the area of currency and coin transportation. The Fed's original proposal for pricing principles and a schedule of fees (*Federal Register* 1980) included the following statement:

> To assure that the public serviced by institutions in more remote locations receive an adequate level of service, the proposed prices for transportation to depository institutions located in more remote areas (over-the-road endpoints) have a ceiling imposed for the per stop portion of the cash transportation charge. The proposed price to mail endpoints has the same ceiling. In the proposed pricing structure, the ceiling is set at $32.

The MCA's universal service objective is clearly manifested in the Fed's original proposal for the pricing of currency and coin transportation. The total transportation charge consisted of a volume charge and charge per stop, the latter of which varied by zone. The proposed $32 cap on the per-stop charge most likely amounted to a cost shift in favor of institutions located in remote areas.

But the tension in this context between the provision of universal service and the MCA's cost-recovery mandate came to light early in the public comments received by the Board of Governors on the proposed fee schedule. In reviewing the comments received, the Fed noted the following concern (*Federal Register* 1981):

Several commentators also were concerned that full cost recovery for these services would result in significant increases in charges for rural and remote endpoint deliveries as urban institutions drop the services.

These commentators apparently anticipated that the price relief for rural areas would, under full cost recovery, necessitate prices above cost for urban areas and thereby open the door for bypass and cream skimming.[5] Consistent with this interpretation, the final fee schedule for currency and coin transportation that became effective in January of 1982 established a $75 ceiling on the per-stop charge, significantly higher than the $32 cap initially proposed by the Fed (*Federal Reserve Bulletin* 1981). It turned out that financial institutions generally established their own transportation arrangements once the Fed prices became effective.

2. The Model

The following develops a voter model of payment system regulation. We couch the political economy aspects of our model in terms of voting behavior in appreciation of the influence of individual banks on regulatory policy, both through the legislative process and, perhaps more importantly, through the process of public comment that accompanies significant regulatory changes.

2.1   Consumers

A population of financial institutions, referred to here as consumers, is assumed with perfectly inelastic demand for a particular payment service, S. A wealth constraint places an upper limit on price. The notion of a fundamentally necessary service motivates the assumption of inelastic demand.

2.2   Firms

Let $0 \leq c \leq 1$ denote the cost of providing S to individual consumers, with cumulative density function $F(c)$ and $f = F'$. Attention generally is restricted to strictly concave, linear, and strictly convex functions. Fixed costs are not considered explicitly.[6] In the monopoly case, technological or regulatory constraints lead to a sole provider. In an alternative case, perfect competition is introduced to the low-cost segment of the industry ($c \leq c^l$). The model then becomes one of undercutting and limited monopoly.

2.3   Regulation

Regulation emerges as a way to affect P^s, the price of S. Under social regulation, all consumers are charged the same price ($P^s = P^*$), even when the cost of providing the service varies, and the monopolist is restricted to earn zero economic profits overall. The associated per capita administrative costs are denoted as δ. An alternative, which we refer to as marginal cost regulation, sets price equal to cost on a consumer-by-consumer basis ($P^s = c$), also at the per capita cost of δ. A third policy option is no regulation at all.

The wealth constraint is specified so as to ensure each of the policy options is technically feasible. In particular, each consumer's initial endowment is equal to

$$\max(c) + \delta = 1 + \delta.$$

2.4   Politics

Consumers assume a political role as voters. In this role, they determine the form of regulation. In voting for policy alternatives, consumers seek to minimize the cost of S and thereby maximize end-of-period wealth. Majority rule is assumed, so that a policy alternative prevails when it receives more than one half of the vote. If no alternative prevails in the first vote, then the two alternatives with the most votes enter a runoff. The proportions of the population with first-best choices of $P^s = P^*$, $P^s = c$, and no regulation are denoted as V^{P^*}, V^C, and V^{NR}, respectively.

2.5   The monopoly case

Suppose $c^l = 0$ and social regulation ($P^s = P^*$) successfully requires the monopolist to charge the same price to all consumers, while earning zero economic profits. The corresponding regulatory constraint is given by

$$\int_0^1 (P^* - c)\, dF(c) = 0. \tag{1}$$

Consumers for whom $P^* > c$ pay a higher than competitive price. If these consumers could obtain the service at competitive prices from an alternative provider, then they would exit the regulated system.

Proposition 1: When $c^l = 0$, social regulation occurs if and only if F is strictly convex.

Proof: When $c^l = 0$, $V^{P*} = 1 - F(P*)$, $V^C = F(P*)$, and social regulation occurs if and only if $F(P*) < 0.5$. From (1),

$$P^* = \int_0^1 cf(c)\,dc. \tag{2}$$

When F is strictly convex, Jensen's inequality implies

$$\int_0^1 F(c)\,f(c)\,dc > F(P^*). \tag{3}$$

Integration by parts for the left side of (3) gives 0.5. Hence, $F(P*) < 0.5$. When F is strictly concave, the inequality in (3) is reversed, so that $F(P*) > 0.5$. Linearity implies $F(P*) = 0.5$.

2.6 Monopoly with undercutting

Now suppose new technology or a reduction of regulatory constraints allows low-cost consumers $(c \leq c^l)$ to purchase the service at marginal cost from someone other than the former monopolist, so that competitors undercut the regulated price and "cherry-pick" in the low-cost (high-profit) areas of the market. As low-cost consumers bypass the regulated system, the social regulatory constraint covering those remaining becomes

$$\int_{c^l}^1 (p^* - c)\,dF(c) = 0. \tag{4}$$

Proposition 2: When $c^l > 0$, social regulation occurs if and only if $V^{P*} > V^C$ and $V^{NR} \leq 0.5$.

Proof: When $c^l > 0$, $V^{P*} = 1 - F(P*)$, $V^C = F(P*) - F(c^l)$, and $V^{NR} = F(c^l)$. If $F(P*) < 0.5$, then over half the population is characterized by $c > P^*$, and $V^{P*} > 0.5$. If $F(P^*) \geq 0.5$, then $V^C + V^{NR} \geq 0.5$. If $V^C = F(P*) - F(c^l) > 0.5$ or $V^{NR} = F(c^l) > 0.5$, then the corresponding policy alternative prevails. If $V^C \leq 0.5$ and $V^{NR} \leq 0.5$, but $\min(V^C, V^{NR}) \geq V^{P*}$, then the regulatory option of $P^s = c$ and the no-regulation option enter a runoff. Because consumers who had voted for social regulation in the initial vote would now band together with the supporters of marginal cost regulation, the regulatory regime with $P^s = c$ prevails. If $\min(V^{NR}, V^{P*}) \geq V^C$, then consumers who had voted for marginal cost regulation in the initial vote would band together with the supporters of social regulation, and the regulatory regime with $P^s = P^*$ prevails. If $\min(V^{P^*}, V^C) \geq V^{NR}$, then consumers who had voted for no regulation in the initial vote do not participate in the runoff, as they have no stake in its outcome. As a result, max (V^{P^*}, V^C) determines the regulatory regime.

2.7   Deregulation

What is the effect of undercutting on the viability of social regulation? Extensive undercutting ($V^{NR} > .5$) leads to complete deregulation, as shown in the proof of Proposition 2. However, whether or not undercutting has the capacity to induce a shift to the alternative regulatory regime ($P^s = c$) before this point remains to be seen. If not, then once social regulation is established in equilibrium under monopoly, increases in undercutting associated with rising competition in the low-cost segments of the market eventually lead to complete deregulation, and marginal cost regulation never emerges. In this case, relatively long lags may occur between the inception of competitive pressures and the dissolution of social regulation.

Proposition 3: An increase in c^l leads to an increase in P^* if and only if $f(c^l) > 0$.

By pushing up P^*, increases in c^l reduce support for social regulation, since $V^{P^*} = 1 - F(P^*)$. However, as shown in Proposition 2, this effect cannot precipitate the dissolution of social regulation prior to the point when $F(c^l) > 0.5$ unless it causes V^C to exceed V^{P^*}. Because P^* rises, bypass hurts those consumers remaining in the regulated system. This result for universal service regulation contrasts with the more general regulatory context analyzed by Laffont and Tirole (1990), where the effect of bypass on low demand customers is ambiguous.

Proof: (4) implicitly defines P^* as a function of c^l. The implied relationship is

$$\frac{dP^*}{dc^l} = (P^* - c^l) h(c^l), \tag{5}$$

where $h(c^l)$ denotes the hazard rate. Because $P^* > c^l$, (5) is positive when $h(c^l) > 0$, indicating that the regulated price must rise as low-cost consumers exit the system.

Proposition 4: If F is strictly convex, marginal cost regulation never occurs.

Proof: By Proposition 1, social regulation occurs when $c^l = 0$. When $F(c^l) > 0.5$, deregulation occurs. By Proposition 2, if $0 < F(c^l) \leq 0.5$, then social regulation occurs if and only if $V^{P^*} > V^C \Rightarrow 1 - F(P^*) > F(P^*) - F(c^l)$. Let $F^*(c) = [F(c) - F(c^l)]/[1 - F(c^l)]$ and $f^*(c) = f(c) / [1 - F(c^l)]$. For $c^l > 0$,

$$P^* = \int_{c^l}^{1} cf^*(c)\, dc. \tag{6}$$

Since F is strictly convex, F^* must be also, and Jensen's inequality implies

$$\int_{c^l}^{1} F^*(c)f^*(c)\, dc > F^*(P^*). \tag{7}$$

Integration by parts for the left side of (7) gives 0.5, so that $F^*(P^*) < 0.5$. Rearranging terms gives $1 - F(P^*) > F(P^*) - F(c^l)$.

2.8   Strategic voting

The discussion above entertains switching of voting blocks to second best outcomes in the context of runoffs, but leaves unconsidered true strategic voting (see Eckel and Holt 1989), by which consumers vote for second-best alternatives in the first round with the purpose of influencing second round results. Below we show this form of strategic voting does not arise in our model.

Under the assumption that voters cannot coordinate to split their votes among several alternatives, there is no gain to strategic voting in our model. Voters who prefer no regulation are indifferent between social regulation and marginal cost regulation, and so obviously have no incentive to vote strategically. Those who prefer marginal cost regulation over the other alternatives also prefer social regulation over no regulation. They would not want to vote for no regulation in the first round; and they would have no incentive to vote for social regulation either, since in any event max (V^{P^*}, V^C) would determine the outcome in the second round, given $V^{NR} \leq .5$. The same argument applies to voters preferring social regulation.

3.   The Case of Check Processing

Our model of regulation entails clear predictions for the Fed's experience in check processing under the MCA, and these predictions are consistent with broad trends in various check-related data.

3.1   Model predictions for Fed check pricing under the MCA

We would expect the MCA's universal service objective initially to promote a relatively flat fee schedule, in parallel with the model's social regulation regime. The added element of the MCA's cost-recovery mandate would then be expected to foster entry by alternative check processors specializing in delivery to low-cost presentment points, in parallel with the vulnerability of the model's social regulation regime to price undercutting. That is, the cost shifting implied by the combination of a relatively flat fee structure and full cost recovery would be expected over time to give rise to bypass of the Fed in the provision of check-processing services directed toward low-cost presentment points. Such a bypass, in turn, would eventually pressure the Fed to price in closer accordance with the varying costs associated with the geographic locations of different presentment points, thereby relaxing, while not departing from, the MCA's universal service objective, in a manner similar to the eventual deregulation occurring within the model.

3.2   Trends in Fed check pricing

Given the MCA's universal service objective and its emphasis on small institutions located in remote areas, we expect the Fed would have designed its fee structure for check processing so as to promote the provision of check-processing services for rural institutions. And there is anecdotal support for this view. In forums hosted by the Rivlin Committee in the mid-1990s, a taskforce designed to assess the role of the Fed in providing retail payment services, private-sector participants expressed the view that small remote institutions would face higher prices for check processing if the Fed were to exit the business (Committee on the Federal Reserve in the Payments Mechanism 1997).

In this regard, given the relatively low volumes and greater geographic distances associated with rural presentment points, it seems safe to assume that incremental costs are relatively high for the presentment of checks to institutions located in rural areas. Given the higher costs associated with rural presentment, an approximately flat fee schedule would imply that rural presentment was priced lower relative to costs than urban presentment. Therefore, if the fee schedule was approximately flat, rural banks would benefit from Fed participation, as the Rivlin Committee found, if rural banks depend more heavily on rural presentment than urban banks. Even considerable geographic differentiation in pricing could be consistent with the view that rural institutions are more dependent on rural presentment and benefit from Fed cost shifting, so long as the differentiation does not fully compensate for underlying geographic differentials in incremental cost.

Supporting the view that rural institutions depend more heavily on rural presentment, the fees charged by the Reserve Banks for check-processing services were fairly uniform in the early years of the MCA. While a higher fee was already charged earlier on for presentment in a remote location, over time the degree and complexity of geographic differentiation increased substantially.

As of 1990, only two Reserve Banks—Kansas City and Minneapolis—used a tiered fee schedule, whereby different prices were set for low- and high-cost presentment points within the same check collection zone, as shown in table 10.1. The Federal Reserve Board approved tiered pricing as a permanent fee structure for these offices in 1986 and specified as one of the criteria for the adoption of tiered pricing at other offices the requirement that clear cost differences exist between groups of present-ment points within the check collection zone under consideration.[7] By 1998, all the Reserve Banks except Atlanta and Dallas had moved to a tiered fee structure within Regional Check Processing Center (RCPC) zones.[8] Assuming each of these movements to tiered pricing satisfied the Federal Reserve Board's requirement that clear cost differences should exist within check collection zones, we can infer that prior to the move to tiered pric-ing, a constant price had been charged across endpoints with significantly different costs.

In addition, several other features of the Fed's fee schedule for check collection services also conform to the model's implications. Interestingly, in many cases the move to tiered pricing in RCPC zones was accompa-nied by a reduction in prices in the corresponding city zones. Moreover, four Reserve Banks moved to tiered pricing in the city zone as well. These events are consistent with our view that heated competition and cream skimming focused on high-volume low-cost presentment points led the Fed to reduce over time the degree of cost shifting associated with the uni-versal service objective of the MCA. Other features of the fees charged for check clearing services, such as the emergence of volume discounts, also conform to our theory.

We note that the passage of the Check Clearing for the 21st Century Act in October 2004 significantly reduced check items collected in paper form throughout the check industry. Today, almost 99 percent of checks are processed as images (Financial Services Policy Committee, 2010).[9] The processing of images has significantly reduced processing costs and elimi-nated geographic cost differences. As a result, the Federal Reserve reduced the number of offices where paper checks were processed from 45 in late 2003 to a single site in Cleveland.

Table 10.1 Check-processing fees for Federal Reserve cities and associated regional check processing centers (RCPCs), cents per item[a]

	City		RCPC[b]	
	1990	*1998*	*1990*	*1998*
Atlanta	1.1	1.2	1.8	2.0
				1.2
Boston	1.7	1.4	2.2	2.0
				2.6
				2.9
Chicago	2.2	2.0	3.3	3.1
				3.3
				2.1
Cleveland	1.6	1.9	2.0	2.7
		2.3		3.3
Dallas	1.6	1.6	2.2	2.2
				1.5
Kansas City[c]	1.7	1.5	2.2	2.4
			3.2	4.1
				1.1
Minneapolis	1.7	1.3	2.0	2.4
		1.8	2.8	3.2
				2.0
New York[d]	2.7	2.0	2.4	3.5
		5.0		5.0
				1.7
Philadelphia	1.5	1.0	1.9	1.9
		1.6		2.2
				1.9
Richmond	1.6	1.6	2.1	2.5
				3.2
				1.5
St. Louis	1.8	1.4	2	2.4
				3.1
				2.2
San Francisco	1.7	1.9	2	2.4
				2.6

[a] The fee data are taken from the *Interdistrict Check Manual*, 1990 and 1998. Where only one price is shown, the processing bank charged a single price for all checks within the zone; where multiple prices are shown, the processing bank charged a tiered price. The total fee for check processing also includes a cash letter fee, which is not shown above. Prices shown are for "unsorted regular" cash letters.

[b] RCPC zones are designated areas within the territories of Federal Reserve offices but outside Federal Reserve cities.

[c] Because the Kansas City territory did not employ an RCPC zone, prices for country zone items are shown instead.

[d] Checks for New York were processed at East Rutherford, NJ, or Jericho, NY.

3.3   An alternative view

Our perspective takes on increased importance in light of the controversy surrounding the prices charged by the Fed for retail payment services. Lacker and Weinberg (1998) argue that that the movement toward greater differentiation in check-processing fees might reflect certain legal privileges bestowed upon the Fed. In particular, Reserve Banks can present checks to a paying bank until 2:00 p.m. and still receive payment the same day, whereas private-sector participants must present by 8:00 a.m. in order to insist on same-day funds. For relatively remote present-ment where transportation time is significant, the six-hour monopoly enjoyed by the Fed could represent a significant competitive advantage. The possibility then arises that the increasing differentials observed in the Fed's pricing structure might reflect efforts to shift costs to pro-tected market segments for presentment in rural areas, thereby leaving room to maintain relatively low fees in the more closely contested city markets.

In support of our view that a good part of the observed changes in fees reflects underlying cost differentials, we have pointed to the rela-tively flat cost structure that initially was adopted under MCA, together with the Board's requirement that the adoption of tiered pricing at the Reserve Bank offices must be supported by the demonstration of clear cost differences between groups of presentment points. Assuming the widespread movement to tiered pricing satisfied the Federal Reserve Board's requirement that clear cost differences should exist within check collection zones, we can infer that prior to the move to tiered pricing, a constant price had been charged across endpoints with significantly dif-ferent costs. Moreover, squaring the alternative view that prices for rural presentment have been set artificially high with the findings of the Rivlin Committee—that the Fed followed the universal service objective by favoring rural institutions—would require that rural institutions actually tend to present a lower share of their collected checks to rural institutions than do their urban counterparts.

In summary, our analysis suggests costs historically were partially shifted to city presentment, but then over time were aligned more closely with underlying cost differentials for rural presentment, whereas Lacker and Weinberg focus on the possibility that changes in prices have gone beyond this point, so that now costs actually are partially shifted to rural presentment. While we cannot rule out this possibility, our findings are nevertheless significant, in that they show that at least part, if not all, of the movement toward greater complexity and geographic differentiation in prices could be expected as a natural outcome of the MCA.

4. Conclusion

Our analysis supports the view that the Fed's movement away from its initial relatively flat fee structure for check processing to a less-uniform schedule reflects to a significant degree an effort to curtail undercutting and cream skimming by pricing access in closer accordance with geographically determined costs, ultimately reflecting a resolution of the underlying tension between the MCA's cost recovery and universal service provisions.

The universal service objective is no longer politically supported in our model once cream skimming has subsumed half the market, while the alternative regulatory regime that ensures the equality for individual banks of service fees and costs is never selected by the voting mechanism. These results from our model suggest the MCA's universal service provision, while still in effect, may continue to become a less prominent feature of the Fed's role in retail payments. At the same time, other potential motivations for the Fed's presence as a provider of retail payment services, not considered directly in our model, may come to have greater visibility.

*The authors are, respectively, Senior Economist at the Federal Reserve Bank of Chicago; Vice President of the Federal Reserve Bank of Dallas; and Research Officer at the Federal Reserve Bank of Dallas. The authors wish to thank Vadim Anshelevich, Hesna Genay, Gautam Gowrisankaran, Preston McAfee, Marci Rossell, Bruce Smith, Joanna Stavins, Ed Stevens, James Thomson, David Van Hoose, John Weinberg, and participants at the 1998 Southern Economic Association meetings in Baltimore and the Federal Reserve Financial Services Research Group Workshop for comments and suggestions. The views expressed may or may not coincide with the positions of the Federal Reserve Banks of Chicago or Dallas, or the Federal Reserve System.

Notes

1. Regarding structural change, Stavins (2004) suggests that declining Fed check volume in 1994 partly reflected the introduction of same-day settlement. The same-day settlement rule allowed correspondent banks to compete more effectively with the Federal Reserve Banks.
2. The MCA specified that "over the long run, fees shall be established on the basis of all direct and indirect costs actually incurred." In practice, the Board of Governors has set fees with the goal of covering costs on a year-by-year basis (*Federal Reserve Regulatory Service, 7–135*).
3. See *Federal Reserve Regulatory Service, 7–147* for a description of the accounting system used to calculate the costs associated with the Fed's provision of payment services.

4. The MCA specified the following services as requiring explicit fees: currency and coin, check clearing and collection, wire transfer, automated clearinghouse, settlement, securities safekeeping, float, and any additional services initiated after the MCA was passed.
5. Because the Fed paid private couriers to provide it with currency and coin transportation services, bypass would involve an institution establishing a direct relationship with a courier at a lower price than the price charged for the indirect relationship provided through the Fed.
6. For simplicity, and also to isolate cross-subsidization, we consider only attributable costs and not common costs. While not a subsidy in economic terms, the allocation of fixed costs could also yield prices that potentially result in cream skimming.
7. For a brief history of the advent of tiered pricing, along with a statement of the associated criteria established by the Federal Reserve Board, see the *Federal Register* (1990).
8. The Kansas City Reserve Bank did not employ an RCPC zone, but used tiered pricing in its country zone, as shown in Table 1. RCPC zones are designated areas within the territories of Federal Reserve offices, but outside Federal Reserve cities. Country zones generally are exterior to RCPC zones. Of the five Reserve Banks that designated country zones in both 1990 and 1998, four employed a flat country zone fee, rather than a tiered price. Each of these four Reserve Banks raised the country zone fee from 1990 to 1998.
9. Financial Services Policy Committee (2010), "Federal Reserve Banks Complete Check Processing Infrastructure Changes," press release, March 2.

References

Committee on the Federal Reserve in the Payments Mechanism (1997), *Summary of Input from Payments System Forums*. Washington, D.C.: Board of Governors of the Federal Reserve System, September.

Eckel, Catherine, and Charles A. Holt (1989), "Strategic voting in agenda-controlled committee experiments." *American Economic Review* 79 (September): 763–73.

Federal Register (1980), Proposed fee schedules and pricing principles, 45 FR 58689, September 4.

――――― (1981), Adoption of fee schedules and pricing principles for Federal Reserve Bank services, 46 FR 1338, January 6.

――――― (1990), Approval of a private sector adjustment factor and fee schedules for Federal Reserve Bank priced services for 1991, 55 FR 46720, November 6

Federal Reserve Bulletin (1981), Announcements, adoption of fee schedules, transportation services, November, p. 854.

Federal Reserve Regulatory Service (1994), Policy statement on surpluses and shortfalls that arise from the provision of Federal Reserve priced services, 7–135, March.

―――――, Standards related to priced-service activities of the Federal Reserve Banks, 7–137, March.

————— , Provision of payment services to all depository institutions, 7–143, March.

—————, Methodology for computing Federal Reserve Bank costs and fees, 7–147, March.

Interdistrict Check Manual (1990, 1998), Federal Reserve Bank of Philadelphia.

Lacker, Jeffery M., and John A Weinberg (1998), "Can the Fed be a payment system innovator?" *1997 Annual Report*, Federal Reserve Bank of Richmond.

Laffont, Jean-Jacques, and Jean Tirole (1990), "Optimal bypass and cream skimming," *American Economic Review* 80: December, 1042–61.

Stavins, Joanna (2004), "Do bank mergers affect Federal Reserve check volume?" *Public Policy Discussion Papers No. 04-7*, Federal Reserve Bank of Boston, October.

11

Estimating the Volume of Counterfeit U.S. Currency in Circulation Worldwide: Data and Extrapolation

*Ruth Judson and Richard Porter**

Abstract

The incidence of currency counterfeiting and the possible total stock of counterfeits in circulation are popular topics of speculation and discussion in the press and are of substantial practical interest to the U.S. Treasury and the U.S. Secret Service. This chapter assembles data from Federal Reserve and U.S. Secret Service sources and presents a range of estimates for the number of counterfeits in circulation. In addition, the chapter presents figures on counterfeit passing activity by denomination, location, and method of production. The chapter has two main conclusions: first, the stock of counterfeits in the world as a whole is likely on the order of 1 or fewer per 10,000 genuine notes in both piece and value terms; second, losses to the U.S. public from the most commonly used note, the $20, are relatively small, and are miniscule when counterfeit notes of reasonable quality are considered.

Introduction

In a series of earlier papers and reports, we estimated that the majority of U.S. currency is in circulation outside the United States and that that share abroad has been generally increasing over the past few decades.[1] Numerous news reports in the mid-1990s suggested that vast quantities of counterfeit dollars might be circulating overseas as well; these reports contrasted sharply with information from official sources indicating that counterfeiting is relatively rare.[2] In this chapter, we attempt to place an upper bound on the quantity of counterfeit in circulation based on samples of counterfeit data collected by the U.S. Secret Service (USSS) and Federal Reserve together with our understanding of circulation patterns for genuine and counterfeit currency.[3] This paper differs from previous work in that the magnitude of the counterfeiting problem is examined for all denominations now being issued rather than just for $100s, as in our earlier work.[4]

We have very good sampling data from two sources that can be considered independent in various dimensions. In order to develop appropriate confidence bounds for extrapolation, we compare the data from these two sources. Both sources suggest that the incidence of counterfeits in the population is quite small, in the neighborhood of one note in 10,000 for the denominations now being issued. The nature of these data flows also allows us to estimate the degree to which the currency received by the Federal Reserve System is likely to represent the total population of currency outstanding.

In addition, we argue that it is unlikely that small areas containing large numbers of counterfeits can exist for long outside the banking system, and that the total number of counterfeits circulating is at most a couple of times what the sampling data indicate. In particular, we find that an upper bound on the stock of counterfeit currency in circulation, as a share of the genuine, would still be less than 3 in 10,000. Finally, we present evidence that, for the denominations most commonly handled by U.S. consumers, the incidence of counterfeits that cannot be detected with minimal authentication effort is smaller, probably on the order of about three in 100,000.

The chapter proceeds as follows. The first section provides a brief overview of dollar usage outside the United States and counterfeiting within and outside the United States. Section 2 reviews the data sources used for this analysis. The third section presents our estimates of the likely total value of counterfeit dollars in circulation. The fourth section presents estimates of how representative the notes that pass through the banking system are. The fifth section presents a model of currency circulation that demonstrates that it is quite unlikely that a large pool of counterfeits can circulate undetected. The sixth section concludes.

1.   Background

Out of the approximately $759 billion in U.S. dollars held in U.S. currency in the form of banknotes (paper currency) in circulation outside the U.S.

Treasury and the Federal Reserve at the end of 2005,[5] the Secret Service reported that about $61 million in counterfeit currency was passed to the public worldwide.[6] Of the counterfeit currency passed, the majority, $56.2 million, was passed in the United States, with the remainder passed abroad. While the loss associated with a counterfeit to the individual who mistakenly accepts it can be significant, the aggregate loss of $56.2 million in 2005 amounts to about 20 cents per U.S. resident, a minor amount. Losses from counterfeiting have also been very small relative to the cost of check fraud and other forms of fraudulent transactions. For example, in 2005, the cost of check fraud to commercial banks was estimated to be about $1 billion, or nearly 20 times the cost of counterfeiting.[7]

1.1   U.S. Dollar usage around the world

The Federal Reserve supplies currency on demand. In practical terms, Federal Reserve Banks provide currency at face value to banks that have accounts with them. Banks that do not have accounts with the Federal Reserve can purchase currency through their correspondent banks that do have Federal Reserve accounts. Individuals and nonfinancial firms typically obtain currency from banks or currency exchanges.

As a share of the monetary aggregates, currency is relatively small: it makes up just over a third of the narrow monetary aggregate, M1, and about a tenth of the broader monetary aggregate, M2. However, there is a great deal of currency outstanding. Currency held outside depository institutions at the end of 2005 amounted to about $759 billion, or about $2,500 for every U.S. resident.[8]

Although a great deal of U.S. currency is in circulation per U.S. resident, not all U.S. currency is held within the United States.[9] Cash U.S. dollars are used widely overseas. The U.S. dollar is the leading international currency in many regions, and our estimates from earlier studies suggest that between half and two-thirds of all U.S. currency in circulation is held outside the United States.[10] People outside the United States have a wide range of motivations for holding and using dollars and a correspondingly wide range of habits for managing their dollar holdings. Generally, dollars are held when other assets are inferior in reliability, liquidity, anonymity, or compactness. In highly volatile economic and political conditions, dollars can virtually drive out other assets, including domestic currency. Moreover, once people lose faith in their local currency, they tend to hold dollars for a long time before the local currency is able to regain credibility. Beyond these situations, dollars are the currency of choice for travelers headed for destinations outside Western Europe, and are favored as a store of value or as a medium of transaction for large purchases in areas with moderate instability and underdeveloped financial services. U.S. currency provides individuals in these countries with a vehicle for savings and transactions that they would not otherwise have. For the U.S. taxpayers, there are benefits, too: total currency outstanding has yielded seignorage income of $20 billion to $32 billion per year in recent years, and the estimated portion of this revenue derived from overseas dollar holdings is in the range of $10 to $20 billion per year.[11]

For the purposes of this paper, we group currency abroad outstanding into three categories: currency hoarded, or held for long periods in one place; currency that circulates, but stays outside the United States and the banking system in general; and currency that is used largely for tourism or otherwise circulates back to the Federal Reserve through the banking system. The currency in circulation abroad that is most readily analyzed with existing data sources is that in the last category.

1.2   The economics of counterfeiting

Both theoretical studies and the little empirical information we have suggest that high-quality counterfeiting is expensive and only effective when few counterfeits are passed relative to the amount of genuine currency in circulation. Producing high-grade counterfeits requires access to presses, inks, and high-grade paper. The last item is the most important element because cashiers and bank tellers often rely on touch to detect counterfeits. In addition, the notes must then be either passed or distributed to others for passing, which is a complicated undertaking when large volumes of notes are produced.[12] A bank or an individual might be fooled into accepting a batch of counterfeits once, but it seldom happens more than that. Thus, the notes must be ever more widely dispersed. Informal discussions with the Secret Service indicate that the full cost of producing and *distributing* high-grade counterfeit $100s can be in excess of $50 per counterfeit.[13]

The few theoretical papers on currency counterfeiting also conclude that the only long-run equilibria are for two alternate states, either very low or very high levels of counterfeiting. Lengwiler (1997) finds that, in fact, the only possible equilibria are for zero counterfeiting or a high level of counterfeiting. In his model, the equilibrium that actually occurs is a function of the note's production cost (i.e., difficulty of counterfeiting) and its face value. The monetary authority is more likely to invest in higher-cost notes and thus insure a zero-counterfeiting equilibrium the higher the cost of counterfeiting and the higher the value of the note. The U.S. dollar, especially its pre-1996 series, had significantly fewer counterfeit protection devices than many other industrialized countries and was relatively low in value.[14] However, as Green and Weber (1996) point out, the technology embedded in the new-design 1996-series $100 approached that of other countries' currency at that time. The technology of euro banknotes, which were introduced in 2002, is generally higher than the 1996-series U.S. dollar, but the new-design $20 issued in October 2003 has comparable security to the euro.

2.   Data Sources

We have two primary sources of data from the USSS and the Federal Reserve. In addition, we have institutional knowledge collected from both continuing contact and periodic visits to banks, currency dealers, banknote shippers, and other officials responsible for currency distribution and counterfeit detection around the world. Both sources of data suggest that the incidence of counterfeiting among actively circulating U.S. banknotes is quite low.

2.1   Secret Service data on counterfeiting

The USSS is responsible for investigating, prosecuting, and preventing counterfeiting activity. They record counterfeit currency seized (i.e., found at the point of production, before it enters circulation) and passed (i.e., found in circulation) by denomination, location, and production method. We focus on the data for notes passed for two reasons: first, only notes passed were ever in circulation; second, only passed counterfeits generate an economic loss to the public.

The Secret Service data are in principle complete, and should provide representative figures. That is, if twice as many counterfeits are found in Country X than in Country Y, one would in principle conclude that Country X had twice as many counterfeits as Country Y. However, these data are incomplete for two major reasons. First, while U.S. law requires that all counterfeits be turned over to the Secret Service, local treatment and reporting of counterfeits outside of the United States varies considerably. Counterfeit U.S. dollars found abroad may be retained by banks, returned to customers, or held by local law enforcement authorities without being reported to the Secret Service. In some countries, counterfeiting of foreign currency is not illegal, or counterfeits presented at banks or exchange offices are routinely returned to the holder or retained by the bank or exchange office. Teams from the Treasury's International Currency Awareness Program (ICAP) visit banks and other cash handlers in various countries, and when teams visit, it is not at all uncommon for the banks visited to produce substantial caches of counterfeits that they have accumulated and

Table 11.1   Data on counterfeit currency received by the U.S. Secret Service, fiscal years 1999–2005 (millions of dollars)

Year	Passed			Seized		
	Domestic	Foreign	Total	Domestic	Foreign	Total
1999	39.2	1.4	40.6	13.7	126.6	140.3
2000	39.7	1.4	41.1	20.9	190.8	211.7
2001	47.5	1.5	49.0	12.6	54.0	66.6
2002	42.9	1.4	44.3	9.7	120.4	130.1
2003	36.6	1.5	38.1	10.7	52.2	62.9
2004	43.6	1.2	44.7	10.3	33.6	43.9
2005	56.2	4.8	61.0	14.7	37.9	52.6

Note: "Seized" refers to counterfeit currency that was detected before being circulated, while "passed" indicates currency that was determined to be counterfeit after entering circulation. Only passed currency represents a loss to the public; seized counterfeits represent an averted threat.

held, either because they wish to use the notes to train their cashiers or because, prior to meeting the ICAP teams, they had little idea that the USSS considers it useful to at least examine and ideally retain passed counterfeits for investigative purposes. The banks are not necessarily obligated to turn the counterfeits over to the USSS as the USSS has no jurisdiction outside the United States and its territories. Second, the capacity of the USSS itself to detect and seize counterfeit U.S. currency overseas is directly related to its ability to develop working relationships with the appropriate agencies and officials overseas: detection of counterfeits is generally higher in countries in which the Secret Service has better ties with local law enforcement agencies. As shown in the top panel of table 11.1, in the fiscal year 2005, the Secret Service recorded $56.2 million in counterfeit currency passing in the United States, but only $4.8 million in passing activity outside the United States. Because of the reporting and data problems described above, the Secret Service agrees that the true quantity of U.S. notes passed abroad is considerably larger than the reported quantity and is likely similar in magnitude to U.S. passing activity.[15]

2.2   Federal Reserve processing data

Each of the roughly three dozen Federal Reserve Cash Offices collects data on its cash processing activities, including counterfeit detection. These data are useful in three ways. First, the Federal Reserve Bank of New York, which is the major port of entry and exit for overseas shipments of U.S. dollars, can often identify the source country of the counterfeits it receives. These data complement the data collected by the Secret Service in several respects. First, these data measure counterfeiting in dollars that circulate differently. The Secret Service data cover notes that were detected abroad, or, in the taxonomy mentioned in the introduction, are circulating but remain outside the Federal Reserve. The Federal Reserve data, in contrast, capture notes that by definition have been returned to the United States. Thus, the correlation between these two sources can be used to calculate confidence bounds for the population of notes in circulation as a whole.

The second use of Federal Reserve processing data for this paper comes from the fact that separate statistics are recorded for pre-1990 series notes, 1990-series notes, and 1996-series notes.[16] Notes circulating within the United States are likely to return to Cash Offices more quickly, while overseas notes in remote areas and areas where dollars are used more as a store of value than as a medium of exchange are likely to circulate to Cash Offices only infrequently.[17] The information on the series status, however, can be exploited to obtain estimates of how much of the total currency population is in "active" circulation and how much might be hoarded.[18]

The third use of Federal Reserve processing data is the most direct: from counterfeit detection rates and total processing figures, we can estimate confidence intervals for the true incidence of counterfeits among the stock of dollars circulating actively.

2.3   Institutional information

The final sources of information, albeit not hard data, are the observations made during the ICAP's visits to dollar-using economies, in which both authors have participated. Locations visited by the authors of the current paper included Argentina, Bahrain, Belarus, Bolivia, Bulgaria, Cambodia, Chile, China, Colombia, the Dominican Republic, Ecuador, El Salvador, Egypt, Greece, Hong Kong, Kazakhstan, Latvia, Lithuania, Mexico, Panama, Peru, the Philippines, Poland, Romania, Russia, Saudi Arabia, Singapore, South Africa, Switzerland, Taiwan, Thailand, Turkey, Ukraine, the United Arab Emirates, the United Kingdom, and Vietnam. Other team members visited Brazil, Indonesia, Japan, South Korea, and Paraguay. In addition to providing a great deal of information about how and why U.S. currency circulates in other countries, discussions during ICAP team visits indicate that most currency returns to the banking system with surprising regularity, that internal counterfeit detection statistics at commercial and central banks worldwide fall into a fairly narrow and low range, that counterfeit detection skills are remarkably high wherever dollars are used extensively, and that counterfeit detection practices are very responsive to market forces.[19]

3.   Estimating the Total Quantity of Counterfeit Dollars in Circulation Worldwide

The worldwide estimates of counterfeiting rely on a variety of data sources with differing characteristics. Specifically, we have made three sets of calculations to estimate the total amount of *counterfeit* currency now in circulation. First, we generate a lower bound for the total number of counterfeits by denomination based on Federal Reserve cash processing data, reported in table 11.2. Second, we generated an upper bound for counterfeits by denomination by extrapolating from Federal Reserve data to cover counterfeits found outside the Federal Reserve. Third, we generate a range of plausible estimates for all denominations based on the relative incidence of $100 counterfeits and lower-denomination counterfeits. We conclude that the total value of counterfeits in circulation at any moment is in the order of $60 to $80 million, or less than $1 for every $10,000 outstanding, and is highly unlikely to exceed $220 million, or less than $3 for every $10,000 in circulation. Further, we conclude that the incidence of counterfeits is roughly the same inside and outside the United States, and thus the distribution of counterfeits follows the estimated distribution of genuine currency, which is estimated to be about 55 to 60 percent abroad with the remainder located within the United States.

3.1   Estimating the minimum stock of counterfeits in circulation

We estimate a lower bound on the number of counterfeits in circulation by extrapolating from the concentration of counterfeit notes in notes processed by Federal Reserve Banks. The Federal Reserve keeps records on the origin (domestic or international) of counterfeit U.S. notes it detects. Table 11.2

Table 11.2   Counterfeiting rates in deposits at Federal Reserve banks, 2005

Denomination	Total notes processed (millions)	Value of counterfeits detected (millions of dollars)	Counterfeits detected per million notes processed
$1	12,729.5	0.01	1.1
$2	20.8	0.00	1.2
$5	2,709.4	0.08	5.6
$10	2,162.4	0.17	7.8
$20	15,355.9	1.70	5.5
$50	1,274.2	0.31	4.9
$100	2,210.6	9.75	44.1
Total	36,462.8	12.02	6.4

presents figures on note processing, the value of counterfeits detected, and the rate of counterfeits detected per million notes processed. Table 11.3 presents similar information, but for a ten-year period for $100s.

Given these figures, the calculation is straightforward: the estimated number of counterfeits in circulation is estimated as the product of the number of notes in circulation and the rate of counterfeit detection in notes processed by Federal Reserve Cash Offices. Table 11.4 presents estimates of the value of $100 counterfeits in circulation based on the assumption that the notes processed at the Federal Reserve represent a random sample of $100 notes in circulation and by using a broad range of assumptions on the share of total U.S. currency held abroad.[20] As seen in the table, the Federal Reserve processing data suggest that the total stock of $100 counterfeits outstanding in 2005 was in the range of about $20 million to $30 million, a figure we consider a lower bound for several reasons. First, the notes sent to Federal Reserve Cash Offices are a relatively "clean" sample of the population of all notes in circulation because such notes have already passed through several detection "screens" before reaching the Federal Reserve. If a counterfeit is deposited at a commercial bank, the probability that it will remain in the stock of notes sent on to the Federal Reserve is less than one, and most likely substantially less than one. Four possibilities for disposal await a counterfeit that arrives at a commercial bank. First, if undetected it could be recirculated or sent to the Federal Reserve. In the

Table 11.3   Counterfeit $100 notes detected in deposits processed at Federal Reserve Banks 1996–2005

Period	Counterfeits detected (millions of dollars)			Notes processed (billions of dollars)			Counterfeits detected per million notes processed		
	Total	NY, LA, Miami	All Other	Total	NY, LA, Miami	All Other	Total	NY, LA, Miami	All Other
All Designs									
1996	6.8	3.6	3.3	112.9	59.2	53.7	60.5	60.2	60.9
1997	7.2	3.9	3.4	108.3	52.9	55.4	66.6	73.0	60.5
1998	6.3	3.5	2.8	107.5	51.3	56.2	58.9	69.1	49.6
1999	5.8	2.8	3.0	112.3	51.9	60.4	51.8	54.2	49.9
2000	6.5	2.8	3.6	161.7	72.7	89.0	39.9	39.2	40.5
2001	7.4	3.3	4.1	154.0	70.7	83.3	48.1	47.1	48.9
2002	5.0	2.4	2.6	162.7	71.9	90.8	30.7	33.1	28.9
2003	4.3	2.1	2.3	173.7	79.3	94.5	24.8	26.0	23.9
2004	4.1	2.0	2.2	200.7	96.5	104.2	20.6	20.6	20.7
2005	9.7	6.7	3.0	221.1	112.0	109.1	44.1	60.2	27.6
Total, 1996–2005	**63.3**	**33.1**	**30.1**	**1512.3**	**718.4**	**796.6**	**41.8**	**46.1**	**37.8**

Table 11.4 Counterfeit $100 stocks implied by Federal Reserve processing data, assuming varying shares of currency held abroad

Year	Stock of $100s ($ billion)	Assumed Share Abroad	Domestic			Foreign			Total implied counterfeits ($ millions)
			Detection rate (notes per million)	Assumed $100s in circulation ($ billions)	Implied counterfeits ($ millions)	Detection rate (notes per million)	Assumed $100s in circulation ($ billions)	Implied counterfeits ($ millions)	
1996	261	40%	60.9	156.8	9.5	60.2	104.6	6.3	15.8
		80%		52.3	3.2		209.1	12.6	15.8
1997	292	40%	60.5	174.9	10.6	73.0	116.6	8.5	19.1
		80%		58.3	3.5		233.3	17.0	20.6
1998	320	40%	49.6	192.1	9.5	69.1	128.0	8.8	18.4
		80%		64.0	3.2		256.1	17.7	20.9
1999	386	40%	49.9	231.7	11.6	54.2	154.5	8.4	19.9
		80%		77.2	3.9		308.9	16.7	20.6
2000	378	40%	40.5	226.6	9.2	39.2	151.1	5.9	15.1
		80%		75.5	3.1		302.1	11.8	14.9
2001	421	40%	48.9	252.6	12.4	47.1	168.4	7.9	20.3
		80%		84.2	4.1		336.9	15.9	20.0
2002	459	40%	28.9	275.4	8.0	33.1	183.5	6.1	14.0
		80%		91.7	2.7		366.9	12.1	14.8
2003	488	40%	23.9	292.7	7.0	26.0	195.1	5.1	12.1
		80%		97.6	2.3		390.2	10.1	12.5
2004	517	40%	20.7	310.0	6.4	20.6	206.7	4.3	10.7
		80%		103.3	2.1		413.4	8.5	10.7
2005	545	40%	27.6	327.0	9.0	60.2	218.0	13.1	22.1
		80%		109.0	3.0		436.0	26.2	29.3

latter case, it would appear in the Federal Reserve processing data.[21] Second, it could be detected as a counterfeit by the bank, and reported to the police and the Secret Service. In this case, the note would appear in the Secret Service's statistics but not in the Federal Reserve's statistics. Third, it could be detected and returned to the depositor, an illegal and highly unlikely outcome within the United States. Fourth, a counterfeit could be detected and confiscated but either not reported to the police and USSS or not released. Banks are often eager to retain a few counterfeits for use in training their own tellers. In some countries, banks are permitted to report counterfeits and then retain the notes. This set of notes thus does not appear in the Federal Reserve statistics but may or may not appear in the Secret Service statistics, generally depending on whether the Secret Service has had an opportunity to examine the notes. Counterfeit detection at commercial banks is generally quite good, so we believe that the majority of counterfeits that arrive at banks do not get shipped to the Federal Reserve. The observation that the Secret Service receives five times as many passed counterfeits as the Federal Reserve would seem to bear this out.

We believe that a counterfeit arriving at a foreign bank is less likely than a counterfeit arriving at a U.S. bank to be delivered to the Secret Service or to make it into a Federal Reserve deposit for two reasons. First, U.S. banks are much more likely than their foreign counterparts to contact the Secret Service directly. Second, on average, overseas banks appear to check their dollar shipments more carefully for counterfeits than do U.S. banks, partly because labor costs are generally so much lower in many foreign countries with heavy dollar traffic.

Table 11.5   Counterfeit $50, $20, $10, $5, and $1 stocks implied by 2005 Federal Reserve processing data assuming all currency held within the United States

Denomination	Detection rate (notes per million)	Value of genuine notes in circulation (billions of dollars)	Implied counterfeits (millions of dollars)
$50	4.9	62.1	$0.30
$20	5.5	115.4	$0.63
$10	7.8	15.5	$0.12
$5	5.6	10.3	$0.06
$2	1.2	1.5	$0.00
$1	1.1	8.8	$0.01
Total	. . .	195.3	$1.13

Note: . . . Not applicable.
Source: Federal Reserve Bank of New York; U.S. Treasury.

Table 11.5 displays lower-bound estimates of the stock of lower-denomination counterfeits in circulation based on Federal Reserve processing data. The Federal Reserve does not provide the same domestic-foreign breakdown for these denominations, but, based on the $100s data, it is safe to say that the detection rates for lower denominations held overseas should be at or below the domestic levels, making these estimates more likely on the high side.

It is interesting to note that the incidence of counterfeits detected in processing is substantially lower for lower denominations than it is for $100s. We believe that the lower incidence can be explained by the overall poorer quality of lower-denomination counterfeits. Poorer-quality counterfeits are easier to detect and are thus more likely to be detected before they are returned to a Federal Reserve Bank. Table 11.6 displays Secret Service data on counterfeits passed in the United States by denomination and method of production. "Circular" notes are those that are assigned classification numbers by the USSS for further investigation. They are typically of higher quality than the other categories of counterfeit notes, which include those printed on office copiers or computer printers or other relatively rudimentary methods.

The data in table 11.6 indicate that circular notes are nearly three-quarters of $100 counterfeits passed, but less than one-fifth of $50 counterfeits passed and less than 5 percent of $20 and smaller counterfeits passed.[22] At the domestic consumer level, the breakdown between circular and other notes is significant. A noncircular counterfeit note is

Table 11.6 Counterfeits passed in the United States by denomination and method of production, fiscal year 2002

Denomination	Circular	Other (Printer, Copier, Raised**)	Total	Circular Share
$100	$22,995,600	$8,263,500	$31,259,100	73.6%
$50	$402,750	$1,689,650	$2,092,400	19.2%
$20	$186,420	$5,500,720	$5,687,140	3.3%
$10	$28,470	$1,033,740	$1,062,210	2.7%
$5	$2,345	$160,870	$163,215	1.4%
$2	$0	$114	$114	0.0%
$1	$535	$14,425	$14,960	3.6%
Total*	$23,616,120	$16,663,019	$40,279,139	58.6%

*Excludes denominations above $100.
**Raised notes are high-denomination counterfeits that are constructed from genuine lower-denomination notes. For example, raised notes often feature one or more corners of a high-denomination note attached to the body of a lower denomination note.
Source: U.S. Secret Service.

usually of minimal quality: a person with minimal training in counterfeit detection and currency authentication should be able to detect it readily with the naked eye, and successful passing occurs only when the recipient of the note fails to give it much scrutiny at all. Over 95 percent of the notes in the $20 and smaller denominations, which are those most commonly used by U.S. consumers, fall into the noncircular category. As can be seen in table 11.6, the value of circular counterfeits passed in the $20 and smaller denominations in 2002 was less than $220,000.

There is a policy implication to these figures that deserves to be highlighted: for U.S. residents, a minimal level of vigilance is sufficient to virtually rule out losses from accepting counterfeit notes. Consumers can easily familiarize themselves with the authentication features of genuine currency, including the distinctive feel of the paper, watermark, security thread, and color-shifting ink.[23] Similarly, retail outlets can provide authentication training to cashiers and might even consider the purchase of low-cost authentication devices such as black lights if they are handling large quantities of cash.

We now return to the estimate of the total stock of counterfeits. As noted above, a lower bound for the estimate of $100 counterfeits in circulation is $20 million to $30 million and a lower bound for the number of other denominations in circulation is $1 million, for a total of $21 to $30 million. Within the United States, about five or six counterfeit $100 notes are detected outside the Federal Reserve for *each* note found by the Federal Reserve. An estimate of total counterfeit $100s in circulation based on such ratios would be about $120 million ($20 million multiplied by 6) to $210 million ($30 million multiplied by 7). For the lower denominations, the ratio of notes found outside the Federal Reserve to those found inside ranges from seven or eight to one for $50s to less than one for one for $1s, as reported by the U.S. Treasury (2003); these findings generate a range of $1 million to $11 million for the estimated stock of smaller-denomination counterfeits in circulation. Thus, the range of estimates for the total quantity of counterfeits in circulation becomes $120 million to $220 million.

This range, however, should be viewed as an upper bound, for reasons similar to those discussed above. The counterfeits found outside the Federal Reserve are generally of lower quality and more easily detected (hence their detection outside the Federal Reserve). Thus, they likely do not circulate for as long as the counterfeits that survive until reaching the Federal Reserve.[24] Since we believe that both the upper-bound and lower-bound estimates are relatively far from the true stock of counterfeits in circulation, a middle-range value of about $60 to $80 million, or less than $1 worth of counterfeit for every $10,000 in circulation, is most likely.

4.   How Representative Are Our Datasets?
Comparing the Datasets

4.1   Country-level comparisons

In principle, the country-by-country Federal Reserve Cash Office processing data on counterfeits should be a subset of the Secret Service data. Under certain conditions, moreover, the proportions of counterfeits detected by country and region should be similar in both datasets. However, neither of these conditions holds exactly in the data we present here and as a result, the ratios do not exactly coincide, though most observations do fall within two standard deviations of the mean absolute deviation.

There are two conditions that would need to hold for the country-specific counterfeit datasets to exactly match both each other and the underlying true country distribution of counterfeits. First, the Secret Service's ability to detect counterfeits would have to be exactly uniform across countries. This condition is surely not the case given variation in staff size, relations with local law enforcement, and other local factors. Second, the notes processed by the Federal Reserve would have to be a random sample of the notes in circulation in a given country. This condition is somewhat more likely to hold. While some currency is held for long periods and some currency is selected for return to the United States because it is extremely worn or dirty, our estimates below on hoarding suggest that notes circulate fairly randomly.

The Secret Service data used here cover only notes passed to the public in the fiscal year 2002; they do not include notes seized, since these notes by definition were never in circulation. Since the Secret Service dataset includes counterfeits found by the Federal Reserve, the Secret Service's figure for each country should exceed the Federal Reserve's figure. Countries are dropped if the Secret Service shows fewer counterfeits than the Federal Reserve.

Each point in Figure 11.1 represents one country's share of the counterfeits detected in each data set. Thus, a point at (5,10) would indicate that 5 percent of the counterfeits detected at the New York Federal Reserve Cash Office came from that country while 10 percent of the counterfeits detected by the Secret Service did. These points would all lie on the 45-degree line if the relative detection rates between the two data sets agreed and if the samples of notes processed were exactly representative of the notes in circulation. The dotted lines represent a 95 percent confidence interval around the 45-degree line. Since all of the points associated with the individual country pairs lie within the confidence band, we cannot reject the hypothesis that the relative detection rates in the two datasets are not significantly different from one another.

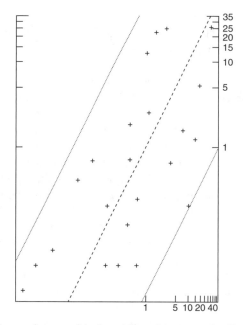

Figure 11.1   Shares of counterfeits found in various countries, financial year 2002

4.2   Secret Service data and counterfeit stock estimates

We now return to the estimate of the total stock of counterfeits. Recall that extrapolation from Federal Reserve cash processing data yields an esti-mated minimum *stock* of $20 to $30 million in counterfeits of all denomi-nations in circulation. In contrast, the Secret Service data for 2005 indicate that the total value of counterfeit currency passed on the public in 2005 was about $60 million, roughly two to three times what the Federal Reserve data would suggest, but in the range of our "mid-range" estimate and well below our upper bound. It is not clear what this discrepancy implies. Most notably, we do not know how long a typical counterfeit circulates before being detected. If, for example, the average counterfeit only circulated for one month before being detected, then the annual Secret Service statistics could be consistent with as little as $5 million in counterfeit currency circu-lating at any given time.[25] Thus, if we were willing to assume that the Secret Service on average finds counterfeits within three or four months of their first appearance, the Federal Reserve and Secret Service figures would be consistent with each other.

In fact, our circulation data can help resolve this issue. Assume first that we are in counterfeit equilibrium in which the stock of counterfeits as a share of genuine currency in circulation is roughly constant. Then the number of counterfeits that is detected and removed from circulation each year should be roughly equal to the number that are placed into circulation.[26] The questions are then how rapidly the stock of counterfeits turns over and what share of total counterfeits detected are reported to the Secret Service.

Consider the circulation lives of $100 notes. Genuine notes circulate, return to Reserve Banks, and sometimes recirculate; their average lifespan is about eight years.[27] In contrast, counterfeits end their lives when they are detected, which at the very latest is on their first (and only) trip to a Federal Reserve Cash Office. Cash processing data from the first year following the introduction of the 1996-series $100 note indicate that about one-third of the total notes outstanding at the beginning of the period were replaced, which means that one-third of the notes visited the Federal Reserve at least once. If counterfeits circulate at least as fast as genuine notes, which we benchmark with observations on $100s after the introduction of the 1996-series notes, then on average counterfeits should remain in circulation at most about three years before facing certain detection at a Federal Reserve Bank. However, the average lifespan of a counterfeit $100 is probably only a small fraction of three years for three reasons. First, as noted earlier, more than 80 percent of $100 counterfeits are detected prior to reaching a Federal Reserve Bank. Second, we have reason to believe that, if anything, counterfeits circulate faster than genuine notes: all other things equal, if an individual has two notes and considers one of them "suspicious" or possibly counterfeit, the individual is likely to try to get rid of that note first. Thus, we assume that, on average, counterfeits could remain in circulation at most for one year, with a few months being much more likely.[28]

Next, the question is what share of notes that are detected as counterfeit appears in the Secret Service's statistics. For domestic notes, this figure is almost surely near 100 percent. For counterfeits detected overseas, this figure is surely well below 100 percent, but whether it is 10 percent or 70 percent is difficult to say. In any case, using domestic figures as a benchmark, we estimate that about $40 million worth of $100 notes were passed within the United States in fiscal year 2005. Using the figure of an average lifespan of a counterfeit note of one year and the assumption of constant shares of counterfeit activity, we arrive at an estimate of domestic steady-state stock of counterfeit $100s of about $40 million.

We can extrapolate to the rest of the world in a couple of directions; Table 11.7 presents the calculations. Depending on how much of the stock of $100s we assume is held outside the United States and how long we think the average counterfeit $100 survives before being detected, there could be anywhere from $7 million to $133 million in counterfeit $100s outstanding worldwide. These calculations rest critically on the assumption

Table 11.7 Stocks of $100 counterfeits for various longevity and share abroad assumptions

Longevity	Implied counterfeits in U.S. ($ million)	Share of genuine notes abroad (%)	Implied counterfeits abroad ($ million)	Implied total counterfeits ($ million)
1 month	3	50	3	7
		70	8	11
3 months	10	50	10	20
		70	23	33
6 months	20	50	20	40
		70	47	67
1 year	40	50	40	80
		70	93	133

Note: Total counterfeit currency detected within the United States by the Secret Service in 2005: $56 million. Based on the distribution of counterfeits by denomination in earlier years, we estimate the value of $100 counterfeit U.S. currency passed within the United States in 2005 at about $40 million.

Table 11.8 Stocks of $20 counterfeits for various longevity and share abroad assumptions

Longevity	Implied counterfeits in U.S. ($ million)	Share of genuine notes abroad (%)	Implied counterfeits abroad ($ million)	Implied total counterfeits ($ million)
1 month	0.8	5	0.0	0.9
		50	0.8	1.7
3 months	2.5	5	0.1	2.6
		50	2.5	5.0
6 months	5.0	5	0.3	5.3
		50	5.0	10.0
1 year	10.0	5	0.5	10.5
		50	10.0	20.0

Note: Estimated counterfeit $20s detected within the United States by the Secret Service in 2005, based on total counterfeits detected within the United States of $56.2 million and denomination breakdown for all counterfeit U.S. currency reported to the U.S Secret Service in 2002 (refer to U.S. Treasury 2003): $10 million.

of the lifespan of a counterfeit. As noted above, we consider the one-year assumption to be a very realistic or conservative upper bound.

Table 11.8 displays the results of similar calculations for $20s. We have not formally estimated how many $20s are in circulation outside the United States, but we consider 50 percent to be a reasonable upper bound. In addition, $20s circulate much more rapidly than $100s: in 2002, about three times as many $20s were processed by Federal Reserve Banks as were in circulation, so on average a $20 circulates for only a few months before certain detection at a Federal Reserve Bank. The average life of a counterfeit $20 is likely even shorter than a few months, but we show the same range of time possibilities as for $100s just for comparison. The results for $20s, as for $100s, have a very wide range, but the value is substantially lower: from less than $1 million to about $20 million. Note that the upper bound estimate of $20 million amounts to two counterfeit $20 notes for every 10,000 notes in circulation. For this denomination, though, we consider the most likely estimate to be much closer to the lower end of the range given the rapid turnover for the $20 denomination, probably in the range of $2 million, or one counterfeit $20 note for every 50,000 $20 notes in circulation. Since the volume of counterfeiting among the remaining denominations is in a range similar to or much smaller than that of $20s, we omit tables for those denominations.

We now return to our comparisons of Federal Reserve and Secret Service data. Recall that the Secret Service found about twice as many notes as the Federal Reserve data would suggest are outstanding. This finding is consistent with either a lifespan of just a few months for the average counterfeit, or with a longer lifespan for each note and more detection outside the Federal Reserve, or with some combination of these two factors, which we believe to be the case. We do consider the range of estimates to be bounds on the true number of counterfeits in circulation at a given time: the two data sources on counterfeits, plus what we know about circulation, suggest that it is very unlikely that more than $31 million in counterfeit $100s is in circulation within the United States. Extrapolation to the stock of notes circulating outside the United States is similarly ambiguous, but does yield an upper bound figure of $104 million. Estimates for $20s would add $11 million to that total, and estimates for the remaining denominations would add at most another $10 million, for a total of at the very most $125 million for all notes in circulation. Note that this figure, which we consider to be extremely conservative (i.e., very much on the high side of the truth) still represents less than 1/50 of 1 percent of all currency in circulation.

5.   The Next Step: How Unrepresentative Are Our Data?

The estimates constructed above rely heavily on the assumption that currency, both genuine and counterfeit, circulates with some frequency, which we generally believe to be true.[29] However, it is sometimes asserted that counterfeit notes somehow find their way into isolated "pools" of currency that never reach the banking system.

Below we present two models that show why it is unlikely that notes can remain outside the banking system indefinitely. The first model shows that notes in active circulation almost surely return to the banking system after a relatively small number of transactions, which *on average* translates into a relatively short period. The second model exploits cash processing data to estimate the shares of currency at home and abroad that might be hoarded, or out of circulation for more than a year at a time. Both of these models suggest that it is extremely unlikely that large quantities of counterfeits that have been passed can hide anywhere for very long.

5.1   *Hoarding*

In some countries and circumstances, U.S. dollars are used as a store of value and can be held for a very long time without circulating. We exploit the processing data from the Federal Reserve Cash Offices to estimate the parameters of a simple model of hoarding. In this model, a share h of the currency stock is hoarded in a given year, and a share α of the hoarded stock is turned over every year. The currency processed is a random sample of the active notes only. The key ingredient in this model is the fact that a new-series \$100 note was introduced in 1991. After this date, all old-series \$100s arriving at Cash Offices were replaced with new-series notes. We have six years of data, 1991 to 1996, and two unknowns, h and α. If the population of notes is n and notes are drawn (processed) randomly with replacement, then the probability that a note gets processed in one draw is $1/n$. The probability that a note is drawn after p draws is thus

$$1 - \left(1 - \frac{1}{n}\right)^p$$

Observe that the only notes that can be processed are in the active share of the pool, A. Thus, the right figure to use in the denominator of the equation above is not n but An. Since the draws are independent, the number of notes replaced, say r, is just equal to An times the probability that one note will be replaced:

$$r = An\left(1 - \left(1 - \frac{1}{n}\right)^p\right)$$

Dividing both sides by n, we obtain an expression in terms of R, the share of notes replaced, as a function of A, the active share of the population, n, the total note population, and p, the number of notes processed. This is our basic equation:

$$R_t = A\left(1 - \left(1 - \frac{1}{n_t}\frac{1}{A}\right)^{p_t}\right)$$

The stock of $100s outstanding grew fairly rapidly in this period. We assume, however, that the *share* of notes hoarded remained constant. After the first year, R is defined net of note growth. Moreover, one must account for the fact that some notes enter the active pool and some leave. If α is the share of inactive notes that re-enter the active pool each period, R after the first period is defined as

$$R_{t>1} \equiv \left(I - G_{n_t}\right)\left(\frac{1}{m^a}\right)$$

where I is the number of new notes issued, G is the growth rate of the stock of notes, and m^a and m^h are active and hoarded stocks of new-series notes, with m^a defined as follows:

$$m_t^a \equiv m_t - m_t^h \equiv m_t - (m_{t-1}^h - \alpha \, m_{t-1}^h + \alpha \, (1+G_t)\left(\frac{m_t / n_t}{A}\right)$$

Since there are two parameters, we conduct a grid search to find the best fit. We estimate the parameters separately for notes circulating within and outside the United States. Since we do not know the total number of notes circulating in each area, we estimated the parameters for a range of assumptions about the share of notes held abroad. As in previous work (Porter and Judson 1996), we treated the New York Cash Office as the "foreign" office since we know that it handles the bulk of foreign shipments.

The objective functions are well-behaved but fairly flat. In general, they indicate that hoarding is unlikely to be important for very long, and that turnover is likely to be high. For example, for the case of 50 percent of currency stocks assumed abroad, we find that α, the turnover rate for inactive currency, is 0.6 for domestic currency and 0.99 (corner solution) for overseas dollars. We find that the share hoarded at home is 0.19 and is effectively zero (again a corner solution) overseas.[30] For other assumptions, the highest share of hoarding found is 0.69 and the lowest turnover is 0.47. We conclude that it is highly unlikely that large quantities of notes are likely to stay out of circulation (and hidden from counterfeit detection) for very long.

5.2 *"Pools" of undetected counterfeits*

One often-cited possibility is that there are isolated "pools" of circulating currency with high concentrations of counterfeits that do not circulate to Cash Offices. Although such an idea is in principle plausible, we are able to show that it is in practice highly unlikely.

This idea that notes could circulate outside the banking system indefinitely is based on several assumptions, including some variation on the following:

(a) Currency overseas endlessly recirculates without being processed by any banking entity, thus counterfeit is not detected and continues to circulate, or

(b) Currency is processed by banking entities that lack detection capability, thus counterfeit is not detected and continues to circulate, or

(c) Currency is processed by banking entities that detect the counterfeit, but choose to recirculate the currency to avoid losses, thus counterfeit continues to circulate,

(d) Currency continues to circulate overseas without routinely being repatriated, thus counterfeit is not detected and continues to circulate.

When we visited central and commercial banks and authorities charged with stopping counterfeiting in a large group of countries, we were able to observe counterfeit detection capabilities and the condition of the currency. Based on what we observed, it was apparent that currency does not endlessly recirculate in any of the markets we visited. Currency is used for a wide range of transactions, but even in gray- or black-market economies it will eventually find its way into a commercial banking institution, most likely after being used in relatively few transactions.[31]

The logic behind our conclusion that notes cannot remain in circulation very long is readily laid out. Since transactions are usually between unrelated individuals, it is plausible to assume that successive transactions are statistically independent of one another. To make the analysis tractable, also assume that there is a constant probability, say μ, that after any transaction a given banknote will not be returned to a financial institution. There is a presumption that μ should be relatively small. After all, apart from transactions between individuals, most currency transactions are with retail establishments and most retailers generally accumulate nearly all of the currency they receive and deposit/sell all but "seed" cash—in particular, all large-denomination notes—at financial institutions or exchange houses on at least a daily basis. Survey evidence suggests that currency circulating both within and outside the United States turns over (is exchanged) on average about once a week.[32] If the probability is μ that the note recirculates, the note is used in one transaction per week, and successive transactions are independent, the probability that the note will continue to recirculate after θ weeks has a joint binomial distribution with probability μ^θ. Thus, the complementary event that a given note is returned to a financial institution after θ transactions is $1-\mu^\theta$. Clearly, this probability will approach unity after a relatively short interval of time even if μ is close to unity because it is raised to the power θ. For example, consider the extreme case where $\mu = 0.9$ so the odds are 9 to 1 that a note will recirculate; even in this case after seven weeks, the probability is greater than one half that the note will hit the banking system; and after 22 weeks, the probability is greater than 0.95 that the note will stop recirculating. A more plausible assumption would be to assume $\mu = 0.1$ so that most transactions are with retail vendors and not with "hand-to-hand transactors." In this case, the probability that the note will be returned to a financial institution approaches one almost immediately.

If notes turn over more frequently than one time per week, the time of the first passage to the financial institution would be even sooner. In some countries, cash dollars are the dominant medium of exchange even for small daily purchases; in this case, notes could turnover as fast as once per day on average. If currency turned over on a daily basis, the twenty-two week period for the first passage of a note to a financial institution in the extreme case with $\mu = 0.9$ would be cut to one-seventh of the time, or approximately three weeks.

Once currency hits the banking system, it naturally flows to regional financial processing centers, and is routinely repatriated in large quantities. Thus, currency does not generally recirculate in large amounts, most probably not in amounts any greater than is found in Federal Reserve deposits from foreign sources. Further, it is quite unlikely that banks recirculate counterfeits either to other banks or to their customers. While the bank pays no additional penalty if another bank or the Federal Reserve finds a counterfeit, its reputation can suffer if customers find the bank giving out counterfeits.

In sum, we find it unlikely that counterfeits can circulate for long outside the banking system, and thus outside reasonably sophisticated counterfeit detection, for very long. These figures thus suggest that notes are unlikely to circulate outside banks for much more than a year.

6. Conclusion

We develop upper- and lower-bound estimates for the quantity of counterfeit dollars in circulation. Processing data from the Federal Reserve Bank of New York suggest a lower bound of $20 to $30 million in value terms. Using denomination-specific weights to scale up the lower-bound estimate to account for the counterfeits passed outside the Federal Reserve yields an upper-bound estimate of $120 to $220 million, or about $1.50 to $3 per

$10,000 in circulation. We believe that an estimate in the neighborhood of $60 to $80 million, or 80 cents to $1 per $10,000 in circulation, is the most plausible, and is consistent with a relatively short average lifespan for a given counterfeit note. These figures are relatively small, but for U.S. consumers, the threat from high-quality counterfeits is even smaller: for the $20 and smaller denominations, counterfeiting losses are minuscule, at $7 million in 2002, of which less than $220,000 were notes that could not be detected by users with minimal hand inspection.

We further find that while it is indeed possible that a large number of counterfeits could be injected into the financial system, it is quite unlikely that they would remain there in use and undetected. We find the close correlation between the country distribution of the counterfeits detected by the Federal Reserve and the Secret Service particularly intriguing; we believe it is strong evidence that both counterfeit detection and incidence fall within a small range of about one note in 10,000 throughout countries where dollars are in circulation.

*The authors are, respectively, an Economist at the Federal Reserve Board and Vice President and Senior Policy Advisor at the Federal Reserve Bank of Chicago. The authors thank colleagues in the U.S. Secret Service Counterfeit Division, the Cash Function of the Federal Reserve Bank of New York, and the Division of Reserve Bank Operations and Payment Systems for assistance in compiling and obtaining data and for valuable discussions and comments. Members of the Divisions of Monetary Affairs and International Finance also contributed helpful comments. The views presented are solely those of the authors and do not necessarily represent those of the Federal Reserve Board, the Federal Reserve Bank of Chicago, or their respective staffs.

Notes

1. Judson and Porter (2001, 2004), Porter (1993), Porter and Judson (1996), U.S. Treasury (2000, 2003, 2006), and Porter and Weinbach (1999). Portions of the material here, which were written by the authors, appear in U.S. Treasury (2000, 2003, 2006).

2. The reports of counterfeiting led to a congressional hearing on counterfeiting issues in February 1996, which resulted in a legislation requiring overseas audits of U.S. currency. (Refer to "Counterfeit U.S. Currency Abroad: Observations on Counterfeiting and U.S. Deterrence Efforts," Statement of JayEtta Z. Hecker before the Subcommittee on General Oversight and Investigations, Committee on Banking and Financial Services, House of Representatives, February 27, 1996. In testimony leading up to this legislation, the Government Accountability Office (GAO) argued that the evidence about the true dimensions of the counterfeiting problem facing the United States

overseas was mixed. In particular, the GAO could not verify the claims of the Treasury that the problem was economically insignificant nor those of Secret Service about the actual extent of the counterfeiting. In part because of these concerns, the Congress passed the Anti-Terrorism and Effective Death Penalty Act of 1996, which obligated the Secretary of the Treasury, in consultation with the interagency Advanced Counterfeit Deterrence group, see http://www.treasury.gov/offices/domestic-finance/acd/about.html, to make several reports to the Congress on the use and counterfeiting of U.S. currency abroad, including U.S. Treasury (2000, 2003, 2006).

3. The Treasury and Federal Reserve work together on currency design. Currency is produced by the Bureau of Engraving and Printing, a branch of the Treasury. The Federal Reserve distributes currency. The Secret Service, formerly a branch of the Treasury but as of 2003 a branch of the Department of Homeland Security, is charged with the responsibility of detecting and arresting any person committing any offense against the laws of the United States relating to currency. From 1996 to 2006, the Federal Reserve and Treasury were legally required to provide estimates of genuine and counterfeit currency circulating outside the United States.

4. Data coverage for the $2 denomination is not as complete as it is for the other denominations, and so some of the analysis is not possible. However, the volume of $2 notes in circulation is tiny, about 0.2 percent of the value of currency held outside banks.

5. Currency in circulation is measured in several different ways, depending on whether currency is held in the vaults of depository institutions ("vault cash") and Treasury currency, which includes Treasury notes and coin, are included. The Federal Reserve's data on money stock currency, reported in the H.3 statistical Release, include Treasury currency and vault cash. On a monthly average basis, vault cash ranged from $45 billion to $51 billion during 2005. The value of coin in circulation at the end of 2005 was $35.2 billion. The Treasury figures on currency in circulation, which include vault cash but exclude coin, are used in this report.

6. The Secret Service reported that additional quantities were "seized," or confiscated before they entered circulation. In this chapter we focus on the figures for "passed" counterfeits. While seized notes posed some threat prior to the seizure, passed notes clearly caused losses to the banknote-using public. Moreover, the fact that they were passed at least once suggests that they passed a "quality control" by fooling at least one person.

7. Board of Governors of the Federal Reserve System, 2007. Notably, this figure does not include overall losses from check fraud to consumers and businesses.

8. Weekly figures on the quantity of currency held by the public are reported on the Federal Reserve's H.4.1 and H.6 statistical releases. Quarterly figures are reported by the U.S. Treasury in the Treasury Bulletin.

9. The observations in this section are drawn from first-hand visits to dozens of economies by both authors since the mid-1990s under the auspices

of the International Currency Awareness Program (ICAP) run jointly by the Federal Reserve, U.S. Treasury, U.S. Secret Service, and Bureau of Printing and Engraving; refer to U.S. Treasury (2006), Table 3.1 for a list of countries visited. The authors also participated in a precursor program to the ICAP. During these visits, the authors spoke with hundreds of senior officials from central banks, commercial banks, cash handlers, and law enforcement agencies about currency usage and counterfeiting outside the United States.

10. Judson and Porter (2001), Porter (1993), Porter and Judson (1996), U.S. Treasury (2000, 2003, 2006).

11. For every dollar in currency obtained, individuals must give the Federal Reserve an asset worth a dollar. The Federal Reserve purchases Treasury securities with these assets. As long as the dollar remains outstanding, the Federal Reserve earns interest on its Treasury securities. Such interest earnings are rebated to the Treasury after deducting Federal Reserve expenses. In the nine years from 1999 to 2007, the Federal Reserve returned between $19.0 and $32.3 billion to the Treasury each year (Economic Report of the President 2003 and 2009, Table B-81.) For analysis of earlier years, refer to Jefferson (1998).

12. Transportation of large quantities of currency across international borders is generally regulated. In addition, in very large quantities, currency is bulky: $1 million in $100 notes weighs about 20 pounds (or about 10 kg.) and fills a briefcase.

13. The fixed costs of producing high-grade counterfeits are relatively high. In addition, the costs of (successfully) passing more than a few notes into circulation can escalate quickly as victims who have accepted counterfeit currency become aware of the new threat and increase their level of scrutiny.

14. The highest denomination now issued is $100. In contrast, many other countries issue denominations valued between $500 and $1,000, and a few countries issue notes whose value exceeds $1,000.

15. U.S. Treasury (2000, 2003, 2006).

16. 1990-series notes were first issued in 1991 and include a security thread and microprinting. 1996-series notes were first issued in 1996 and include a larger portrait, a reflective security thread, a watermark, additional microprinting, optically variable ink, and other features to prevent counterfeiting. A 2004-series $20 design was unveiled in May 2003. As new series are added, the data flow is adjusted. At any time, separate figures are maintained on the current series, the most recent prior series, and all other earlier series. Thus, when the issuance of the 2004-series notes began, figures for pre-1990 series and 1990-series notes were combined.

17. Depository institutions bear the cost of transporting currency for deposit in Federal Reserve Banks. For U.S. depository institutions, the volumes of currency are typically relatively large and the nearest Federal Reserve Bank is typically not very far away, so the transportation costs are relatively minor. For overseas institutions, however, the costs of transporting currency to the nearest Federal Reserve Bank can be considerably higher, providing an incentive for these institutions to try to recirculate currency rather than return it.

18. This question is beyond the scope of the current chapter.
19. Banks displayed varying counterfeit detection practices depending on local labor costs, local counterfeiting activity, and the relative cost of missing a counterfeit.
20. Although the estimates in Porter and Judson (October 1996) and U.S. Treasury (2000, 2003, 2006) put the estimated overall share of currency abroad between 55 and 70 percent, Feige (1996) presents estimates as low as 40 percent.
21. It is assumed that the Federal Reserve detects all counterfeits in shipments it receives. For a discussion of this assumption, see Allison and Pianalto (1997).
22. For this table as well as for several later tables, it was not possible to obtain 2005 figures that were comparable to the 2002 figures presented in U.S. Treasury (2003).
23. Existing $1 and $2 denomination notes do not have the watermark, security thread, or color-shifting ink.
24. Appendix B in U.S. Treasury (2000) takes up the issue of estimating the life-span of a counterfeit.
25. That is, if each month $5 million in counterfeits entered circulation, were then detected by the Secret Service in that month, and were then replaced with new counterfeits, the Secret Service could find $5 million x 12 = $60 million in counterfeit currency each year, even though at any moment only $5 million was in circulation.
26. More precisely, assuming that counterfeits represent a constant percentage of currency in circulation, the number of new counterfeits entering circulation would be equal to the number of counterfeits leaving circulation multiplied by the overall growth rate of currency in circulation.
27. The estimate is probably on the high side. A 1991 Federal Reserve survey found such an estimate but the rate at which $100s have been received from circulation has increased significantly since then. This suggests an average age more in the neighborhood of 5 years might be more appropriate now.
28. Appendix B.2 in U.S. Treasury (2000) addresses this issue in more detail. In informal discussions, agents from the U.S. Secret Service have repeatedly noted that their investigations point to very short active lives for counterfeits in active circulation; they consider one year beyond a reasonable upper bound for the average lifespan of a counterfeit note. Based on the calculations in U.S. Treasury (2000) and the input from the U.S. Secret Service, we would place the probability that the true average lifespan of a counterfeit dollar exceeds a year at well below 1 percent.
29. Counterfeit currency likely circulates more rapidly than genuine currency, but with rare exceptions, all currency moves into the market occasionally.
30. At first blush, it might seem counterintuitive that overseas notes emerge from the hoarding state with a greater propensity abroad. A 1989 survey of notes circulating domestically and internationally found that the turnover rates of foreign and domestic notes were similar in that they had similar age-degree of use profiles where use was measured by the quality and degree of soil on the notes. Such a pattern indicates that the notes were active to about the same degree both domestically and overseas. Since currently a large portion of United States is held abroad in rather undeveloped economies where currency

is used extensively, the turnover rate may be higher abroad simply because currency is a relatively more important source of payment than in the United States and is therefore used more often.

31. There is an important exception to this argument. For years, stories have circulated that some government(s) hostile to the United States had obtained plates to print currency and were going to produce a flood of counterfeits in an effort to destabilize the dollar. It was argued that these counterfeits could circulate endlessly and freely within the bounds of such countries. We have no way of confirming or denying such stories. If "closed" countries (e.g., North Korea) do indeed have many counterfeits in circulation, it is impossible to know as long as the system remains closed. The evidence and model we present here apply to *open* markets and economies. Moreover, in a closed system where nobody is being fooled about the genuineness (or lack thereof) of the currency, it is not clear that there is a loss to consumers and, as long as the counterfeits remain confined to the closed economy, they do not affect the value of genuine dollars.

32. See Porter and Judson (1996) and Feige (1996).

References

Allison, Theodore E., and Rosanna S. Pianalto (1997). "The issuance of Series-1996 $100 Federal Reserve notes: Goals, strategies, and likely results." *Federal Reserve Bulletin* 83:7 (July): 557–64.

Board of Governors of the Federal Reserve System (2007). "Report to the Congress on the check clearing for the 21st Century Act of 2003." April.

Economic Report of the President (2003). Washington, D.C.: United States Government Printing Office.

Economic Report of the President (2009). Washington, D.C.: United States Government Printing Office.

Feige, Edgar L. (1996). "Overseas holdings of U.S. currency and the underground economy." In *Exploring the Underground Economy: Studies of Illegal and Unreported Activity,* ed. Susan Pozo, pp. 5–62. Kalamazoo, Michigan: W.E. Upjohn Institute for Employment Research.

Green, Edward J., and Warren E. Weber (1996). "Will the new $100 bill decrease counterfeiting?" *Federal Reserve Bank of Minneapolis Quarterly Review* (Summer): 3–10.

Jefferson, Philip N. (1998). "Seignorage payments for use of the U.S. dollar: 1977–1995." *Economics Letters* 58:2 (February): 225–30.

Judson, Ruth A., and Richard D. Porter (2001). "Overseas dollar holdings: What do we know?" Wirtschaftspolitische Blatter 4.

——— (2004). "Currency demand by Federal Reserve Cash Office: What do we know?" *Journal of Economics and Business* 56:4 (Special Issue, July-August): 273–85.

Lengwiler, Yvan (1997). "A model of money counterfeits." *Journal of Economics* 65(2): 123–32.

Porter, Richard D. (1993). "Estimates of foreign holdings of U.S. currency—An approach based on relative cross-country seasonal variations." In *Nominal*

Income Targeting with the Monetary Base as Instrument: An Evaluation of McCallum's Rule, Finance and Economics Discussion Series Working Study 1. Board of Governors of the Federal Reserve System, March.

Porter, Richard D., and Ruth A. Judson (1996). "The location of U.S. currency: How much is abroad?" *Federal Reserve Bulletin* 82:10 (October): 883–903. Addendum to the Treasury Audit Plan on the Uses and Counterfeiting of U.S. Currency, April 1997, Department of the Treasury.

Porter, Richard D., and Gretchen C. Weinbach (1999). "Currency ratios and U.S. underground activity." *Economics Letters* 63:3 (June): 355–61.

U.S. Department of the Treasury (2000). The Use and Counterfeiting of U.S. Currency Abroad (February).

———— (2003). The Use and Counterfeiting of U.S. Currency Abroad, part 2 (March).

———— (2006). The Use and Counterfeiting of U.S. Currency Abroad, part 3 (March).